Gateway ok

2nd Edition

David Spencer

B1

macmillan
education

Contents B1

Listening	Speaking	Writing	✓ Exam success
▶ **Family dinners**	▶ **Asking for personal information**	▶ **An informal email**	Reading: Multiple-choice activities
Teenagers' responsibilities	Family arguments	Making a timetable	Speaking: Information role-plays
Asking for personal information	Family dinners		
▶ **Describing an incident**	▶ **Apologising**	▶ **A blog post**	Listening: True/False/Not Mentioned activities
Doing the right thing	Discussing crime stories	A questionnaire	Writing: Knowing evaluation criteria
Apologising	Telling stories		
▶ **Languages**	▶ **Asking for information**	▶ **A language biography**	Use of English: Multiple-choice cloze activities
Speaking in public	Talking about social networks	Preparing a presentation	Speaking: Knowing evaluation criteria
Asking for information	Discussing definitions		
▶ **Action scenes**	▶ **Describing photos**	▶ **Notes and messages**	Reading: Matching activities
Giving first aid	Discussing health tips	Writing a quiz	Writing: Content and style
Describing photos	Talking about past experiences		
▶ **TV today**	▶ **Negotiating**	▶ **A review**	Listening: Identifying the speaker activities
Talking about fame	Discussing Slow TV	A video message or email	Speaking: Negotiating
Negotiating	Giving opinions on TV and films		

Listening	Speaking	Writing	✔ Exam success
▶ **Sustainable energy** Reducing your carbon and water footprint Making arrangements	▶ **Making arrangements** The future of the planet Talking about your future	▶ **A formal letter** A video or a poster	Use of English: Sentence transformation activities Writing: Writing in exam conditions
▶ **Film and TV extras** Transferable skills Making polite requests	▶ **Making polite requests** Discussing unusual jobs Giving advice	▶ **A letter of application and CV** A description of transferable skills	Reading: True/False activities Listening: Multiple-choice activities
▶ **Discover your secret self** Making friends at university Reporting a past event	▶ **Reporting a past event** Talking about friendship Discussing interests	▶ **An email of advice** A leaflet or a webpage	Speaking: Reporting activities Writing: Answering the question
▶ **Book vs. film** Book descriptions A presentation	▶ **A presentation** Favourite books Reporting interviews	▶ **A story** Organising a book club	Reading: Missing sentences activities Listening: Completing notes
▶ **Wikipedia** Internet security Comparing and contrasting photos	▶ **Comparing and contrasting photos** The importance of the Internet Trivia quiz	▶ **Text messages** Preparing a presentation	Use of English: Cloze activities Speaking: Speculating about photos

 Irregular verbs **p149**   Writing bank **p150**

1 Family life

Vocabulary

Ages and stages of life

1 Work with a partner. Match these words to the photos. What ages go with each stage of life?

> baby • child • middle-aged (man/woman)
> senior citizen • teenager • young adult

e   baby, 0 to 3 approximately

 a
 b
 c
 d
 e
 f

2 Put the stages of life in order. Begin with *birth*.

> adolescence • birth • childhood
> death • middle age • old age

3 🔊 01 Listen, check and repeat.

The family

4 Divide these words into three lists as below.

> aunt • brother-in-law • cousin • ~~daughter~~
> grandfather • grandson • ~~husband~~ • nephew
> niece • stepfather • uncle • wife

Male	Female	Male or Female
husband	daughter	

5 Match the words in 4 with these descriptions.

1 the man that a woman is married to
   husband
2 the brother of one of your parents
3 your mother's new husband in a second or later marriage
4 a daughter of your brother or sister
5 the son of one of your children
6 the brother of your husband or wife

6 **SPEAKING** Work with a partner. Take it in turns to define the other words in 4. Can your partner say the family member?

> It's the son of your brother or sister.

> Nephew.

7 Complete the sentences with the words in the box.

> born • divorced • one-parent
> only child • partner • single

1 If you are _____, you aren't married.
2 An _____ doesn't have brothers or sisters.
3 The word _____ describes your husband, wife, or the person that you live with.
4 If you are married and then you end the marriage, you are _____ .
5 In _____ families only the father or the mother lives with the children.
6 Approximately 800,000 babies are _____ every year in the UK.

8 **LISTENING** 🔊 02 Listen to three people talking about their families. Choose the correct alternatives.

1 Joshua is *a child/a teenager*. He has a *big/small* family.
2 Olivia is *a child/a teenager*. She has got a *big/small* family. She lives with her *father/grandfather*. She spends a lot of time with her *aunt/cousin*.
3 Jessica is a senior citizen. She's got *four/twelve* grandchildren. She is *married/divorced*.

9 **SPEAKING** Work with a partner. Tell them about your family using words from this page.

Reading

1 **Work with a partner. What types of things do teenagers argue about with their parents? Make a list.**

clothes, music ...

2 **Read this post on a website that helps teenagers with problems. Does Zoe talk about any of the things in your list in 1?**

| HOME | POPULAR | **ASK OUR EXPERT** | SIGN IN |

ZOE, 14 years old, London

Q I'm writing to you because of my problems at home. I'm having a really hard time at the moment. I have arguments with my parents about everything! For example, my mum and dad never knock before coming into my bedroom! When I'm sitting at my desk doing my homework, my mum interrupts me. She tells me how untidy my room is and says that I need to clean it. She doesn't understand that I have a lot of things to do. Later on she comes back to tell me to turn my music down. I don't think it's loud. But then we start shouting. She says that it's impossible to do homework and listen to music at the same time and tells me to switch it off completely. But she doesn't realise that the music helps my concentration. Please help. I don't know what to do!

3 **Work with a partner. Think of good advice to give Zoe.**

4 **Now read advice from an expert. Do they mention any of your ideas in 3?**

Our expert says ...

A You want your parents to treat you with respect. But show them respect, too. You say you have a lot to do but I'm sure your mother is also busy. You don't want to tidy your bedroom when you're doing your homework. So, decide on a time that is convenient for you. Tell your mum what time that is. Then make sure you do it! As for the music, parents and teenagers always argue about music. Speak to your mum calmly. Explain that it helps you to study. But keep it to a reasonable volume or use headphones. And finally, your bedroom. Maybe your parents don't realise that you're not a little child any more. Explain why you think it's important to have a private space. Maybe you're spending a lot of time in your bedroom and your parents don't see you or get a chance to speak to you. When you talk to parents it makes a big difference. Tell them what's happening in your life.

✔ **EXAM SUCCESS**

Here is a multiple-choice reading activity. In this type of exercise you have three or four options. You choose the option that is best according to the information in the text. If you aren't sure of the correct answer, what can you do?

➤ EXAM SUCCESS page 144

5 **Read the text again and choose the best answers.**

1 Zoe is angry with her mum because she says her mum doesn't ...
   a tidy Zoe's bedroom.
   b realise how busy Zoe is.
   c want Zoe to do her homework.

2 Zoe's mum has a problem with Zoe's music because she ...
   a doesn't think it helps Zoe concentrate.
   b doesn't like the style of music.
   c can't do her work with loud music.

3 The expert thinks that Zoe's mum ...
   a is right to tell Zoe to tidy her room.
   b is right to stop Zoe in the middle of her homework.
   c is right to decide what time Zoe should clean her room.

4 The expert thinks that Zoe can do what she likes with her music ...
   a because parents are never happy with their children's music.
   b if she talks to them about it.
   c within certain limits.

5 The expert says that ...
   a it's normal for Zoe's parents to enter her bedroom without knocking.
   b maybe Zoe's parents want her to communicate with them more.
   c Zoe's parents don't want her to have a private space because she's too young.

6 ⚙ **CRITICAL THINKING**

   Think! Then compare ideas with your class.
   ■ What do you think is good advice for when you have disagreements with your parents?

7 **What do the underlined words in the text mean? Guess and then check in your dictionary.**

8 SPEAKING **What about *you*?**

Do you ever argue with your parents? What about?

Present simple and present continuous

1a Look at these sentences. Which sentences are in the present simple and which are in the present continuous?

1 I'm writing to you because of my problems at home.
2 My mum and dad never knock before coming into my bedroom!
3 Parents and teenagers always argue about music.
4 I don't know what to do.

1b Match the sentences in 1a with the explanation of their uses in a–d.

a With certain verbs like *love*, *like*, *hate*, *think*, *believe*, *know*, *understand*, *want*, *need*.
b For regular or routine actions.
c For things that are always or generally true.
d For actions that are happening now or temporary actions.

1c Complete the sentences with the correct form of *study*.

Present simple

Affirmative: He ......*studies*...... history.

Negative: He .... physics.

Question: .... he .... English?

Present continuous

Affirmative: She .... English now.

Negative: She .... maths now.

Question: .... she .... French?

GRAMMAR REFERENCE ➤ PAGE 16

2 Look at the picture. Write sentences about what the different members of the family are doing or not doing. Use the present continuous form of the verbs in the box.

cry • drink • laugh • listen • play • read • sit • sleep • stand • talk • watch

The daughter is talking on the phone.

3 Complete the dialogue about the picture using the present simple or present continuous form of the verbs given.

Molly: Hi, Julia. What (a) .... you .... (do)? Are you at home?

Julia: Yes. I never (b) .... (go) out on Wednesdays.

Molly: (c) .... you .... (watch) TV?

Julia: No, right now my mum (d) .... (watch) her favourite series. She always (e) .... (watch) it on Wednesdays.

Molly: What's that sound? (f) .... somebody .... (cry)?

Julia: Yeah. It's my baby cousin.

Molly: (g) .... she always .... (cry) like that?!

Julia: No, she (h) .... (i) .... you .... (know) what my dad (j) .... (do) at the moment?

Molly: No, I (k) ....

Julia: He (l) .... (listen) to loud music because he (m) .... (hate) the sound of crying! And the amazing thing is that now my grandfather (n) .... (sleep). He usually (o) .... (sleep) in the afternoon. I don't know how he's doing it!

4 Find these words and phrases in the dialogue in 3. Which go with the present simple and which go with the present continuous?

1 at the moment   5 now
2 never   6 right now
3 normally   7 usually
4 on Wednesdays

at the moment = present continuous

5 Complete the sentences with the present simple or present continuous form of the verbs in the box.

help • lie • need • not understand • shout • work

1 I can't come out at the moment because I .... my sister with her homework.
2 Why .... you ....? My grandfather can hear you.
3 My cousin always .... in a restaurant on Saturday afternoons.
4 Can you say that again? I ....
5 Can I help you, Dad? .... you .... anything?
6 My sister .... down right now because she doesn't feel well.

6 Write questions for these answers.

1 *What do you do on Fridays?*
 I play basketball on Fridays.
2 ....
 My mum is working at the moment.
3 ....
 My uncle and aunt live in Liverpool.
4 ....
 No, my cousin isn't studying at university.
5 ....
 My grandparents go for a walk in the mornings.
6 ....
 My family and I usually go to the cinema at the weekend.

7 SPEAKING Use the questions in 6 to interview your partner. When you finish, think of similar questions to ask.

What do you do on Fridays?

I go out with my friends.

Noun suffixes *-ment, -ion, -ence*

1 Look at these words from the text on page 7.

argu**ment** • concentrat**ion** • differ**ence**

The parts of the word in **bold** are suffixes. Suffixes change the type of word, e.g. from an adjective or a verb to a noun.

2 Complete the words in the table and then use your dictionary to check the words.

-ment	
Verb	Noun
1 *argue*	argument
move	2 ....
improve	3 ....
4	retirement

-ion	
Verb	Noun
concentrate	5 ....
6	information
describe	7 ....
8	discussion

-ence	
Adjective	Noun
9	difference
10	adolescence
11	independence
confident	12 ....

3a Choose the correct alternative.

1 How can you *improve/improvement* your English this year?
2 Do you think you are an *independent/independence* learner?
3 Have you got a lot of *confident/confidence* when you speak in English?
4 Are there many *different/differences* between English and your language?
5 Do you like having *discuss/discussions* in English?

3b SPEAKING Work with a partner. Ask and answer the questions in 3a.

Contributing to FAMILY LIFE

LIFE SKILLS OBJECTIVES	KEY CONCEPTS
■ To think about rights and responsibilities in a family. ■ To learn about different ways of helping with family life. ■ To decide positive steps to take to contribute to family life.	**right, rights [n]:** *We all have a right to express our opinions.* **responsibility, responsibilities [n]:** *When you have a pet, you must take responsibility for what it does.* **respect [v]:** *Children need to respect their parents and grandparents.* **independent [adj]:** *She's very independent. She is able to make her own decisions.*

1a SPEAKING **Work with a partner. Ask and answer these questions.**

1 Who prepares your school bag each morning?
2 Who makes your dinner?
3 Who buys the food you have for dinner?
4 Who puts clean towels in the bathroom?
5 Who cleans the table after you eat?
6 Who empties the rubbish bin in your bedroom?
7 Who provides the money if you need some to go out?

> We all have rights. Sometimes we feel angry if people don't respect our rights. Teenagers usually feel strongly that they have a right to say what they think. Or they have a right to choose what they do in their free time. Maybe they feel that they have a strong right to privacy.
>
> These rights are all important. They are part of becoming an independent adult. But, when we are changing from a child into an adult, it is easy to forget that there are two sides to this. We have rights, but we also have responsibilities at home. Can we demand our independence if other people do the shopping for us, make our meals, clean the bathroom and give us pocket money to go out?
>
> As we get older, we feel we have more rights. And we want others to respect our rights. But to become an independent adult we need to accept our own responsibilities and begin to do things for ourselves. After all, parents have rights, too.

3 SPEAKING **Answer these questions.**

1 Do you agree with the examples of rights in the first paragraph? Why/Why not?
2 What other rights do you think teenagers have at home? Make a list.
3 Look at the question at the end of the second paragraph. What is your answer to this question? Explain.
4 What rights and responsibilities do you think parents have?

1b Count how many times your answer was 'I do' in 1a.

2 READING **Read the essay. Choose the best title.**

a Teenagers have rights AND responsibilities.
b Teenagers have the power.
c Wait until you are an adult.

4 LISTENING ▶ 03 **Three teenagers talk about their special responsibilities. Watch the video or listen and write down each person's special responsibility.**

Grace ....

Louis ....

Jessica ....

5 ▶ 03 **Watch or listen again and write the name of the person who says these things.**

1 I'm an only child. ....

2 I chose to take on my responsibility.

  ....

3 I have a new opinion about my mum.

  ....

4 I can do more in my free time because of my responsibility. ....

5 I can now have something I want. ....

6 I have to help because my mum is busy studying. ....

6a **Work with a partner. Look at the list of jobs around the house. Check that you understand the words in the list. Use a dictionary if necessary.**

		A Who usually does this in your house?	B How often do you do this?
1	clean the kitchen	....	....
2	clean the bathroom	....	....
3	cook	....	....
4	do the shopping	....	....
5	do the washing	....	....
6	lay the table	....	....
7	make your bed	....	....
8	take the rubbish out	....	....
9	tidy your bedroom	....	....
10	wash the dishes	....	....

6b SPEAKING **Interview your partner to find out who usually does these jobs in their house.**

Who usually cleans the kitchen in your house?

6c SPEAKING **Now find out how often your partner does these jobs (*every day, once/twice/three times a week, at the weekends, never*).**

How often do you clean the kitchen?

LIFE TASK

You want to contribute more to your family life.

Follow this plan:

1 *Work in a small group. Apart from the list of jobs in 6 and the ideas in the videos, make a list of any other ideas, big or small, to help at home.*

2 *Individually, make a list of things that you think **you** could do to make a positive contribution to your family life.*

3 *Make a 'Helping out' timetable in your notebook to plan when you can do these things. Use your school timetable to help.*

4 *Compare and comment on your timetables.*

5 *Tell your family about your plans!*

a

b

1 SPEAKING **Work with a partner. Describe the photos.**

2 LISTENING ▶ 04 **Listen to a radio programme about family dinners. Match the people with their situations.**

1 Mike ☐   3 Sally ☐   5 Jennifer ☐
2 Chris ☐   4 Alice ☐   6 Daniel ☐

A eats with the family just once a week

B eats with the family but they don't talk

C makes dinner for the family every day

D never arrives home in time for dinner

E eats and talks with the family every day

F usually eats with the family but isn't eating with them today

G always eats alone because their parents work

H has to order pizza because nobody has time to cook

3 LISTENING ▶ 04 **Answer these questions. Listen again if necessary.**

1 How many hours a week does Mike work?

2 Where does he go in his job?

3 What does Chris usually eat?

4 When does Sally eat?

5 How many children and grandchildren does Alice have?

6 When does Alice eat with her family?

7 Where are Jennifer's parents tonight?

8 What's the problem with Daniel's family dinners?

4 SPEAKING **What about *you*?**

Do you think it's important to eat with your family? Why/Why not?

Articles

1 **Look at these sentences and then complete rules 1–5 with *a/an*, *the* or no article.**

a I think family dinners are great.

b Family dinners are an important moment for us.

c The dinner I'm eating today isn't good.

d The government talks a lot about family dinners.

e I'm a computer technician.

1 We use ___no article___ when we talk about things in general.

2 We use .... to talk about a singular, countable person or thing for the first time, or to say that the person or thing is one of a number of things or people.

3 We use .... to talk about a specific person or thing or a person or thing mentioned before.

4 We use .... to talk about someone or something that is unique.

5 We use .... to say what somebody's profession is.

GRAMMAR REFERENCE ➤ PAGE 16

2a PRONUNCIATION ▶ 05 **Listen to how we pronounce *the* in List A and List B below. What is the difference in pronunciation? Why is this?**

List A: *the problem   the dinner   the government the weekend*

List B: *the end   the important thing   the evening the afternoon*

2b ▶ 05 **Listen again and repeat.**

3 **Complete the sentences with *the* if necessary.**

1 Today on .... programme we're talking about .... family dinners.

2 I'm going to .... fridge to see if there's anything to eat.

3 I think .... communication is essential.

4 In my house .... breakfast isn't an important meal.

5 Adults can't always arrive on time because of .... work.

6 I don't like .... food at school.

7 In .... films they often show .... families eating together.

4 Read the text and choose the correct alternative.

(a) *A/The* report by the National Literacy Trust in the UK says that talking at home during meals can help (b) *the/–* children to be more confident and to communicate well. (c) *A/The* report says that 87% of (d) *the/–* young people sit down with their family at mealtimes. But 7.1% of those young people never or rarely talk to their family while they are eating. (e) *A/An* interesting thing the Literacy Trust discovered is that talking at mealtimes makes you more confident about speaking in (f) *the/–* class discussions or in front of your classmates. Most young people who talk at mealtimes think that (g) *the/–* good communication skills are important for finding (h) *a/the* good job. (i) *A/The* British Government is interested in this report because they want to improve children's speaking and listening skills. And (j) *the/–* families can help to do this just by talking at dinnertime.

5 Find and correct a mistake with articles in each sentence.

1 I'm a vegetarian. I never eat the meat.
2 My mum is the doctor in a big hospital.
3 Could you pass me potatoes?
4 I had a cat but a cat disappeared last month.
5 He's a student at University of Edinburgh.
6 She's got a brother and the sister.
7 I haven't got a watch – can you tell me a time?

6a Look at these questions. Add *a, an, the* or – if no article is necessary.

1 Do you think .... family dinners are important?
2 Are .... family dinners .... important part of life in your country?
3 Do you think .... children and .... parents talk a lot in your country?
4 Do you talk about .... important things when you have .... dinner?
5 Do you listen to .... music at dinnertime?
6 Do you think .... food you eat makes a difference to your school marks?
7 Do you like .... food at your school?

6b SPEAKING **Interview your partner using the correct questions in 6a.**

Do you think family dinners are important?

Yes, I do. You can talk and find out how everybody is.

Asking for personal information

1 Complete with information about you and your brothers, sisters or best friend.

> Brothers/sisters/best friend:
> Age:
> What they do:
> How often you see them:
> What you usually do on Saturdays:
> What you usually do on Sundays:
> Your likes/dislikes:

2 SPEAKING Look at these four people and their personal information files. Tell your partner which people are similar to you. Explain why.

> *Oliver is similar to me because he's got one brother and he does sport on Sundays.*

Liam
- one brother, one sister
- brother at university, sister works
- goes out with friends on Saturdays
- plays tennis on Sundays

Oliver
- no brothers or sisters
- best friend studies at school
- goes out with friends on Saturdays
- does sport on Sundays

Emma
- one brother
- brother at school
- watches films on Saturdays
- doesn't like sport

Phillipa
- one sister
- sister lives in the US
- plays tennis on Saturdays
- plays computer games on Sundays

3 LISTENING ▶ 06 Listen to two teenagers meeting for the first time. Look at the information in 2. Which two people are talking?

4 Work with a partner. Complete the dialogue with the correct questions. Look at the Speaking bank for help.

A: (a) ....

B: Yes, I've got one brother.

A: Me too. (b) ....

B: He's 22.

A: (c) ....

B: No, he doesn't. He's at university in Manchester.

A: (d) ....

B: About once a month, when he comes home for the weekend.

A: That's good! I see my brother every day because he's only 14. (e) ....

B: I usually go out with my friends on Saturdays and we sometimes play football on Sundays. (f) ....

A: My brother and I often go to the cinema on Saturdays. But I never play football because I don't like sport.

💬 SPEAKING BANK

Useful questions to ask for personal information

- Have you got any brothers or sisters?
- What do you do at the weekend/in the evenings/ on Wednesdays?
- What about you?
- Do you like ...?
- What do you think of ...?
- How often do you ...?

5a PRONUNCIATION ▶ 07 Which questions in the dialogue go with diagram A? Which go with diagram B? Listen again and check.

diagram A   diagram B

5b ▶ 07 Listen and repeat the questions.

6 SPEAKING Practise the completed dialogue in 4 with your partner. Pay special attention to the correct intonation in questions.

PRACTICE MAKES PERFECT

7a SPEAKING Work with a partner. Do this role-play using the dialogue in 4 and the Speaking bank to help you.

You meet an English boy/girl at a summer camp.
- Find out if he/she has brothers or sisters.
- Tell him/her about your family.
- Find out what he/she does at the weekend.
- Tell him/her what you do in your free time.

7b SPEAKING Change partners and repeat.

✓ EXAM SUCCESS

In information role-plays, how can you keep the conversation going?

➤ EXAM SUCCESS page 144

Developing writing

An informal email

Category	Language – English
Main aim	Find an international e-pal
I speak	English and a little Spanish
My interests	Music, books, travel
Message ✎	Hi! I'm from Dublin. I've got two brothers, two sisters and two pets; a cat and a dog! I love travelling and discovering new countries, new music and new books. If you want to practise your English and make new friends, write to me.

Name	Alanna
My country	Ireland
My age	15

1 Look at this advert from a teenager called Alanna. What does Alanna want? Would you be interested in contacting her? Why/Why not?

2 Read this reply to Alanna's advert. Do you think this person is a good e-pal for Alanna? Why/Why not?

e)pal.com **New message!** ✎

Hi Alanna!

1 I'm Isabel. I'm from Alicante in Spain. Let me tell you about myself.

2 I'm from quite a big family. I've got two brothers and a sister. My sister and I are almost the same age and we go everywhere together. My father is a teacher and my mother works in a hospital. My dad teaches at my school. That's often a good thing, but sometimes it can be really bad ☺.

3 I love listening to all types of music, but especially pop and rock. My favourite group is Imagine Dragons. Do you know them? Right now I'm listening to their latest album.

4 English is my favourite subject at school. This year I'm doing extra classes and I also read books in English. At the moment I'm reading a book by John Green. Do you know him?

5 Anyway, that's all for now. Write back soon if you'd like to be my e-pal.

Best wishes
Isabel ☺

3 Look again at the email in 2 and complete the information in the Writing bank.

✎ WRITING BANK

Useful words and expressions in informal emails

- To begin an informal email we usually use *Dear (Alanna)* or just *Hi*.
- We use contractions like *I'm* or ....
- We can use emoticons like ☺ or ....
- We can use the word .... to change the subject.
- To finish an informal email we can use:
  That's .... *for now, Bye for now!, Write* .... *soon, All the best* or *Best* ....

4 Match the paragraphs in Isabel's email with their content.

Paragraph 1 — favourite subject at school
Paragraph 2 — main interest or hobby
Paragraph 3 — basic personal information
Paragraph 4 — asking for a reply
Paragraph 5 — family

PRACTICE MAKES PERFECT

5 Look at the task and write an email. Use Isabel's email and the Writing bank to help you. Follow the paragraph plan in 4.

Write an email with information about yourself to a new e-pal. Tell your e-pal:
- basic personal information
- information about your family
- information about your main hobby
- information about your favourite subject at school.

WRITING BANK ➤ PAGE 150

Grammar reference

Present simple

FORM	
Affirmative	I/You/We/They understand. He/She/It understands.
Negative	I/You/We/They don't (do not) understand. He/She/It doesn't (does not) understand.
Question	Do I/you/we/they understand? Does he/she/it understand?
Short answers	Yes, I/you/we/they do. No, I/you/we/they don't. Yes, he/she/it does. No, he/she/it doesn't.

Time expressions we often use with the present simple: *always, usually, normally, often, sometimes, rarely, never, once/twice/ three times a day/week/month/year, on Mondays/Tuesdays*

USE

We use the present simple to talk about:
- regular habits and routines.
  We walk to school every day.
- permanent situations.
  They live in France.
- general and scientific facts.
  Birds fly.

Present continuous

FORM	
Affirmative	subject + am/are/is + verb + -ing. *We're working.*
Negative	subject + am not/aren't/isn't + verb + -ing. *She isn't working.*
Question	Am/Are/Is + subject + verb + -ing? *Are they working?*
Short answers	Yes, subject + am/are/is. No, subject + am not/ aren't/isn't. *Yes, I am. No, they aren't.*

Time expressions we often use with the present continuous: *now, right now, at the moment, today, this week*

USE

We use the present continuous to talk about:
- actions that are happening now.
  She can't go out. She's studying for an exam.
- temporary actions.
  Jim is studying in the UK.

NOTE: Some verbs are not usually used in the present continuous because they describe states not actions:

believe, hate, have (=possess), hear, know, love, mean, need, prefer, see, seem, think (=have an opinion), understand, want

Articles

A/An

We use *a/an* with singular, countable nouns. We use it when we mention something for the first time, or to say that the thing is one of a number of things.

I've got a bike. It's a mountain bike.

We use *a/an* to describe somebody's profession.

He's a teacher.

We use *a* before a consonant and we use *an* before a vowel sound.

She's an engineer.

The

We use *the* with countable (singular and plural) and uncountable nouns. We use it to refer to something or somebody previously mentioned.

I've got a problem. The problem isn't serious.

We also use *the* to talk about specific things or people.

The film I saw was good.

We also use *the* to talk about something unique.

the sun, the government, the world

No article

We do not use an article with plural, countable nouns or uncountable nouns when we are talking about people or things in general.

Education is important.   I love oranges.

Vocabulary

1 Ages and stages of life adolescence • baby • birth • child • childhood • death • middle age (n) middle-aged (man/woman) • old age • senior citizen • teenager • young adult

2 The family aunt • born • brother • brother/sister/father/mother-in-law • cousin • daughter • divorced grandfather/mother • grandson/daughter • husband • nephew • niece • one-parent family • only child • partner single • sister • son • stepfather/mother • uncle • wife

3 Noun suffixes -ment, -ion, -ence adolescence • argument • concentration • confidence • description difference • discussion • improvement • independence • information • movement • retirement

4 Other words and phrases ➤ page 136

Grammar revision

Present simple and present continuous

/ 16 points

1 Write the third person singular form and -ing form of the verbs below.

Verb	Third person singular	-ing form
1 have		
2 lie		
3 write		
4 cry		
5 get		
6 watch		
7 do		
8 sit		

2 Choose the correct word to complete the sentences.

1 He's .... a new pair of jeans today.
  a wears   b carries   c wearing   d carrying

2 When .... your sister have English lessons?
  a is   b do   c does   d has

3 I'm not sure if he .... French or German right now.
  a studies   b are studying c study   d 's studying

4 I'm sorry, I .... what you're telling me.
  a 'm not understanding   b not understand
  c are understanding   d don't understand

5 Where's your cousin? He normally .... on time.
  a come   b is arriving   c arrives   d is coming

6 Ah! Now I .... what you mean.
  a see   b 'm seeing   c 'm knowing
  d 'm not understanding

7 Stop talking to her because she .... to you.
  a don't listen b listens   c 's listening d never listens

8 Why .... she doing anything?
  a hasn't   b isn't   c doesn't   d don't

Articles

/ 8 points

3 Choose the correct alternative.

1 It's a/the/– beautiful day and a/the/– sun is shining.

2 A/The/– young girl walks into a restaurant. A/The/– girl sits down and orders a pizza.

3 My cousin loves a/the/– books. He's a/the/– writer.

4 Pete's uncle is a/the/– doctor. He says a/the/– exercise is good for you.

Vocabulary revision

AGES AND STAGES OF LIFE – THE FAMILY

/ 8 points

1 Complete the text with the appropriate words.

'My name's Harry. I'm not married yet, I'm still **(a)** .... My mum and dad are middle-**(b)** .... – I think they're both 50 this year. I'm an **(c)** .... child. I haven't got any brothers or sisters but I spend a lot of time with my **(d)** ...., Tara. She's my Uncle Jack's daughter. She's young. I remember when she was born. In fact, I was there at the hospital on the day of her **(e)** .... My Aunt Angela, Uncle Jack's **(f)** ...., is really nice, too. My dad's mum, my **(g)** ...., is really special. She says I'm special for her too, maybe because I'm her only **(h)** ....'

NOUN SUFFIXES -MENT, -ION, -ENCE

/ 8 points

2 Complete the sentences with the correct form of these words.

> adolescent • concentrate • describe • different
> excite • improve • independent • inform

1 She usually gets 50% or 60% in her exams but in this exam she got 90%. That's a big ....

2 Can you give me a .... of your sister? I don't know who she is in this photo.

3 Good food helps your .... at school.

4 There's a lot of .... about the famous actor's visit to the school.

5 There are two or three .... between the present simple and the present continuous.

6 She wants to be a secondary school teacher because she likes working with ....

7 A dictionary gives you .... about new words.

8 He's very .... – he doesn't need anybody to help him.

2 Who did it?

Vocabulary

Crimes and criminals

1 Work with a partner. Complete the sentences with these words. Use a dictionary if necessary.

> burglary • fraud • mugging • piracy
> robbery • shoplifting • theft • vandalism

1 A _____ is when somebody steals something.

2 A _____ is when somebody breaks into a house and steals things from it.

3 A _____ is when somebody steals from a bank or a person.

4 _____ is when somebody damages public property.

5 _____ is when somebody takes things from a shop without paying.

6 _____ is when somebody copies software such as CDs and DVDs illegally.

7 _____ is when somebody takes a person's money or possessions using violence.

8 _____ is when you trick somebody to get money or something from them.

2 Complete the words for the person who does each of the crimes in 1. Use a dictionary if necessary.

1 b _____ g _____   5 r _ b _____
2 m _____ g _____   6 s _____ l ____ t _____
3 f ____ u ___ s ____ r   7 t _____ f
4 p _____ t _____   8 v _____ d _____

3 ▶ 08 Listen, check and repeat.

4 LISTENING ▶ 09 Listen to four radio news items. What are the crimes?

1 _____   3 _____
2 _____   4 _____

Detective work

5 Complete the definitions with the expressions in the box.

> accuse a suspect • analyse evidence • arrest a suspect
> charge a suspect • collect evidence • investigate a case
> prove something • question a suspect

When detectives …

1 _____, they try to find out what really happened.

2 _____, they ask them things.

3 _____, they take them to a police station because they think they have done something bad.

4 _____ with something, they make an official statement that they think the suspect did something bad.

5 _____ of something, they say that they did something bad.

6 _____, they get DNA samples or something that can help to show that somebody did something bad.

7 _____, they give evidence or proof that something is true.

8 _____, they study it in detail.

6 What is the noun form of each verb in 5? Remember that some noun forms are identical to the verb form.

Verb: accuse ➤ Noun: accusation
Verb: analyse ➤ Noun: analysis

7 SPEAKING Work with a partner. Ask and answer this question.

Would you like to do detective work? Why/Why not?

1 Look at these pictures. They illustrate three newspaper stories. Can you match the titles of the stories with the pictures? There is one title you do not need.

1 **POLICE! DON'T MOVE!**

2 The bank that's always open.

3 **ARREST THAT DETECTIVE!**

4 A thief? Or just thirsty?

2 Work with a partner. From the titles and pictures, what do you think happens in each story? Guess.

3 Read the stories. Which picture and title goes with each one?

POLICE FILE

A

Tommaso Bonardi, 78, and Vittorio Laudani, 70, are a pair of experienced thieves. Last weekend, they tried to steal from a luxury fashion shop in Rome.

They went into the shop in the middle of the night wearing smart suits. At 4 am they were putting clothes and accessories worth €100,000 into a bag when the police arrived. But the criminals didn't run away. They stood completely still and pretended to be part of the fashion display. The police looked for them but didn't see them. Then one of them moved. The police arrested them immediately, and not for the first time!

B

Police in Devon, UK, had a difficult case to investigate last week. A work of art disappeared at a literary festival. The work of art was a bottle of water.

It was special because the water came from melted Antarctic ice. An American artist called Wayne Hill brought back two litres of the special water and made a bottle for it. The work represented the problem of global warming. It had a value of over £42,000, so Hill wasn't very happy about its disappearance. Did an art thief take it? Or maybe somebody came across the bottle, thought it was rubbish and threw it in the bin. Or was somebody just very thirsty? The police looked into the case but no evidence turned up.

C

Banks use complicated systems to stop bank robbers. So what happened last weekend at a bank in Easingwold was very surprising.

It was Saturday lunchtime. British banks don't usually open on Saturday afternoon. Daniel and Alison Pettigrew were outside their local bank with Oliver, their 5-year-old son. Oliver disappeared for a minute. When he came back, he said: 'Dad, the bank's open.' Daniel didn't believe his son at first. But he found out it was true. The door was open! Nobody was inside, but they saw computers and other things, all unprotected. Daniel called 999 and waited for the police to arrive. The bank worked out that there was a problem with the door and sent somebody to lock it. They thanked Oliver for doing the right thing and opened an account for him.

4 Read the stories again and answer these questions.

1 How did Bonardi and Laudani try to escape the police?
2 Why didn't their plan work?
3 What was the work of art that disappeared at a literary festival in Devon?
4 What different theories could explain the disappearance of the work?
5 Why were the Pettigrews surprised the bank was open?
6 Who discovered the problem and what did they do about it?
7 How did the bank thank Oliver?

5 **⚙ CRITICAL THINKING**

Think! Then compare ideas with your class.

- How serious are the crimes in stories A and B? Why?

6 What do the underlined words in the text mean? Guess and then check in your dictionary.

7 SPEAKING What about *you*?

Which story do you prefer and why?

Grammar in context

Flipped classroom: watch the grammar presentation video.

Past simple

1a Look at these sentences. Which sentences are in the present simple and which are in the past simple?

a The police arrested them immediately.

b Did an art thief take it?

c Banks use complicated systems to stop bank robbers.

d The work of art was a bottle of water.

e They went into the shop in the middle of the night.

f British banks don't usually open on Saturday afternoon.

g The police didn't see them.

h Hill wasn't very happy.

1b In 1a, find a sentence with ...

1 a form of be in the past simple affirmative. _d_

2 a form of be in the past simple negative. _____

3 a regular verb in the past simple affirmative. _____

4 an irregular verb in the past simple affirmative. _____

5 a past simple question. _____

6 a verb in the past simple negative. _____

1c Complete the sentences with the past simple form of be, walk and go.

Affirmative: He (a) _was/walked/went_ there yesterday.

Negative: He (b) _____ there yesterday.

Question: (c) _____ he

(d) _____ there yesterday?

GRAMMAR REFERENCE ➤ PAGE 28

2a PRONUNCIATION **Look at the three lists below. How do we pronounce the -ed ending in each list?**

List A: finished   watched   liked   passed
List B: wanted   needed   painted   started
List C: stayed   arrived   discovered   planned

2b ▶ 10 **Listen, check and repeat.**

2c In which list is the -ed ending pronounced /id/? Which letters come just before -ed in the words in this list?

3 Work with a partner. Write an A to Z of irregular past simple forms with one verb for each letter. Omit any difficult letters. How many can you think of in five minutes?

A – ate, B – bought, C –

4 Complete the text with the past simple form of the verbs given.

In 2013, in New York, there (a) _____ (be) a terrible crime. Somebody (b) _____ (mug) a 16-year-old boy in the street and (c) _____ (steal) his smartphone. Then he (d) _____ (run) away. The boy (e) _____ (not know) the criminal but, soon after the mugging, he (f) _____ (get) a surprise. The mugger (g) _____ (not be) very clever. He (h) _____ (take) a photo of himself on the phone and accidentally (i) _____ (email) it to the boy! The boy (j) _____ (print) the photo and (k) _____ (go) to the police. The police (l) _____ (find) the criminal easily and (m) _____ (arrest) him. He (n) _____ (have) other stolen things at home, too, so the police (o) _____ (be) happy to catch him.

5 Complete these questions about the text in 4 with the past simple form of the verbs given.

1 Who _____ a criminal _____ (mug) in 2013 in New York?

2 What _____ the criminal _____ (steal)?

3 _____ the boy _____ (know) the criminal?

4 _____ (be) the criminal clever?

5 What _____ the criminal _____ (do)?

6 _____ the photo _____ (help) the police?

7 _____ (be) it difficult to find the criminal?

8 How _____ this story _____ (end)?

6 SPEAKING **Work with a partner. Take it in turns to ask and answer the questions in 5.**

7a SPEAKING **Work in pairs. Student A: look at the information below in 7b. Student B: turn to page 147. Prepare questions to ask your partner to find the missing information.**

(a) When was Sir Arthur Conan Doyle born?

7b SPEAKING **Interview your partner.**

Student A

Sir Arthur Conan Doyle was the creator of the world-famous detective, Sherlock Holmes. He was born in **(a)** .... in Edinburgh, Scotland.

Conan Doyle was a **(b)** .... He began writing stories when he was at university. When he began work he didn't have many patients. He started writing stories again.

Conan Doyle wrote his first Sherlock Holmes novel in 1886. The title was **(c)** .... The idea for Sherlock Holmes came from one of Conan Doyle's teachers at university. The teacher's name was **(d)** .... Apart from Sherlock Holmes, Conan Doyle created another interesting character, Sherlock's great friend, Doctor Watson.

Sherlock Holmes was always a very popular character. He appeared in over 50 short stories and **(e)** .... novels. Conan Doyle tried to kill the character in a story in 1893. But the public wanted more Sherlock Holmes stories and Conan Doyle started writing them again in 1903.

Conan Doyle died when he was **(f)** .... years old. But his famous character Sherlock Holmes is still very much alive. He continues to appear in **(g)** ....

Sherlock Holmes and Doctor Watson

Phrasal verbs connected with investigating and finding

1 **Find the phrasal verbs in the stories on page 19 and match them with the definitions below.**

> come across • find out • look for
> ~~look into~~ • turn up • work out

1 investigate *look into*

2 find by accident ....

3 solve a problem by considering the facts ....

4 try to find ....

5 discover ....

6 arrive or appear unexpectedly ....

2 **Make new sentences using the correct form of the phrasal verbs in 1.**

1 Detectives are trying to find the fraudster.

Detectives *are looking for the fraudster.*

2 The CIA began to investigate the case.

The CIA ....

3 They found the keys by accident in the garden.

They ....

4 The shoe appeared unexpectedly in the garden.

The shoe ....

5 Sherlock Holmes used logic to solve crimes.

Sherlock Homes ....

6 After their investigation, they soon discovered where the thief was.

After their investigation, they ....

3 **Work in a group. You have three minutes. How many sentences can you make with the words in the table? Your sentences must include the phrasal verbs in 1.**

I looked for the key.

I	looked found came worked	out for across	the key. the answer. the identity of the criminal.

Thinking about RIGHT & WRONG

LIFE SKILLS OBJECTIVES	KEY CONCEPTS
■ To consider what your values are. ■ To give advice to people in difficult situations. ■ To decide the right way to behave in a variety of situations.	**values [n]:** *Your values are the ideas that help you decide the way you live.* **lie [v, n]:** *Is he lying or telling the truth?* **beliefs [n]:** *People from different cultures sometimes have different beliefs.* **hurt [v]:** *When you use violence, you can hurt someone.* **stand up for [v]:** *You've got to stand up for what you believe in.*

1 SPEAKING **Look at these ideas for how to behave in your everyday life. How much do you agree with them? Write a percentage (20%, 50%, 100%) and then discuss with a partner.**

Back   **Values checklist**   **Edit**

1 Don't lie, always tell the truth. ☐
2 Respect other people's opinions and beliefs. ☐
3 Don't hurt people or animals. ☐
4 Don't steal. ☐
5 Don't damage other people's property. ☐
6 Stand up for what you think is right. ☐
7 Think about others, not just yourself. ☐

3 **Read the explanations in 2 again and answer these questions.**

1 What two things does the writer say about people having different opinions and beliefs?
2 What happens when people don't think about others?
3 What types of stealing does the writer mention?
4 What does the writer say about violence?
5 What is the problem with lying?
6 What does the writer say about public property?
7 What does the writer say about doing what other people want you to do?

2 READING **Read these short explanations for the values in 1. Match the explanations with the values.**

A ☐ We don't all think exactly the same way. That's normal with so many people in the world. The important thing is that everybody has the right to their own opinions and ideas. We all need to respect that right.

B ☐ Part of being human is looking after other people. When we only think about ourselves, the world becomes a cold and difficult place. When we take action, we need to think about the consequences for us and also for others.

C ☐ We can't just take what we want. How do you feel if somebody comes and takes your things? Copying another student's work and piracy are two other examples of the same thing - taking things that aren't yours.

D ☐ Physical violence is never a solution. Violence sometimes brings more violence in the end. When we hurt a person or an animal, we need to be prepared for negative consequences.

E ☐ When we don't tell the truth, we can make life difficult, especially for ourselves. When somebody finds out that we're lying, they lose confidence in us. They never know when to believe us. Sometimes even small lies can cause big problems.

F ☐ We need to remember that public property belongs to all of us. So we shouldn't damage it. After all, there's no reason for us to break or destroy things that other people can use and enjoy.

G ☐ You see somebody doing something that you think is bad. If you don't agree with that, do something about it. Never do things that you believe are wrong because somebody tells you to. It can be easy to go against what you think is right but there are usually negative consequences in the end.

4a Look at the photos. What can you see? What do you think happened?

a

b

4b LISTENING ▶ 11 James and Jessica talk to a friend on a video call about a problem they had recently. Watch or listen. Match the teenager to the photos. Which value in 1 does each teenager have a problem with?

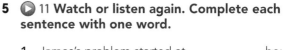

5 ▶ 11 **Watch or listen again. Complete each sentence with one word.**

1 James's problem started at .... house.

2 The clock was special to his ....

3 James said .... broke the clock.

4 James is worried because his mum and Oliver's mum are ....

5 Jessica and Kayla had a .... exam.

6 Jessica .... go out at the weekend.

7 Jessica didn't let Kayla copy because she didn't think it was .... and she was worried about what the .... might think.

8 Jessica now has problems with .... and her friends.

6a What do you think is good advice to give James and Jessica? Think and make notes.

6b Work in a group. Compare your ideas. Do you have similar opinions?

7 Work with a partner. Read about these two situations and choose the best answer.

1 You need money to buy your friend a birthday present. You find £20 on the classroom floor. Do you …
   a use the money today to buy the present?
   b keep the money but wait a few days to see if anybody asks for it?
   c give the money to the teacher to find out who it belongs to?
   d do something else? What?

2 A friend wants you to tell her mum that you were together on Saturday afternoon. You weren't. Do you …
   a agree to do it without asking any questions?
   b ask her to explain first and then you'll do it?
   c say no, you don't want to lie?
   d do something else? What?

LIFE TASK

You want to do the right thing.

Follow this plan:

1 *Think of three situations similar to the ones in 7. Write questions and suggestions using some of the values in 1.*

2 *Ask another group of students your questions. Make a note of their answers.*

3 *Work in your initial group again. Do you agree with the answers? Do you think people are doing the 'right thing' or not? Why?*

4 *Tell the class your conclusions.*

Listening

1 SPEAKING **Work with a partner. Invent a very short story connecting the four pictures.**

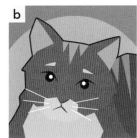

✔ **EXAM SUCCESS**

You are going to do a 'True/False/Not Mentioned' listening activity. What do you think is the first thing to do in this type of activity?

➤ EXAM SUCCESS page 144

2 LISTENING ▶ 12 **Listen to a boy telling his friend about something that happened to him last night. How are the pictures in 1 connected?**

3 LISTENING ▶ 12 **Listen again and decide if each statement is True (T), False (F) or if the information is Not Mentioned (NM).**

1 Daniel was watching a detective film on TV last night.   T / F / NM

2 Jim doesn't like watching detective programmes.   T / F / NM

3 Daniel was enjoying the programme he was watching.   T / F / NM

4 Daniel stopped watching because his parents called him.   T / F / NM

5 Daniel went to the kitchen to see what was happening.   T / F / NM

6 Daniel's new cat was responsible for the scene in the kitchen.   T / F / NM

7 Somebody was crying in the kitchen.   T / F / NM

8 Daniel's parents were really angry with him because of the cat's behaviour.   T / F / NM

4 Compare your answers with your partner.

Grammar in context

Past continuous

1a Look at sentences 1–4 and match them with the explanation of their uses in a–d.

1 Somebody was crying. ....

2 While I was watching the programme, I suddenly heard a loud noise. ....

3 I went towards the kitchen. ....

4 I studied in my room for an hour or two and then I had dinner. ....

a a completed action in the past.

b two completed actions in the past that happened one after the other.

c an activity in progress in the past.

d an activity in progress in the past interrupted by a sudden action.

1b Complete this rule.

We make the past continuous with the past simple of .... + verb -ing

GRAMMAR REFERENCE ➤ PAGE 28

2 What were these people doing yesterday at 6.30 pm? Write complete sentences.

1 Rachel and Kate/buy clothes.

2 Joe's dad/not make the dinner.

3 Kim/run in the park.

4 We/not watch TV.

5 We/do homework.

6 Becky/swim.

7 Sam and Beth/sit in the kitchen.

3 Write the questions and answers.

1 Rachel and Kate/swim?

....

2 Joe's dad/make the dinner?

....

3 What/Kim/do?

....

4 Becky/swim?

....

5 Where/Sam and Beth/sit?

....

4 Have you got good powers of observation and memory? Look at the scene for two minutes. Then work with a partner. Close your book and list all the things that were happening. The pair with most sentences wins.

5 SPEAKING Take it in turns. One of you closes the book and the other asks questions about the scene.

> What was the old man doing?

6 Write complete sentences to answer these questions about the story.

Mystery story

One afternoon a young man was sitting in a café drinking coffee.

a What else was he doing? *He was talking on his mobile phone.*

Suddenly an old man ran into the café and shouted the young man's name.

b What was the young man's name? ....

c What was the old man wearing? ....

d What was the old man carrying? ....

The young man didn't appear to be very happy to see the old man. He immediately started to look inside his bag.

e What was he looking for? ....

f What did he take out of his bag? ....

The old man ran quickly towards the young man.

g Then what did he do? ....

h What did the young man do and why? ....

i How did the story end? ....

Mystery story
One afternoon a young man was sitting in a café drinking coffee.

7 SPEAKING Read your complete story to your partner. Are your stories similar or different? Which story do you prefer?

> *One afternoon a young man was sitting in a café drinking coffee. He was talking on his mobile phone. His name was …*

Apologising

1 SPEAKING Work with a partner. Look at the pictures. Describe what you can see. How do you think the people feel?

a

b

c

2 SPEAKING Discuss these questions with your partner.

1 When was the last time you apologised to someone? Who did you apologise to and why?

2 When was the last time somebody apologised to you? Who apologised and why?

3 How easy or difficult do you find it to say that you're sorry?

3 LISTENING ▶ 13 **Listen to two dialogues. In each dialogue, why does the person apologise? Does the other person accept the apology or not?**

4 ▶ 13 **Listen again and complete the expressions.**

1 I'm ....

2 It .... matter.

3 It's .... (water).

4 .... me (get you a new bottle in the break).

5 I'll .... it up to you.

6 That's the .... time (I lend you anything).

7 I .... terrible.

5 **Where do the completed expressions go in the Speaking bank?**

> ### 💬 SPEAKING BANK
>
> **Useful expressions for apologies**
> ■ *Making apologies*
> I'm sorry.
>
> ....
> ....
>
> ....
>
> ■ *Responding to apologies*
> It's OK.
> Don't worry about it.
> Never mind.
>
> ....
> ....
>
> ....
> It's not that important.

6 **Work with a partner. Think of different situations where somebody needs to make an apology. Look at the examples and think of two more.**

1 You were going to go out with your friend on Saturday, but now you remember that you have to go somewhere with your family.

2 Your friend lent you their favourite DVD. Now you can't find it.

3 Your friend told you a secret. You told somebody else and your friend knows it.

4 ....

5 ....

PRACTICE MAKES PERFECT ▰▰▰▰▰▰▰

7a **Work with a partner. Choose one of the situations in 6. Create a dialogue for the situation. Use expressions from the Speaking bank.**

7b SPEAKING **Practise the dialogue. Act it out for the class.**

7c SPEAKING **Now choose another situation and create and practise the dialogue.**

A blog post

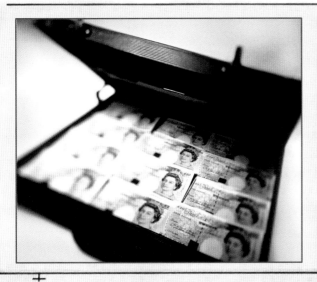

1 **SPEAKING** Work with a partner. Look at the photos above from a newspaper. What do you think happened?

2 Read a blog post from Tom. Were your ideas in 1 correct?

TOM'S WORLD

Posted on August 21, 2014

MY AMAZING DISCOVERY!

Did you see me in the newspapers yesterday?!

Yesterday evening I went out with my friend Max. We were going home when we came across a bag at the bus station. At first, we didn't know what to do. But then we decided to open it, to see who it belonged to. When we opened it, we couldn't believe it. It was full of money! There were also passports and plane tickets. We found out that there was £7,000 in there!

We went to the local police station but it was closed. Suddenly, we saw a police car. We decided to stop it as it was passing by. We explained the whole story. The police were a bit surprised, but very grateful. They contacted the owner. He was happy, too. In the end, he didn't give us a reward, but that doesn't matter because Max and I knew we did the right thing.

3 Look at the words and expressions in the Writing bank. Tick (✓) the ones which appear in the text.

✏ WRITING BANK

Useful words and expressions of sequence and time

- At first ✓
- First of all
- Then
- Next
- In the end
- Finally
- Suddenly
- A few minutes/hours/days later
- The next day

4 Imagine that you found something unusual last week. Make notes answering the questions.

1 When did you find it?
2 Where were you?
3 Who were you with?
4 What did you find?
5 Why was it unusual?
6 What did you do with the object?
7 What happened in the end?

PRACTICE MAKES PERFECT

5 Look at the task and write your blog post. Use your notes from 4 and the words and expressions in the Writing bank to help you.

Last week you found something unusual. Write a blog post about what you found. Tell them:

- what you found and where
- why the object was unusual
- what you did next and what happened in the end.

WRITING BANK ➤ PAGE 150

✓ EXAM SUCCESS

What are the criteria for getting a good mark in your English writing exams?

➤ EXAM SUCCESS page 144

Language checkpoint: Unit 2

Grammar reference

Past simple of to be

FORM	
Affirmative	I/He/She/It was here yesterday. You/We/They were here yesterday.
Negative	I/He/She/It wasn't (was not) there last week. You/We/They weren't (were not) there last week.
Question	Was I/he/she/it in this school last year? Were you/we/they in this school last year?
Short answers	Yes, I/he/she/it was. No, I/he/she/it wasn't. Yes, you/we/they were. No, you/we/they weren't.

Past simple of regular and irregular verbs

FORM	
Affirmative	I/You/He/She/It/We/They worked yesterday. I/You/He/She/It/We/They began yesterday.
Negative	I/You/He/She/It/We/They didn't (did not) work yesterday. I/You/He/She/It/We/They didn't (did not) begin yesterday.
Question	Did I/you/he/she/it/we/they work yesterday? Did I/you/he/she/it/we/they begin yesterday?
Short answers	Yes, I/you/he/she/it/we/they did. No, I/you/he/she/it/we/they didn't.

USE

We use the past simple to:

- describe finished actions or situations in the past.
  I went to Mexico last year.

- to say that one thing happened after another.
  When mum came home, we had dinner.

Past continuous

FORM	
Affirmative	I/He/She/It was working. You/We/They were working.
Negative	I/He/She/It wasn't (was not) playing. You/We/They weren't (were not) playing.
Question	Was I/he/she/it listening? Were you/we/they listening?
Short answers	Yes, I/he/she/it was. No, I/he/she/it wasn't. Yes, you/we/they were. No, you/we/they weren't.

USE

We use the past continuous to:

- talk about activities in progress at a moment in the past.
  At four o'clock this afternoon we were reading.

- describe scenes in a story or description.
  The old man was wearing a suit and he was singing an old song.

- talk about an activity in progress when another, shorter activity happened or interrupted it. It tells us that an action was in progress, but not that the activity was finished.
  I was watching the TV when somebody knocked at the door.

We often use *while* and *as* with the past continuous.

While/As I was watching him, he turned and looked at me.

Remember that some verbs are not usually used in the continuous (see page 16 for some examples of state verbs).

I had a green bike. not *I was having a green bike.*

Vocabulary

1 Crimes and criminals break into (v) • burglar (n pers) • burglary (n) • burgle (v) • copy (v) • damage (v) fraud (n) • fraudster (n pers) • mug (v) • mugger (n pers) • mugging (n) • piracy (n) • pirate (n pers) • rob (v) robber (n pers) • robbery (n) • shoplift (v) • shoplifter (n pers) • shoplifting (n) • steal (v) • theft (n) • thief (n pers) vandal (n pers) • vandalise (v) • vandalism (n) • violence (n)

2 Detective work accusation (n) • accuse (v) • analyse (v) • analysis (n) • arrest (v, n) • case (n) • charge (v, n) collect (v) • collection (n) • evidence (n) • investigate (v) • investigation (n) • proof (n) • prove (v) • question (v, n) suspect (n)

3 Phrasal verbs connected with investigating and finding come across • find out • look for • look into turn up • work out

4 Other words and phrases ➤ page 136

Grammar revision

Past simple
/ 8 points

1 Change these sentences and questions from present simple to past simple.

1 Richard and I are students at this school.

_____

2 What's the problem?

_____

3 We leave school at five o'clock.

_____

4 She catches the bus at that stop.

_____

5 What time do you finish work?

_____

6 She doesn't teach English.

_____

7 Running makes me tired.

_____

8 They've got a problem.

_____

Past continuous
/ 8 points

2 Complete the sentences and questions with the past continuous form of the verbs in the box.

cry • listen • read • sit • sleep • tidy • wait • write

1 At 9 pm last night I _____ a novel.

2 Which CD _____ you _____ to?

3 He _____ a letter, it was an email.

4 _____ you _____ at 2 am?

5 I _____ my room at 8.15 this morning.

6 They _____ for the bus, it was a taxi.

7 Which chair _____ you _____ in?

8 My baby brother _____ because he was very tired.

Past continuous and past simple
/ 8 points

3 Choose the correct alternative.

1 While I _travelled/was travelling_ to work, my phone suddenly _rang/was ringing_.

2 The boy _stole/was stealing_ the apple while nobody _looked/was looking_.

3 Craig _drove/was driving_ home when he _remembered/was remembering_ it was his mum's birthday.

4 Sam _broke/was breaking_ the window and then he _ran/was running_ away.

Vocabulary revision

CRIMES AND CRIMINALS
/ 6 points

1 Complete the sentences with some of the words.

burglary • burgle • mug • mugger • piracy pirate • steal • theft • thief • vandal

1 When you _____ someone, you attack them for money.

2 When you _____ from a person or a place, you take money or objects illegally.

3 _____ is a general word for somebody who takes other people's things or money.

4 _____ is entering a house to take things.

5 A _____ is someone who damages and destroys things for no reason.

6 Making illegal copies of DVDs is _____ and it's a crime.

DETECTIVE WORK
/ 4 points

2 Choose the correct alternative.

1 The man made an important _accuse/accusation_.

2 They searched but couldn't find any _proof/prove_.

3 We need to _analyse/analysis_ this evidence.

4 They _charged/questioned_ the people who saw the crime.

PHRASAL VERBS CONNECTED WITH INVESTIGATING AND FINDING
/ 6 points

3 Complete the sentences with prepositions.

1 I looked (a) _____ my keys but I couldn't find them. I hope they turn (b) _____. If you come (c) _____ them, could you tell me?

2 A detective is looking (d) _____ the case to work (e) _____ who the criminal is. It's urgent to find (f) _____ who did it.

Total: / 40 points

Unit 2   29

Reading

> **TIP FOR READING EXAMS**

In multiple-choice reading activities, remember …
If you aren't 100% sure of the correct answer, begin
by taking away any answers which you know aren't
correct.

> EXAM SUCCESS page 144

1   **Look at the picture. When do people usually call an emergency phone number like 911 or 999?**

2   **Read the text and write a title for it.**

....

3   **Read the questions. Are there any answers that you think are definitely not correct? Put X next to them.**

   1   The problem with emergency numbers is that

     a   people don't know what the number is in different countries. ....

     b   people don't always use the service responsibly. ....

     c   not every country has one. ....

   2   Rother McLennon called

     a   to order a sandwich. ....

     b   to give extra information about his order for a sandwich. ....

     c   to complain about his sandwich. ....

   3   The person who answered McLennon's call

     a   found it difficult to believe the call was serious. ....

     b   didn't understand the call. ....

     c   paid no attention to the call. ....

   4   One young boy

     a   made a successful call to 911. ....

     b   called 911 because he didn't have anything to do. ....

     c   rang 911 because of a personal problem. ....

   5   People need to know that calling 911 can

     a   waste a lot of money. ....

     b   stop the police from doing their job. ....

     c   make many people laugh. ....

4   **Now read the text again and choose the best answers in 3.**

I n most countries there is a special emergency telephone number to call the police. This number is 911 in the US but it can change from one country to the next. The only trouble is that some people do not have a very clear idea of what an emergency is.

Take the case of Rother McLennon from Connecticut in the US. In 2012, McLennon rang 911 because of a sandwich. In a local delicatessen, he ordered a sandwich with a lot of cheese and mayonnaise. When they gave him his sandwich, he wasn't happy with it. The police officer who answered the call could not believe her ears. At first, she thought the man was joking. Then she said, 'Don't buy the sandwich, then. Just leave.' But McLennon explained that he didn't want to do that because he wanted to be able to go back to the shop in the future. In the end, the police officer sent somebody to help.

Another woman once called 911 to tell the police that she wasn't happy because her local fast-food restaurant didn't have her favourite dish. One evening, a four-year-old boy was doing his maths homework. He was having a problem with one of the questions and so he called 911. The police officer helped him to answer the maths problem! One man had no job and no friends, so each day he invented a reason to call 911, to stop getting bored. Another woman was sitting in her car and couldn't find her keys to open the car door. She called 911. Of course, the police officer told the woman to try opening the car door manually. It worked.

At first these 911 calls seem to be funny, but really they aren't. Each call takes up the time of the police. They waste their time instead of being free to answer serious calls and to help people with real problems. That explains why the police can, in fact, arrest you for calling 911 without a good reason.

Listening

> **TIP FOR LISTENING EXAMS**

In True/False activities, remember …
Before you listen, read the questions. They can give you ideas about the topic of the text and the vocabulary you are going to hear.

➤ EXAM SUCCESS page 144

5 LISTENING ▶ 14 **You are going to listen to a programme about the British Secret Intelligence Service (SIS). Listen and decide if the statements are True (T) or False (F).**

1   The popular name for the SIS is MI5.   T / F
2   The SIS generally works outside the UK.   T / F
3   The director of the SIS is called M.   T / F
4   In real life, the SIS has a director of technology, like the character Q in the James Bond films.   T / F
5   The headquarters of the SIS are under the River Thames.   T / F
6   You can see inside the headquarters in a James Bond film.   T / F
7   The SIS has a secret nuclear bunker under its headquarters.   T / F

6 ▶ 14 **Correct the false sentences. Listen again if necessary.**

Speaking

> **TIP FOR SPEAKING EXAMS**

In information role-plays, remember …
Use basic question words like *Who? What? When? Where? How? Why?* to think of more questions to keep the conversation going.

➤ EXAM SUCCESS page 144

7 **Look at this situation and make a list of questions that you can ask.**

There is a new student from England in your school.

■   Ask them about their family and a member of their family who is special to them.
■   Find out information about their free-time activities.

Which member of your family is special to you? How often do you see this person? Why?

8 SPEAKING **Work with a partner and act out the role-play. When you finish, change roles.**

Writing

> **TIP FOR WRITING EXAMS**

In writing exams, remember …
It's important to know what the examiners want to see in your answer. Find out how many marks there are and what you need to do to get a good mark.

➤ EXAM SUCCESS page 144

9 **Write an informal email to an e-pal. Describe a good friend at school. Follow this paragraph plan and remember to use typical words and expressions in informal emails.**

Paragraph 1: Basic personal information about your friend (name, age, where they are from)
Paragraph 2: Information about your friend's family
Paragraph 3: Their hobbies
Paragraph 4: Their favourite subject(s) at school
Paragraph 5: Ask for a reply

'CAN DO' PROGRESS CHECK UNITS 1–2   CEF

1   **How well can you do these things in English now? Give yourself a mark from 1 to 4.**

> **1** = I can do it very well.
> **2** = I can do it quite well.
> **3** = I have some problems.
> **4** = I can't do it.

a   I can talk about routines and what's happening now using the present simple and present continuous.   ☐
b   I can ask for and give basic personal information.   ☐
c   I can make nouns using the suffixes *-ment, -ion, -ence*.   ☐
d   I can understand conversations about families and family life.   ☐
e   I can write a basic informal email about myself or somebody I know well.   ☐
f   I can talk about past events using the past simple and past continuous.   ☐
g   I can understand written and spoken texts about crimes and the police.   ☐
h   I can make and respond to apologies.   ☐
i   I can write a blog post about a past event.   ☐
j   I can explain events in the past using expressions of sequence and time.   ☐

2   **Now decide what you need to do to improve.**

1   Look again at my book/notes.
2   Do more practice exercises.
    ➤ WORKBOOK Units 1 and 2
3   Ask for help.
4   Other: ....

3 Universal language

Vocabulary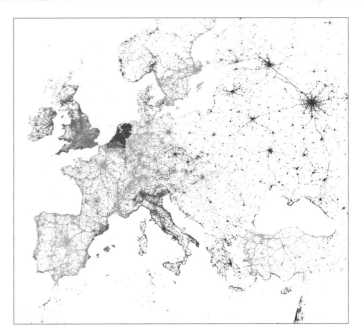

Countries, nationalities and languages

1 Work with a partner. How many countries can you name in this map of Europe?

2 Complete the table of countries around the world with the names for the nationality and the main language(s).

Country	Nationality	Main language
1 Argentina		
2 Austria		
3 Brazil		
4 Bulgaria		
5 Egypt		
6 Japan		
7 Mexico		
8 Poland		
9 Russia		
10 Switzerland		
11 Thailand		
12 Turkey		

3 ▶ 15 Listen and check your answers.

4a PRONUNCIATION Mark the main stress in each word in 2.

Argentina   Argentinian   Spanish

4b ▶ 16 Listen, check and repeat with the correct stress.

5 SPEAKING Work in a small group. Which of the countries in 2 would you like to visit and why?

I'd like to visit Brazil, because I love watching the Brazilian football teams.

Learning a language

6 Look at these words. They are all verbs. What nouns can you make from them?

memorise • practise • revise • ~~study~~ • translate

study – student, studies

7 Look at these words. Decide if we use *do* or *make* with each word. Can you think of other verbs we can use with the words?

English • an essay • an exam
an exercise • homework • a mistake

do English, study English, learn English …

8 SPEAKING Interview your partner with these questions about learning English. Are your answers similar?

1 How do you study English outside school?
2 How do you revise vocabulary before an exam?
3 How often do you translate from and into English?
4 How do you feel about writing in English?
5 How often do you do English homework?
6 When do you take English exams?
7 How do you feel when you make mistakes in English?
8 Do you prefer practising speaking, writing, reading, and listening or doing grammar and vocabulary exercises? Why?

How do you study English outside school?

I do my homework and I sometimes read books in English. I watch films in English, too.

1 Look at the map on page 32. The colours show the languages used on Twitter in different countries. Can you guess what language each colour is?

2 Read the text. How did they create the map on page 32? What other maps do they talk about in the text?

Diolch yn fawr   Σας ευχαριστώ   þakka þér   Gracias   Teşekkür ederim   AITÄH   Grazie

Tak   Dziękuję   Спасибо   Hvala   Dank je wel   Děkuji   Merci

Köszönöm   Dankie   Salamat   Obrigado   Danke

MAPPING
the world's
LANGUAGES

Nowadays there are a lot of different ways to communicate with others. One of these is Twitter. People send millions of Twitter messages, or tweets, every day. One Twitter user, Eric Fischer, likes making maps.

He had an idea. He used data collected from Twitter to show all the languages used in the tweets. He needed some time to collect the data. But once he had it all, it didn't take him long to create the maps. Now we have a collection of maps which show who uses which languages and where. The maps are fascinating and also very beautiful.

In North America there aren't many different colours. English, in grey, is the main language. There's also some pink for Spanish. And there is a little purple for French in Canada. The map of Europe, on the other hand, is like a rainbow. We can see that there are big blocks of colour for languages such as English, French, Spanish, German and Italian. But look closely and you can see there are a few areas where different languages co-exist, such as in Switzerland. But what you can see are only tweets. Some countries are almost invisible because there are only a few Twitter users there. And in some countries, like Russia, the tweets are mainly concentrated in big cities.

There are also detailed maps of specific cities. A map of London in 2012 showed that people were tweeting in 66 languages! 92.5% of all the tweets were in English. Next were Spanish, Turkish and Arabic. The experts were surprised to see that the seventh biggest language appeared to be Tagalog, from the Philippines. At first, they couldn't see any good explanations for this unusual result. They looked into it and found that many of the words were not really Tagalog. They were English terms such as 'hahahahaha', 'ahhhhhhh' and 'lololololol'. The professor in charge of the project said: 'Tagalog wasn't included in the final map but it seems like a fun language!'

3 Read the text again. Are these statements True (T), False (F) or is the information Not Mentioned (NM)?

1 Eric Fischer doesn't send Twitter messages.   T / F / NM
2 Eric Fischer just needed Twitter to make his maps.   T / F / NM
3 The map of North America shows that one language is dominant there.   T / F / NM
4 Fischer decided to make the map of Europe colourful.   T / F / NM
5 On the maps, it is difficult to see countries where people don't use Twitter.   T / F / NM
6 The Twitter map of London showed that 8.5% of tweets there are in Spanish.   T / F / NM
7 Tagalog is a very difficult language to learn.   T / F / NM
8 Tagalog wasn't really the seventh biggest language in London.   T / F / NM

4 ⚙ CRITICAL THINKING

Think! Then compare ideas with your class.
- What do you think a Twitter map of your town, city, region or country would show?

5 What do the underlined words in the text mean? Guess and then check in your dictionary.

6 SPEAKING What about *you*?
1 What do you think about social networks like Twitter and why?
2 How do you communicate with people and which language(s) do you use?

Grammar in context

Flipped classroom: watch the grammar presentation video.

some, any, much, many, a lot (of), a few, a little

1a Look at the words. Are they countable or uncountable?

1	country	3	money	5	area
2	time	4	colour	6	language

1b Look at these sentences. The words in bold all express quantity. Answer questions a–e about the words.

1 **Some** countries are almost invisible.
2 He needed **some** time to collect the data.
3 They couldn't see **any** good explanations for this.
4 Did Fischer make **any** money from the maps?
5 There aren't **many** different colours.
6 He didn't need **much** time.
7 There are **a lot of** different ways to communicate.
8 It doesn't take **a lot of** time.
9 There are **a few** areas where different languages co-exist.
10 They had **a little** knowledge of Tagalog, but not much.

a Which words do we use with uncountable nouns?

  some, any, much, a lot of, a little

b Which words do we use with plural, countable nouns?

c Which words usually appear in negative sentences and questions?

d Which words do we use to talk about large quantities?

e Which words do we use to talk about small quantities?

GRAMMAR REFERENCE ➤ PAGE 42

2a Complete the dialogue with *some* or *any*.

Jamie: Brad, I'm going shopping this afternoon. What do we need to get? Have we got

(a) .... bananas?

Brad: Yeah, we've got (b) .... bananas but we haven't got (c) .... tomatoes or potatoes.

Jamie: What about sugar? Have we got

(d) .... sugar?

Brad: No, we haven't got (e) .... sugar, but we have got (f) .... chocolate. And we need to get (g) .... biscuits too.

Jamie: OK. Listen. I think I'll get (h) .... burgers for dinner tonight.

Brad: Good idea. In that case, get (i) .... tomato ketchup, too. We haven't got

(j) .... at the moment. And get

(k) .... yoghurt for dessert!

2b All the words above in bold are types of food, but they all have something else in common. Can you guess what it is?

3 Choose the correct alternative.

Nobody knows exactly how (a) *much/many* words there are in total in the English language but there are (b) *a lot/a lot of*. One reason why there are so (c) *many/much* is that English takes words from (d) *much/many* other languages. Look at the words for food in exercise 2, for example. There may be (e) *a few/a little* words there that come from your language. (f) *Some/Any* of the words come from South America – potato, tomato and chocolate. There aren't (g) *any/many* words from Chinese in the English language, but ketchup is one of them. Originally, ketchup was the name for a type of fish sauce in China. Teenagers in the UK don't eat (h) *many/much* fish sauce but they do eat (i) *lots/lots of* burgers. There is (j) *some/any* confusion about the origin of the word burger, but (k) *a lot of/much* people think that it comes from German. Because the UK and France are neighbours it is normal that there are (l) *a few/a lot of* French words in English – hundreds in fact. Biscuit is just one example. On the other hand, (m) *a lot of/ many* fruit travels a long way to get to the UK. That explains why the word banana comes from an African language. There are also (n) *a few/a little* words from Turkish, like yoghurt. And, finally, if you ask for (o) *a few/a little* sugar in your coffee, you're using two Arabic words. Just by being in an English kitchen you can travel to (p) *much/many* countries!

4 Work with a partner. Complete these sentences about your language. Use the words in the box for ideas. You may complete each sentence with two or three different ideas.

> English/French/German/Russian words
> irregular past forms • phrasal verbs • prefixes
> prepositions • present tenses • words beginning with Z
> words with more than 12 letters

1 There are some *French words and some German words.*

2 There are a lot of ....

3 There aren't any ....

4 There aren't many ....

5 There are a few ....

5a Work individually. Look at the photos and choose a country. Make notes about things that there are or aren't in this country. Use the ideas in the box.

> animals • bicycles • food • fruit
> modern/old buildings • monuments • mountains
> offices • people • snow • tourism • trees • water

Japan

Brazil

Switzerland

Egypt

5b SPEAKING Work in pairs. You need to discover your partner's country by asking questions with *any, much, many, a few, a little, a lot (of)*. Your partner can only answer 'Yes' or 'No'.

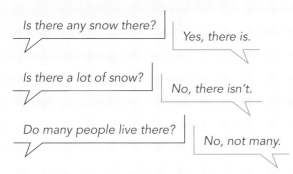

Is there any snow there? / Yes, there is.
Is there a lot of snow? / No, there isn't.
Do many people live there? / No, not many.

5c SPEAKING Now choose different countries not in the photos and repeat.

Negative prefixes *un-, in-, im-, ir-, il-*

1 Look at the words in the box. What do they have in common? What is the opposite of each word?

> illegal • impossible • incorrect
> informal • invisible • irregular
> unhappy • unusual

2 Choose the correct alternative.

1 Many common English verbs, such as *go, do* and *make*, have *a regular/ an irregular* past form.

2 People aren't usually *happy/unhappy* when somebody reads their private messages.

3 'A books' is *correct/incorrect* English.

4 You couldn't see the message. It was *visible/invisible*.

5 'Dear Sir or Madam' is a *formal/ informal* expression.

6 It is *legal/illegal* to steal data.

7 It is *possible/impossible* to read hundreds of messages in just two minutes.

3a PRONUNCIATION 17 Listen to the words in 1. Underline the syllable we stress in each word. Do we stress the prefix in each word?

3b 17 Listen again and repeat the words with the correct stress.

4a Think of an example of something (for example, a word or a situation) for each word in 1.

4b SPEAKING Work with a partner. Say one of your words or situations. Can your partner guess the word?

Climbing Everest in a day.

Impossible.

Public SPEAKING)))

LIFE SKILLS OBJECTIVES	KEY CONCEPTS
■ To consider the importance of body language. ■ To learn useful tips for public speaking. ■ To practise giving a talk to the class.	**gesture [n]:** *He made a gesture with his hand to tell me to stop.* **confident [adj], confidence [n]:** *She was confident about the exam because she studied hard for it.* **(in)secure [adj]:** *I feel secure when I'm speaking in front of my friends.* **(non-)verbal [adj]:** *Animals use non-verbal language because they don't use words.* **audience [n]:** *There were 200 people in the audience for the school concert.* **sincerity [n]:** *An honest way of behaving which shows you really mean what you say.*

1
2
3

1a Work with a partner. Look at the photos. From this person's 'body language', decide if you think the person is:

A secure, confident and in control

B insecure and not very confident

1b Turn to page 147 for an expert's answers.

1c Do you agree with the expert's opinions? Why/Why not? Is any of the body language in the pictures above impolite in your country?

2 READING **Read the text and choose the best title.**

1 Without words, there's no communication

2 Learning to communicate without words

3 Body language – it's the same all over the world

3 Read the text again and answer these questions.

1 Why can non-verbal communication cause problems?

2 What can we learn by doing the TV experiment mentioned in the text?

3 Why do people sometimes put their hand in front of their mouth in a conversation?

4 Is it good or bad to look at somebody directly in the eyes? Why?

5 Why does the writer mention Bulgarians?

6 Is it good or bad to stand very close to the person you are speaking to?

7 In what way is body language similar to verbal language?

WHAT *is* more important – WHAT YOU SAY *or* HOW YOU SAY IT?

Some experts say that up to 70% of decisions made at interviews are based on non-verbal factors. We can communicate a lot just with our body, our face and our gestures. The problem is that we often do this without thinking or realising. Just by the way that we sit, stand or walk we can appear insecure, confident or sometimes overconfident. Other people form opinions about us before we open our mouths.

Do a little experiment. The next time you watch TV, turn down the volume. Watch how people move their arms and hands. Look at their faces and their eyes. Now try to imagine what they are saying and how they feel and turn the volume back up. It's incredible how much we can understand without words.

Look around the room right now. Are people sitting up straight? That probably means they are paying attention. Is anybody folding their arms? That's usually a sign that they are being defensive. Is anybody touching their hair? Maybe they're nervous. When somebody speaks, see if they cover their mouth. If they do, perhaps they're lying. On the other hand, when somebody looks straight into your eyes when they speak to you, it's generally a sign of sincerity and confidence.

There can be problems with body language though. Gestures do not mean the same thing in every country. Even gestures for yes and no can sometimes be different. Bulgarians shake their heads from side to side to mean yes, and they nod up and down to say no. Also, what people believe is polite or impolite can change. Sitting with your hands behind your head is impolite in some countries but not in others. And in some countries it is normal to stand very close to the person you are speaking to. In others, people sometimes feel very uncomfortable when the person speaking to them is very close to them or touching them.

Body language doesn't have grammar or vocabulary, but there are still things we can learn and practise if we want to send the right message!

---

4 Work with a partner. Imagine you are going to speak to a group of people. What do you think is good body language in this situation?

5 LISTENING ▶ 18 Watch the video or listen to two students giving advice about how to speak in public. Do they mention any of your ideas in 4?

6 ▶ 18 Complete the advice with one word in each space. Listen again if necessary.

ADVICE FOR SPEAKING IN PUBLIC

1 .... up straight.
2 Use your .... – but not too much!
3 Look .... at the audience.
4 .... speak with a very loud or soft voice.
5 Speak fluently, without .... frequently.
6 Intonation is when your voice goes up or down and it keeps people ....
7 Always .... your talk before you begin.

7 What do you think of the advice in 6? Why?

LIFE TASK

You want to speak in public.

Follow this plan:

1 Choose one of these statements. Decide if you agree or disagree with the statement and make notes with your ideas.

  a It is essential to learn English in today's world.

  b Films and TV series are always best in the original version.

  c It's bad for our language when people start using English words.

  d Chinese is the language of the future.

  e The whole world should speak just one language.

2 Prepare a one- to two-minute talk with your notes in 1. Decide the best order for your different points and ideas.

3 Give your talk to the class or a group of students. Remember to follow the advice in 6.

4 When you all finish, give each other feedback. Which advice in 6 did you follow? What can you do better next time?

Listening

Grammar in context

Relative pronouns

1a Look at these sentences.

1 Mexico and Argentina are two countries **where** I do a lot of business.

2 Zamenhof was the man **who** created Esperanto.

3 It was a TV series **which** made me want to learn Klingon.

4 He's the character (**that**) I like the most.

5 That was **when** I decided to start learning Japanese.

6 They're comics **that** come from Japan.

7 I don't know **whose** idea it was.

Which words in **bold** refer to:

a people? ......*who*...... and ....

b things? .... and ....

c possessions? ....

d places? ....

e times? ....

1b Look at sentences 4 and 6 in 1a and choose the correct alternative.

We *can/cannot* omit who, which or that when a noun or pronoun comes immediately after.

> GRAMMAR REFERENCE ➤ PAGE 42

1 **SPEAKING** Work with a partner. Look at the five different languages below. What, if anything, do you know about each one? Do you think they are easy or difficult to learn? Why?

a Spanish   c French   e Klingon

b Esperanto   d Japanese

2 **LISTENING** ▶ 19 Listen to four speakers. Match each speaker to the language in 1 that they are learning now. There is one language you don't need.

Speaker 1 ....   Speaker 3 ....

Speaker 2 ....   Speaker 4 ....

3 ▶ 19 Listen again and match the speakers and the correct information. There are two pieces of information for each speaker.

A was not very successful with the first foreign language they learned.

B is learning a language because they like the idea behind the language.

C wants to learn a language to understand more about the people who speak it.

D is learning a language because it helps them professionally.

E started learning a language because of one special person.

F tells people they meet interesting facts about the language they are learning.

G was interested in a language from a TV programme before they started learning a real language.

H knows three or more languages.

Speaker 1 ....   Speaker 3 ....

Speaker 2 ....   Speaker 4 ....

4 **SPEAKING** What about *you*?

Choose one of the languages to learn. Give reasons.

2 **Look at the relative pronouns in these sentences. In which sentences can you omit the relative pronoun?**

1 *The Big Bang Theory* was the series **which** made him famous.

2 That's the language **that** I want to learn.

3 English is a language **which** millions of people speak.

4 A linguist is a person **who** studies and speaks a lot of languages.

Jim Parsons from *The Big Bang Theory*

5 He is the teacher **who** taught me French.

6 She's the person **that** helped me to speak Italian.

7 The first person **who** I met at the hotel was Spanish.

8 She never forgot the people **who** helped her to learn English.

3 Match the sentence halves using appropriate relative pronouns.

Quebec is a part of Canada where they speak French.

1 ~~Quebec is a part of Canada~~
2 Javier Bardem is a Spanish actor
3 Summer is a time
4 JRR Tolkien was the writer
5 Latin was the language
6 Sushi, manga and bento are words
7 Captain Kirk and Mr Spock are characters

a a lot of people go to the UK to study English.
b makes films in English in the US.
c adventures appear in the *Star Trek* films.
d ~~they speak French.~~
e books became a series of very popular films.
f come from Japanese.
g they spoke in Ancient Rome.

4a SPEAKING Choose six words from the Vocabulary sections in Units 1–3. Write definitions of the words using *who, that, which, where, when, whose*.

4b Read your definitions to your partner. Can they identify the words?

> It's a person who attacks you to take money or objects from you.

> A mugger.

> It's the stage of life when you're a child.

> Childhood.

5 Complete these sentences with true information about you.

1 .... is a place where I'm usually happy.
2 .... is an object which is really important to me.
3 .... was a year when something special happened to me.
4 .... is a person who is special to me.
5 .... is a place where I want to go one day.
6 .... is a language that I want to learn.
7 .... is a film that I love.

6 SPEAKING Work with a partner. Compare your sentences in 5 and discuss your answers.

> Home is a place where I'm usually happy.

> Me too. But I wrote 'the swimming pool'. I go swimming every weekend. I love it.

✔ **EXAM SUCCESS**

You are going to do a multiple-choice cloze activity. You have a text with gaps. You must complete each gap with one of three or four words that they give you. Why is it a good idea to read the complete text first, without thinking about the gaps?

➤ EXAM SUCCESS page 144

7 Read about Emilia Clarke. Choose the best answer (A, B, C or D) to complete the text.

Emilia Clarke

Actors have a difficult job. One difficult thing (1) .... they need to do is learn all their words. But imagine how difficult it is when they need to learn words in (2) .... language which doesn't really exist! Emilia Clarke is a British actress (3) .... speaks not one but two fictional languages in the TV series *Game of Thrones*. One of the languages is called Valyrian (4) .... the other is Dothraki. David Peterson is the person who invented all the languages in the series. Peterson went to the University of California, San Diego. That was (5) .... he studied a master's in linguistics. For *Game of Thrones*, he created a (6) .... of words for each language. His wife Erin helped him to create at least one word. She was the person (7) .... name he used to create the adjective for *kind* or *good* in Dothraki. It must be really hard for Emilia (8) .... she needs to film in Dothraki. But there are a (9) .... words that she doesn't need to learn in Dothraki. One of them is 'Thank you'. The Dothraki people are quite aggressive and never use it!

1 **A** that   **B** who   **C** whose   **D** when
2 **A** –   **B** a   **C** the   **D** some
3 **A** –   **B** which   **C** who   **D** whose
4 **A** and   **B** but   **C** because   **D** that
5 **A** that   **B** what   **C** where   **D** which
6 **A** lot   **B** lots   **C** many   **D** few
7 **A** that   **B** which   **C** who   **D** whose
8 **A** that   **B** what   **C** when   **D** which
9 **A** few   **B** little   **C** lot   **D** many

Asking for information

CARDIFF ENGLISH CENTRE:
LEARN ENGLISH IN WALES

As a small school, we can give students the personal care and attention they need. Learn English and have fun, too! Why not contact us to find out more?

1 SPEAKING **Work with a partner. Look at this advert for a school that organises summer courses for students of English. Answer these questions.**

1 Do you think this is a good place to learn English in the summer? Why/Why not?

2 You want to do a summer course to practise English. What factors are important in deciding where to study? Make a list.

2 LISTENING ⏵ 20 **Listen to a student asking for information about the Cardiff English Centre and write the information. Does the student ask about any of the factors you thought of in 1? Which ones?**

Course begins:
Course lasts:
Price:
Other activities:

3 Look at the useful expressions in the Speaking bank. Read the dialogue in 4 and tick (✓) the expressions which appear in it.

💬 SPEAKING BANK

Useful expressions for checking understanding

- Sorry, did you say …?
- Could you repeat that?
- Pardon?
- I'm not sure I understood.

4 Complete the dialogue with the correct information.

Receptionist: Good morning. This is the **(a)** .... English Centre. How can I help you?

Student: Good morning. I'd like some information about your summer courses.

Receptionist: Yes, of course. We have a course for students aged between 14 and 17. It begins on **(b)** ....

Student: Sorry, did you say **(c)** ....?

Receptionist: Yes, that's right. The course lasts **(d)** ....

Student: Do you organise accommodation?

Receptionist: **(e)** ...., we **(f)** ....

Student: How much is the course?

Receptionist: The price of a **(g)** .... course is **(h)** ....

Student: Could you repeat that?

Receptionist: Yes, I said the price is **(i)** ....

Student: Does the price include other activities?

Receptionist: Yes, it does.

Student: What other activities are there?

Receptionist: There are **(j)** ...., **(k)** ...., and sports activities, including **(l)** ....

Student: Oh, that sounds interesting. Can you send me a registration form?

Receptionist: Yes, of course. Can you give me your name and address?

Student: Yes, it's …

5 SPEAKING **Practise the dialogue in 4 with your partner.**

PRACTICE MAKES PERFECT

6a SPEAKING **Work with a partner. Do this role-play using the questions in 4 and the Speaking bank to help you.**

You want to find out the following information about summer courses at a language school:
- the starting date for the course
- the length of the course
- if accommodation is organised or not
- the price
- other activities on the course

Student A: You are the receptionist at the Sydney English Centre. Look at page 147.

Student B: You want information about the Sydney English Centre.

6b Now change roles.

Student B: You are the receptionist at the San Francisco English Centre. Look at page 147.

Student A: You want information about the San Francisco English Centre.

✔ EXAM SUCCESS

What do you need to do to get a good mark in a speaking exam?

➤ EXAM SUCCESS page 144

Developing writing

A language biography

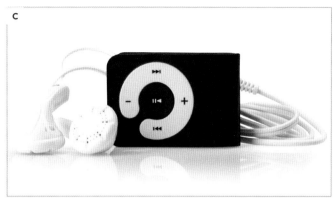

1 SPEAKING **Work with a partner. Look at the pictures. How can each one help you to learn English?**

2 **A language biography is a text where you describe your experiences of learning a different language. Read this language biography written by a student of English. What similarities are there between her experiences and yours?**

We both started learning English at primary school.

My name is Celia Rojas and I'm 16 years old. I'm Mexican and my mother-tongue is Spanish. Apart from Spanish, I can speak English. I started learning English when I was at primary school. I was five years old. Primary school was where we listened to, and sang, a lot of songs in English. We also played games and read some stories. We didn't study a lot of grammar in primary school but we learned a lot of vocabulary and we practised speaking. At the moment I'm studying English at secondary school. We study a lot of grammar and vocabulary, and we do a little speaking. We study vocabulary using an interactive wordlist. From time to time we do vocabulary tests. We don't do many translations in lessons, but we do lots of grammar exercises, sometimes on the computer. Outside school I don't really speak much English. For homework, we often read special English readers which our teacher gives us. When we finish them, we usually write summaries. I listen to a lot of English because I love English and American pop music and I also watch films in English, like The Hunger Games. That's my favourite. When I was thirteen I went to Canterbury to do a summer course. When I was there I met some great people. I'd like to go somewhere else in the UK, to London for example. I like learning English by doing activities and games in pairs. I make a few mistakes when I speak English, but I write the corrections down and revise them from time to time.

3 **The text in 2 is not divided into paragraphs. Read it again and divide it into five paragraphs. Use the plan below to help you. When you finish, read the information in the Writing bank.**

Paragraph 1: Basic personal information

Paragraph 2: Language-learning experiences at primary school

Paragraph 3: Language-learning experiences at secondary school

Paragraph 4: Language-learning experiences outside school, including trips

Paragraph 5: How you prefer to learn a language

4 **Make notes for the paragraphs in 3 with information about yourself and your experiences of learning English.**

✏ WRITING BANK

Paragraphs

We use paragraphs to group similar ideas and information together and express them more clearly. When you write a text in English, brainstorm your ideas and then group those ideas into logical paragraphs.

WRITING BANK ➤ PAGE 150

---

5 PRACTICE MAKES PERFECT **Write your own language biography using your notes in 4. Organise your information into five clear paragraphs.**

Language checkpoint: Unit 3

Grammar reference

Countable and uncountable nouns

Book, mistake, shop, euro are countable nouns. There is a singular and plural form.
Milk, money and bread are uncountable nouns. There is no plural form.
Many nouns can be both countable and uncountable. It depends on the context.
Coffee is bad for you. (uncountable = in general)
Bring me two coffees. (countable = two cups of coffee)
I haven't got much time. (uncountable = in general)
I went there three times. (countable = on three occasions)

We can often make uncountable nouns countable by adding a piece of.
advice, furniture, information (uncountable)
a piece of advice, a piece of furniture, a piece of information (countable)

some, any, much, many, a lot (of), a few, a little

USE

- We use some with uncountable nouns and with plural, countable nouns, in affirmative sentences.
  I've got some books. We've got some free time.
- We use any with uncountable nouns and with plural countable nouns, in negative sentences and questions.
  I haven't got any money.
  He hasn't got any friends.
  Have you got any free time?
  Are there any books?
- We use much, many, a lot (of) to talk about big quantities.
- We often use much in negative sentences and questions, with uncountable nouns.
  I haven't got much time.
  Have you got much water?
- We often use many in negative sentences and questions, with plural, countable nouns.
  I haven't got many books.
  Have you got many books?

- We use a lot of in affirmative and negative sentences and in questions, with countable and uncountable nouns.
  I've got/I haven't got a lot of time/books.
  Have you got a lot of time/ books?
- We use of when a lot comes before a noun. But when there is no noun after a lot we do not use of.
  Have you got any water? Yes, I've got a lot.
  Are there any dictionaries? Yes, there are a lot.
  A lot of and lots of are the same.
  I've got a lot of time. = I've got lots of time.
- We use a few and a little to talk about small quantities.
- We use a few with plural, countable nouns.
  There are only a few problems.
- We use a little with uncountable nouns.
  We've only got a little time.

Relative pronouns

USE

- We use relative pronouns to give information about the person, thing, place or time in the first half of the sentence.
  JRR Tolkien is the person who/that wrote The Hobbit.
  That's the book which/that he translated.
  That's the actor whose film I saw yesterday.

- We use who and that for people, which and that for things, whose for possessions, where for places, and when for times.
- We can omit who, which, or that when a noun or pronoun comes immediately after.
  That's the film that I saw. = That's the film I saw.
  BUT
  That's the film that was popular.

Vocabulary

1 Countries, nationalities, languages   Countries: Argentina • Austria • Brazil • Bulgaria • Egypt • Japan • Mexico • Poland • Russia • Switzerland • Thailand • Turkey **Nationalities**: Argentinian • Austrian • Brazilian • Bulgarian • Egyptian • Japanese • Mexican • Polish • Russian • Swiss • Thai • Turkish
Languages: Arabic • Bulgarian • German • Japanese • Polish • Portuguese • Russian • Spanish • Thai • Turkish

2 Learning a language   do an exercise • do homework • do/study English • do/take an exam • do/write an essay • make a mistake • memorise • memorisation • practice (n) • practise (v) • revise • revision • student • study • translate • translation

3 Negative prefixes il-, in-, im-, ir-, un-   illegal • incorrect • impossible • informal • irregular • invisible • unhappy • unusual

4 Other words and phrases ➤ page 138

Grammar revision

some, any, much, many, a lot (of), a few, a little — / 8 points

1 Complete the sentences with some, any, much, many, a lot (of), a few, a little.

1 I haven't got many magazines, only ....

2 We haven't got .... information about this country – nothing at all.

3 There was only .... milk in the fridge.

4 I haven't got .... money, just five euros.

5 Were there .... people at the concert?

6 We haven't got .... time before the train leaves, only five minutes.

7 He gave me .... good advice.

8 There are only .... people in the library.

Relative pronouns — / 8 points

2 Join the two sentences to make one sentence. Use who, which, that, whose, where, when.

Claudia is a linguist. She teaches German.

Claudia is a linguist who teaches German.

1 David Silva is a football player. He speaks Spanish.

....

2 The park is a beautiful place. You can go there at the weekend.

....

3 Last year was a special year. A lot of important things happened that year.

....

4 That's the teacher. Her classes are brilliant.

....

5 This is a great book. They want to translate it into English.

....

6 Piraha is an unusual language. Only around 400 people speak it.

....

7 George R.R. Martin is an American author. He writes fantasy novels.

....

8 We go to the cinema on Wednesdays. There's a special price on Wednesdays.

....

Vocabulary revision

LEARNING A LANGUAGE — / 8 points

1 Complete the sentences with the words in the box. Use one word twice.

> do • exercise • make • practice
> practise • revision • translation

1 Yesterday we read an English .... of a Russian poem.

2 Before the exam, he did some ....

3 You need to .... to speak English well.

4 Anybody can .... a mistake.

5 Yesterday's exam was just a .... , it wasn't the real one.

6 Did you .... the exercises yesterday?

7 This is the fourth .... on this page.

8 At our school we .... German.

COUNTRIES, NATIONALITIES AND LANGUAGES — / 8 points

2 Complete the sentences with the correct country, nationality or language.

1 Thai people are from ....

2 In Brazil they speak ....

3 People from Turkey are ....

4 Austrians speak ....

5 .... people are from Poland.

6 People from Argentina are ....

7 People from Egypt speak ....

8 People from Egypt are ....

NEGATIVE PREFIXES UN-, IN-, IM-, IR-, IL- — / 8 points

3 Complete the words.

1 sad = un ....

2 wrong = in ....

3 you can't do it = im ....

4 relaxed and friendly = in ....

5 not follow the usual rules = ir ....

6 criminal = il ....

7 strange = un ....

8 you can't see it = in ....

Total: .... / 40 points

Vocabulary

Parts of the body

1a Work with a partner. Look at the picture and point to the parts of the body.

> arm • ear • face • finger • foot • hand • head
> leg • mouth • neck • nose • stomach • toe

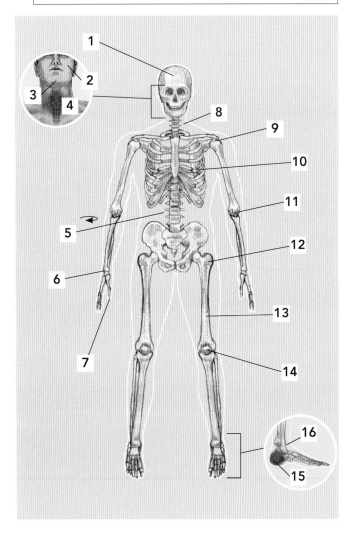

1b Match these words with numbers 1–16.

> ankle • back • cheek • chest • chin • elbow
> forehead • heel • hip • knee • shoulder
> thigh • thumb • throat • wrist • neck

2 ▶ **21 Listen, check and repeat.**

Health problems and illnesses

3 Work with a partner. Complete each phrase with three parts of the body.

1 I've got a broken ..../................................/
....

2 Have you got ..../................................/
.... ache ?

3 My ..../................................/................................ hurts .

4 He injured his ..../................................/
....

4 Complete the texts with the correct form of the words in the box. Use a dictionary if necessary.

> cough • flu • pain • sore • temperature • virus

Karen isn't very well at the moment. She's got a very bad cold, or perhaps it's **(a)** .... She **(b)** .... all the time and so now she has a **(c)** .... throat.

Pete has a very high **(d)** ...., 39.5°C. He's got **(e)** .... in his arms and legs. Perhaps it's a **(f)** .... because a lot of people are ill at school at the moment.

5 LISTENING ▶ **22 Listen to four people. What health problem does each one have?**

Speaker 1 ....   Speaker 2 ....

Speaker 3 ....   Speaker 4 ....

6 SPEAKING **Work with a partner. Discuss the questions.**

1 Do you catch colds easily? What do you do to stop them?

2 Do you ever injure yourself doing sports or other activities? Which sports are the most dangerous?

1 Work with a partner. Look at the titles and photos that go with the articles from a health magazine below. Predict what each article is about.

GOOD HEALTH

January Edition

TEEN HEALTH TIPS

A ANKLES NEED RICE!

Right now there are outdoor ice-rinks almost everywhere in the UK. But many people have never been ice-skating before. That's why hospitals and health centres are preparing for an <u>increase</u> in ankle and wrist injuries. Here's a simple first-aid tip if your injury is not very serious. It's called the RICE method. R is for rest, I for ice, C for compression and E for elevation. So, when you hurt your ankle, for example, stop moving on it and rest it. Put ice on it – not more than 15 minutes and never in direct contact with your <u>skin</u>. Put a <u>bandage</u> on it and keep it <u>tight</u> (not too tight!). And keep your ankle up, on a cushion, for example. But remember, when it's really painful and you think the accident is serious, always see a doctor!

B NO FUN IN THE SUN

Have you ever tried to get a suntan? Be very careful. Doctors say that skin cancer is increasing because of our <u>obsession</u> with the sun. It is now the most common cancer for people between 15 and 34. According to a recent survey of 16- to 24-year-olds, over 70% of them want a suntan when they go on holiday. But the doctors' advice is clear. Don't go out in the sun between 11 am and 3 pm and always wear a T-shirt, hat and sunglasses. And never use sunbeds! They are incredibly dangerous, which is why now in the UK they have made it illegal for under-18s to use them.

C LETTER OF THE WEEK

HOT SOUP FOR COLDS

Answered by Dr Lucy Smith

Dear Lucy,
I've had a bad cold for over a week. I'm taking medicine but it doesn't do anything. My mum says that chicken soup can help me. Is she mad?
Sarah Johnson

Dr Lucy Smith answers: *Your mother's cure for a cold is what we call an 'old wives' <u>remedy</u>'. A lot of people think that it's a mad idea with no scientific basis. But a new study has discovered that many of these 'old wives' remedies' do work. And scientists have found out that chicken soup is a great cure for a cold. All kinds of hot soup can help to <u>get rid of</u> a sore throat. And hot soup also helps to kill viruses quickly. So <u>relax</u>, your mum isn't mad.*

✔ **EXAM SUCCESS**

You are going to do a matching activity for this reading text. In this type of activity, you say which text or part of a text contains a specific piece of information. What do you think is a good way to do this exercise?

➤ EXAM SUCCESS page 144

3 ⚙ **CRITICAL THINKING**

Think! Then compare ideas with your class.

- Why do you think some young people have an obsession with suntans?

2 Which article …

1 talks about a traditional cure for an illness? ....

2 talks about a problem caused by insufficient experience? ....

3 mentions a problem that the law is trying to help with? ....

4 uses a simple word to help people remember their advice? ....

5 gives information to help one person in particular? ....

6 talks about a problem caused by people wanting to enjoy good weather? ....

7 tells you to speak to an expert when there is a real problem? ....

8 mentions a recent discovery in the world of medicine? ....

4 What do the <u>underlined</u> words in the text mean? Guess and then check in your dictionary.

5 SPEAKING **What about *you*?**

1 Do you think the RICE method is useful? Why/Why not?

2 What do you think about the advice in B?

3 Do you know any other traditional remedies like in C? Which?

Present perfect with ever and never

1a Look at these sentences and match them with the explanation of their uses in a–c.

1 **Have** you ever **tried** to get a suntan?
2 **I've had** a bad cold for a week.
3 They **have made** it illegal for under-18s to use sunbeds and now they can't use them.

a an experience or experiences which happened at an unspecified moment in the past.
b a past action which has a result in the present.
c a situation that started in the past and continues to the present.

1b Complete the rule.

We make the present perfect with the present simple of have + the
.... of the main verb.

1c Complete the sentences with the present perfect form of see and visit.

Affirmative: He .... the doctor.

Negative: He .... the doctor.

Question form: .... he .... the doctor?

1d Look at these sentences and choose the correct alternative.

1 Have you *ever/never* tried to get a suntan?
2 Many people in the UK have *ever/never* been ice-skating.

1e Choose the correct alternative.

1 *Ever/never* means at any time in your life.
2 *Ever/never* means at no time in your life.
3 *Ever* and *never* go just *after/ before* the past participle.

GRAMMAR REFERENCE ▶ PAGE 54

2 Complete the sentences with the present perfect form of the verbs given.

1 I *have decided* .... (decide) to study medicine.
2 My friend .... (meet) Dr Lucy Smith.
3 We .... (study) the history of medicine in biology.
4 I .... (not have) any bad accidents.
5 .... your dad .... (work) in a hospital?
6 My sister .... (become) a nurse.

3 Put *ever* or *never* in the correct place in these sentences and questions.

1 Have you had hot soup to stop a cold?

2 I've felt sick in a car.

3 She's taken antibiotics.

4 Has your dad helped anyone in an accident?

5 Sam and I have written a story about doctors.

6 Have you done first aid?

4 Write questions with *ever* to ask your partner.

catch a cold? ➤ *Have you ever caught a cold?*

1 stay in bed because of flu?

2 have a very high temperature?

3 sleep in a hospital?

4 make soup?

5 take medicine that tastes really bad?

6 visit a friend in hospital?

7 break your arm?

8 watch a hospital drama on TV?

5a SPEAKING Work with a partner. Ask and answer the questions in 4.

5b SPEAKING When you finish, tell a different student about your partner.

Adam has never stayed in bed because of flu, but he has broken his arm.

Present perfect with for and since

6a **Look at these sentences and then choose the correct alternative.**

1 I've had a bad cold **for** a week.

2 I've had a bad cold **since** last Friday.

a We use *for/since* for moments in time.

b We use *for/since* for periods of time.

6b **Look at this question and answer.**

Q: How long have you known Andy?

A: For ten months.

Do we use How long to ask about frequency or duration?

GRAMMAR REFERENCE ➤ PAGE 54

7 **Put the time expressions in the box in the correct column.**

6 o'clock • 7th February • 2014 • an hour
five years • Friday • ten seconds
the age of five • the day I met you
three days • ~~20 minutes~~

for	since
20 minutes	

8 **Complete the sentences with information about you. Use the correct form of the present perfect and a time expression.**

1 I ....
(know) my English teacher for
....

2 I .... (live) in this area
since ....

3 I .... (have) this
watch for ....

4 I .... (be) able to
swim since ....

5 I .... (live) in my
home for ....

9a **Guess your partner's answers in 8 and write them down.**

9b **SPEAKING** **Ask your partner questions to find out if you were right.**

How long have you been at this school?

Compound nouns connected with health and medicine

1 **We make compound nouns by joining two nouns or an adjective and a noun. Join words from column A and column B to make compound nouns. Then match them with the correct definitions. Use your dictionary if necessary.**

A		B
1	pain	aid
2	heart	room
3	health	centre
4	waiting	killer
5	food	attack
6	first	poisoning

Definition	
☐ a	a place where people wait, for example to see a doctor
1 b	a medicine that reduces pain
☐ c	basic medical help that you give to someone when they have an accident
☐ d	a building where people can go to see a doctor or nurse
☐ e	when somebody has a lot of pain in their chest and their heart stops working
☐ f	an illness you get from eating food which contains harmful bacteria

2 ▶ **23 Listen and check your answers.**

3a PRONUNCIATION ▶ **24 Listen again to the pronunciation of the compound nouns in 1. Where is the stress in words 1–5? Is it on the first word or the second word? And in 6?**

3b **Practise saying the words with the correct stress.**

4 **Complete the sentences with the compound nouns in 1.**

1 When I'm ill I go to the .... near my house.

2 Please take a seat in the .... The doctor will see you in ten minutes.

3 Salmonella is a type of bacteria which causes
....

4 To help avoid a ...., exercise regularly and eat a healthy diet.

5 I want to learn .... so that I know what to do if there's an emergency.

6 A: My back really hurts.

B: Why don't you take a ....?

Learning some basics of FIRST AID

LIFE SKILLS OBJECTIVES	KEY CONCEPTS
■ To think about why first aid is important. ■ To learn when and how to put somebody in the recovery position. ■ To check understanding of the basics of first aid.	**breathe [v]:** *We breathe through our nose and mouth because we need oxygen.* **(un-)conscious [adj]:** *Her eyes were closed and she wasn't moving so I thought she was unconscious.* **blood [n], bleed [v]:** *I cut my finger and now it's bleeding.* **airway [n]:** *Your airway is the tube that takes air from your mouth to your body.* **recovery position [n]:** *You put somebody into the recovery position to help them breathe when they are unconscious.*

1a Work with a partner. Look at the scene. What dangers can you find in the scene?

1b You are alone. You find somebody in the situation in 1a. What do you think you need to do? Make a list of ideas.

2 READING **Read the text and answer these questions.**

   1 Why is first aid so important?

   2 Were any of your ideas in 1b right?

3 **Look at the steps to take in an emergency. Complete the sentences with the words in the box.**

> 999 • airway • ambulance • breathing
> conscious • dangers • recovery

   1 Check if there are _____ at the scene.

   2 If the scene isn't safe, call _____.

   3 If the scene is safe, check if the person is _____.

   4 If the person is unconscious, check that they are _____.

   5 If they aren't breathing, open their _____.

   6 If they are breathing, put the person in the _____ position.

   7 Call 999 for an _____.

4 SPEAKING **Work with a partner. Prepare and act out the following situation:**

Student A: You are at the scene in 1. Call 999.

Student B: Answer your partner's 999 call. Ask the questions in the text.

1a

WHY LEARN

The simple answer is ... accidents happen, and they happen quite often. Three million people a year go to hospitals because of accidents and injuries. Knowing first aid can help you to help somebody, maybe somebody close to you. Perhaps even in a life and death situation.

Imagine this. You see an accident. Part of a building collapses. One builder is lying on the ground. Another is having problems walking. Meanwhile, something hit a young woman and she is shouting that she has broken her arm. Her baby is crying in its pushchair. In this scene, who do you think is the most important person?

The answer is ... you. Everybody at the moment depends on you. You need to stay calm. And you need to check the dangers. If there is a danger, call 999 immediately.

Look again at the picture in 1. Before you help the boy, you need to look for other dangers. If you hurt yourself, you can't help anybody.

So, assess the dangers of helping. If you think it's OK to help, what do you do next? Firstly, see if the person is conscious. Can they hear you when you ask them a question? Do they respond when you gently shake their shoulder? If they don't answer or respond, shout for help

5 Work with a partner. Look at the five pictures. They show how to put somebody in the recovery position. Try to put them in order.

Step 1: *d*   Step 2: ....   Step 3: ....

Step 4: ....   Step 5: ....

a 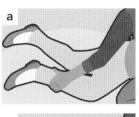   b

c    d

e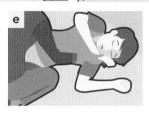

6 Now match the descriptions to the pictures and steps.

1 Pull the knee towards you, keeping the person's hand pressed against their cheek and position the leg at a right angle.

2 Make sure that the airway remains open by gently moving the head back and lifting the chin.

3 Place the arm near you at a right angle.

4 Move the other arm, with the back of their hand against their cheek.

5 Take the knee furthest from you and pull it up until the foot is flat on the floor.

7 LISTENING ▶ 25 **Watch or listen to a teenager explaining how to put somebody in the recovery position. Listen and check your answers in 5 and 6.**

8 Answer these questions with information from the video/listening.

1 Is it a good idea to put somebody who has had a bad fall in the recovery position?

2 Is it important to open a patient's airway before or after putting them in the recovery position?

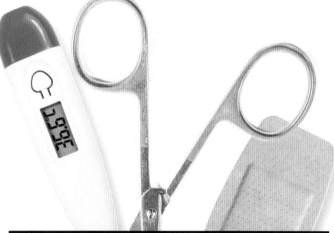

FIRST AID?

Then open their airway to check that they are breathing. If they are breathing, put the person in the recovery position. Call 999 in the UK, or 911 in the US, to ask for an ambulance.

When you call 999, be prepared for the following questions:

✚ Which service do you require? (you say 'Ambulance', they will say 'Connecting you now')
✚ What's your name?
✚ What number are you calling from?
✚ Where are you? (If you aren't sure, describe anything special around you.)
✚ What has happened?
✚ How many people are hurt?
✚ Is anyone unconscious?
✚ Has anyone stopped breathing?
✚ Is anyone bleeding?
✚ Are there any other dangers around?

These are only the first things you need to know. But with just these basics, perhaps you can save somebody's life.

LIFE TASK

You want to explain to people how to put a person in the recovery position.

Follow this plan:

1 Look again carefully at all the information about first aid on pages 48 and 49.

2 Write a quiz to check that people understand and remember the information. Write six questions and use these different question types:

- True-False questions
- Choose the correct alternative
- Questions about pictures
- Comprehension questions
- Your own ideas

3 When you finish, give your questions to other students. Can they answer correctly?

Daniel Craig

1 SPEAKING **Work with a partner and answer these questions.**

1 What can you see in the photo(s)?

2 Do you think actors generally do their own action scenes?

3 Do you think actors often injure themselves?

2 LISTENING ▶ 26 **Listen to two people talking about actors and action scenes. Which two actors do they talk about and why?**

3 ▶ 26 **Listen again. Are the sentences True (T) or False (F)?**

1 'Doubles' usually do all the action in action films.   T / F

2 Jackie Chan injured himself making his new film.   T / F

3 Jackie Chan has broken his nose more than twice.   T / F

4 In 1986 Jackie Chan had a serious accident when he hit his head on a tree.   T / F

5 Sometimes Jackie Chan has made films when he is badly injured.   T / F

6 Daniel Craig never lets other people do the action scenes in the James Bond films.   T / F

7 Daniel Craig has never broken anything.   T / F

8 Chan and Craig prefer their films to look realistic.   T / F

4 SPEAKING **What about *you*?**

1 Do you like action films? Why/Why not?

2 Do you think it's good that actors do their own action scenes? Why/Why not?

Grammar in context

Present perfect with just, yet, already

1a Look at these sentences and complete rules 1–3 with *just*, *yet*, or *already*.

a He's just made a new film.

b He's already had a lot of serious accidents.

c He hasn't stopped making films yet.

d Has he had any accidents yet?

1 We use the present perfect with .... to talk about very recent events.

2 We use .... to talk about something that has not happened, but we think it is going to happen soon.

3 We use .... to talk about something that has happened, possibly before we expected.

1b Choose the correct alternative.

1 We use yet in *affirmative/negative* sentences and questions.

2 Yet usually goes at the end of the sentence, but already and just usually go *after/before* the past participle.

GRAMMAR REFERENCE ➤ PAGE 54

2 What do you think has just happened in these photos? Write sentences with different ideas.

1 ....

2 ....

3 ....

4 ....

1

2

3

4

3a Write six sentences about yourself, two with *already*, two with *yet*, and two with *just*.

I've already done my history homework.

3b Change your sentences into questions to ask your partner.

Have you done your history homework yet?

3c SPEAKING Interview your partner with your questions.

Present perfect and past simple

4 Look at this part of a dialogue and then answer questions 1–4.

Interviewer: *Has he ever had a really serious accident?*
Expert: *Yes, he has.*
Interviewer: *What happened?*
Expert: *It was in 1986. He fell several metres and hit his head on a rock.*

1 Is the presenter's first question in the past simple or the present perfect?
2 Does the question ask about general experience or a specific moment in the past?
3 Is the presenter's second question in the past simple or the present perfect?
4 Does the question ask about general experience or a specific moment in the past?

GRAMMAR REFERENCE ➤ PAGE 54

5 Complete the dialogue with the present perfect or past simple form of the verbs given.

Alan: (a) .... you ever
.... (break) your leg?
Dave: Yes, I (b) .... Two years ago
I (c) .... (go) skiing and I
(d) .... (break) my left leg.
Alan: I (e) .... never ....
(break) my leg but I (f) ....
(have) some bad accidents in the past.
For example, I (g) .... (crash)
my bike at least five times.
Dave: (h) .... you ....
(fall) off your bike last week?
Alan: No, I (i) .... Last week I was
riding a horse and I (j) ....
(fall) off!

6 SPEAKING Ask your partner if they have ever done these things. Ask follow-up questions in the past simple to find out details of their experiences.

a
break an arm

b
ride a motorbike

c
meet a famous person

d
visit the UK

e
swim in the sea

f
be in a race

Have you ever broken your arm?

Yes, I have.

Where were you when you broke it?

Describing photos

a

b
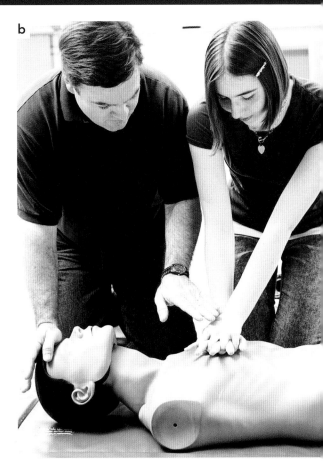

1 SPEAKING **Work with a partner. Look at these photos. What is the connection between them?**

2a LISTENING ▶ 27 **Listen to a boy describing one of the photos. Which photo is he describing?**

2b ▶ 27 **Listen again. Which of these questions does the boy answer? Tick (✓) them.**

1 Where are the people? ☐
2 What type of people are they? ☐
3 What are the people doing? ☐
4 What are they wearing? ☐
5 What things or objects are in the picture? ☐
6 What has just happened before the scene? ☐
7 When is the scene taking place (morning, night, summer, winter, etc.)? ☐
8 Have you ever been in a situation like the one in the picture? When? What happened? ☐
9 What do you think about the picture? ☐

c
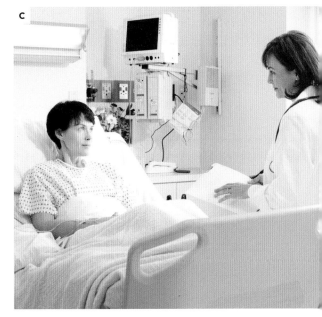

3 SPEAKING **Compare answers with your partner. Do you remember what information the boy gives? Together, practise describing the same photo.**

4 ▶ 27 **Fillers are words or sounds which give you time to think without stopping the conversation. Listen to the boy again. Look at the Speaking bank and tick the fillers he uses.**

💬 SPEAKING BANK

Useful expressions for filling the conversation
- Errr … ✓
- Well … ☐
- The thing is … ☐
- I'm not (really/totally/completely) sure but … ☐
- Maybe … ☐
- You know … ☐
- I think … ☐
- I imagine that … ☐

PRACTICE MAKES PERFECT

5 SPEAKING **Work with a partner. Take it in turns to describe one of the photos, using the questions from 2b and the Speaking bank to help you.**

Choose one of the photos on this page.
- Describe the photo.
- Have you ever been in a situation like the one in the picture? When? What happened?
- What do you think about the picture?

Developing writing

Notes and messages

1 Read these three notes and messages. Write one sentence to explain the situation in each one.

a

> Mum,
>
> My friend Phillip has had an accident. He fell and hurt his knee when we were playing basketball at school. The sports teacher took him to St. Andrew's Hospital. I've gone to see him. Can you come and pick me up there after work?
>
> Kate xxx
>
> PS Can you bring him some magazines, 'Basketball Giants' or something? Phil's really bored.

b

> Jamie,
>
> I wanted to ask you if I could borrow your laptop but you weren't here. I need it to write up a project at school. I've taken it to school but I promise I'll look after it. You don't mind, do you? After all, that's what brothers are for! I'll bring it back asap.
>
> Zara

c

> Jenna,
>
> I was really sorry to hear that you're ill ☹. I only found out yesterday when Martha told me. I know you don't want any visits at the moment, so I'm sending this note and some chocolates. I hope you can eat them! Don't worry about maths, physics, French, etc. I've taken notes for you and I'll give them to you when I see you.
>
> Get well soon!
>
> Sam

2 Look at the notes and messages again and complete the information in the Writing bank.

✏ WRITING BANK

Useful expressions in notes and messages

- In notes and messages it is normal to begin simply with the name of the person we are writing to.
- We often use abbreviations like *PS* or .... to keep messages short.
- We use expressions like *I was really* .... when we are writing about bad news, or *Congratulations!* when you are happy for somebody.
- We use the expression .... to say we want somebody to recover from an illness or accident quickly.

3 Match the abbreviations and their meanings.

1 PS — as soon as possible

here is some additional information to my letter or note (Latin: post scriptum)

2 e.g.

for example (Latin: exempli gratia)

3 NB

and other things of the same type (Latin: etcetera)

4 asap

Please pay special attention (Latin: Nota Bene)

5 i.e.

that is, this is exactly what I mean (Latin: id est)

6 etc.

PRACTICE MAKES PERFECT

4a Look at the task and write the message. Use the expressions from the Writing bank and the abbreviations from 3.

You've just gone to visit your friend at his home because he hasn't been at school for two days. He's just gone out to see the doctor. You don't have your mobile phone so leave him a message. Include this information.

- find out how he is
- find out what he has done in the last two days
- tell him what you've done at school
- tell him some news about one or two of your friends.

WRITING BANK ➤ PAGE 150

4b Give your message to your partner. Write a reply to your partner's message.

✔ EXAM SUCCESS

Look at the instructions for the writing task in 4. Can you write in any way you like? Is the style (formal or informal) important?

➤ EXAM SUCCESS page 144

Grammar reference

Present perfect

FORM

Affirmative	subject + have/has + past participle. *She has taken her medicine.*
Negative	subject + haven't/hasn't + past participle. *We haven't seen the doctor.*
Question	have/has + subject + past participle? *Have you been to the hospital?*
Short answers	Yes, subject + has/have. No, subject + hasn't/haven't. *Yes, I have. No, they haven't.*

USE

We use the present perfect to talk about:

- an experience in someone's lifetime, without saying the exact time when the event occurred. When it happened is not important.

  I've broken my leg twice.

- recent events which have a result in the present.

  She's lost her textbook. (= She hasn't got her textbook now.)

- actions or situations that began in the past but continue in the present.

  Helen's been a doctor for ten years. (= Helen started to work as a doctor ten years ago and she is still a doctor now.)

  Ever, never, for, since, just, already, yet

- We can use *ever* in questions with the present perfect. It means 'at any time in your life'.

  Have you ever appeared in a film?

  Ever comes just before the past participle.

- We can use *never* in negative sentences in the present perfect. It means 'at no time in your life'.

  I've never met a famous person.

  Never comes just after the first verb.

- *For* and *since* are used when the present perfect is describing actions or situations that began in the past and continue in the present. We use *for* with periods of time and *since* with moments in time. With this use of the present perfect we use the question 'How long ...?'.

  How long have you had those glasses?

  I've had them for three months/since January.

  For and *since* go just before the time expression.

- We use *just* with the present perfect to emphasise the fact that something happened very recently.

  We've just had lunch. (= We finished our lunch only a few moments ago.)

  Just goes after the first verb.

- We use *already* to talk about something that has happened earlier than we expected.

  I don't have any homework to do. I've already done it.

  Already usually goes just after the first verb, or at the end of the sentence for emphasis.

- We use *yet* to ask if something we expect has happened, or to say that it hasn't. It is used in questions or negative sentences.

  Have you tidied your bedroom yet?

  I haven't had dinner yet.

  Yet usually goes at the end of a sentence or clause.

Present perfect and past simple

USE

The present perfect describes actions in the past but without saying the specific moment when they happened.
I've won a prize.

If we say the specific moment in the past when something happened we must use the past simple.
I won a prize last year.

Vocabulary

1 Parts of the body ankle • arm • back • cheek • chest • chin • ear • elbow • face • finger • foot • forehead hand • head • heel • hip • knee • leg • mouth • neck • nose • shoulder • stomach • thigh • thumb • throat toe • wrist

2 Health problems and illnesses ache • broken • cold • cough • earache • flu • headache • hurt • injure pain • sore • stomach ache • temperature • virus

3 Compound nouns connected with health and medicine first aid • food poisoning • health centre heart attack • painkiller • waiting room

4 Other words and phrases ➤ page 138

Grammar revision

Present perfect (ever, never, for, since) / 7 points

1 Choose the correct alternative.

1 Matt and I have *took/taken* a lot of photos.
2 *Has/Have* you and Jack started the project?
3 They've been friends *for/since* they were kids.
4 Have you *eaten ever/ever eaten* Indian food?
5 My friend and I have *ever/never* been to Scotland.
6 We haven't had an English test *for/since* ages.
7 How *long/much time* have you known Sam?

Present perfect and past simple / 6 points

3 Are these sentences correct? Correct them if necessary.

1 Danny has been to Bulgaria last year.
2 Have you seen the Eiffel Tower when you were in Paris?
3 Did your sister ever ride a horse?
4 I've seen this film twice.
5 My brother's 18. He went to the US three times.
6 Did you speak to the teacher yesterday?

Present perfect (already, yet, just) / 6 points

2 Lily has to do jobs around the house. Look at her list of jobs and write sentences in the present perfect with *already*, *yet*, and *just* for the things she has and hasn't done. Remember! We use *just* for things done a short time ago.

Jobs
* wash the dishes ✓ – two minutes ago!
* buy the bread ✓
* take the rubbish out ✗
* ring Mum at work ✗
* make the beds ✓ – a minute ago!
* make something for dinner ✓

1 ....
2 ....
3 ....
4 ....
5 ....
6 ....

Vocabulary revision

PARTS OF THE BODY / 7 points

1 Name the parts of the body.

1 .... 2 .... 3 .... 4 ....

5 .... 6 .... 7 ....

HEALTH PROBLEMS AND ILLNESSES / 8 points

2 Look at the pictures and identify the health problems.

1 She's got a ....

2 He's got a .... leg.

3 He's got a .... throat.

4 A lot of people are ill because of a ....

COMPOUND NOUNS CONNECTED WITH HEALTH AND MEDICINE / 6 points

3 Complete the compound nouns with the correct words.

1 Sit in the .... room. The nurse will call you when it's your turn.
2 My sister had an accident but there was someone there who knew first ....
3 She ate something bad and now she's got food ....
4 Take this .... killer three times a day if your back hurts.
5 My neighbour is a doctor at the .... centre down the road.
6 Quickly! Get a doctor. I think this man is having a heart ....

Reading

1 **SPEAKING** **Work with a partner. Ask and answer these questions.**

1 What do you think is good advice for somebody with a stomach virus?

2 How do you think speaking different languages can be good for your health?

3 Do you sometimes feel sick when you travel by car, plane or ship?

2 **Read these newspaper articles. Match each question in 1 with one of the three articles.**

1 .... 2 .... 3 ....

> **TIP FOR READING EXAMS**
>
> In matching activities, remember …
> Read all the text once quickly to get a general understanding. Then read the information that you need to find. Look for the section of the text where you think this information appears and look at it again in more detail.
>
> > EXAM SUCCESS page 144

A *Health matters: This week's news*

SEASICK ON DRY LAND

Have you ever been on a boat or a ship? If you have, you probably know about seasickness, that terrible feeling caused by going up and down non-stop on the sea. But imagine feeling seasick when you're *not* at sea. Mrs Jane Houghton has been seasick since 2001. She was at sea for three days. When she got off the boat, she started to feel seasick and she has never recovered. One unusual thing about her illness is that she only feels OK when she is moving in a car, boat or aeroplane. It's difficult for Mrs Houghton to work because when she sits at her computer she feels terrible. Mrs Houghton has created a website with information about her illness. She wants people to know about it. Perhaps one day doctors will be able to help her.

B ## STAY AT HOME

A large number of people have a stomach virus called norovirus at the moment. This virus can cause stomach ache, high temperatures and pains in your arms and legs. Doctors have told patients to stay at home for two days after the illness has gone. They are also recommending that patients take paracetamol, drink lots of water and, most importantly, that they wash their hands regularly. The Health Protection Agency has said that this year there are twice as many people with the virus as last year. There are between 600,000 and one million cases of norovirus in the UK each year.

C ## BEING BILINGUAL IS GOOD FOR YOUR BRAIN

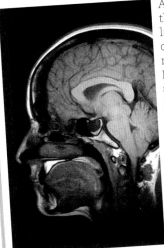

A recent study says that speaking two languages can help old people to stay mentally active. Dr Ellen Bialystok and her team of scientists at York University in Canada did experiments with 104 people between the ages of 30 and 88. They came to the conclusion that being bilingual can help old people to think quickly.

Half of the people who did the tests came from Canada and only spoke English. The other half came from India and could speak English *and* a language called Tamil. The scientists tested vocabulary skills and maths ability. They also checked how fast they did the tests. The ones who could speak two languages did the exercises quickly and well. The people who spoke only one language weren't so good. The British Alzheimer's Society was very interested in the discoveries.

3 **Which article …**

1 talks about an illness which is very bad when the patient isn't moving? ....

2 talks about action that can help older people? ....

3 recommends taking a type of drug? ....

4 mentions one person with problems at work? ....

5 talks about quick answers to questions? ....

6 mentions a new discovery in the world of medicine? ....

7 talks about the usual number of people who suffer a specific illness? ....

8 talks about an unusual illness? ....

9 mentions personal hygiene? ....

4 **SPEAKING** **What about *you*?**

How serious do you think the different illnesses mentioned in the text are? Why?

Use of English

> **TIP FOR USE OF ENGLISH**

In multiple-choice cloze activities, remember …
Read the complete text first without thinking about the gaps. This helps you to get a general understanding of the text.

> EXAM SUCCESS page 144

5 **Read about acupuncture. Choose the best answer (A, B, C or D) to complete the text.**

In China they've used acupuncture for thousands and thousands of years. But now a school in England (1) .... just started to use it with their students. Stanchester Community School is the school (2) .... they have begun this project. At this school they have a teacher who has spent time living in China studying acupuncture with Chinese experts. This teacher has (3) .... acupuncture to a small group of students at the school (4) .... September. A very common problem that the students have is stress, usually stress caused by exams or homework. People (5) .... suffer from stress often have headaches, backache or stomach ache. The students all say that the treatment has (6) .... helped them a lot. In fact, many of the students say that they've started to sleep really well. Luckily they haven't started sleeping in class (7) ....!

1	**A** has	**B** is	**C** have	**D** was
2	**A** that	**B** who	**C** where	**D** which
3	**A** give	**B** gave	**C** gives	**D** given
4	**A** since	**B** for	**C** at	**D** on
5	**A** –	**B** who	**C** when	**D** what
6	**A** yet	**B** for	**C** at	**D** already
7	**A** yet	**B** ever	**C** never	**D** in

Speaking

> **TIP FOR SPEAKING EXAMS**

In speaking exams, remember …
It's important to know what the examiners want to hear. Find out how many marks there are and what you need to do to get a good mark.

> EXAM SUCCESS page 144

6 SPEAKING **Work with a partner. Student A: Look at photo A on page 147. Student B: Look at photo B on page 148. Take it in turns to talk about your photos using the questions below.**

1 Where are the people and what are they doing?

2 Who are the people and what are they wearing?

3 What else can you see?

4 How do you prefer to learn a language?

Writing

> **TIP FOR WRITING EXAMS**

In writing exams, remember …
Include all the information in the instructions or you will lose marks. And don't forget to write in the correct style (formal or informal).

> EXAM SUCCESS page 144

7 **You are staying with an English teenager called Joe. You haven't got a mobile phone. This afternoon you are at home alone but you need to go out to the chemist's to buy some medicine and then take it to a friend. Leave Joe a message. Include this information.**

- Explain where you have gone and why.
- Say who is ill.
- Give the address of the person who is ill and their telephone number.
- Ask Joe to ring you there when he gets home.

'CAN DO' PROGRESS CHECK UNITS 3–4 CEF

1 **How well can you do these things in English now? Give yourself a mark from 1 to 4.**

> **1** = I can do it very well.
> **2** = I can do it quite well.
> **3** = I have some problems.
> **4** = I can't do it.

a I can talk about different quantities. ☐

b I can understand written and spoken texts about different languages. ☐

c I can make negative adjectives by using prefixes. ☐

d I can ask for information about language courses and check that I have understood. ☐

e I can write a text about my experiences of learning a language. ☐

f I can report general and recent experiences in the past using the present perfect. ☐

g I can talk about activities which continue up to now using the present perfect with *for* and *since*. ☐

h I can discuss health problems and illnesses. ☐

i I can describe scenes in photos and pictures using fillers. ☐

j I can write basic notes and messages. ☐

2 **Now decide what you need to do to improve.**

1 Look again at my book/notes.

2 Do more practice exercises.
   > WORKBOOK Units 3 and 4

3 Ask for help.

4 Other: ....

5 TV addicts

Vocabulary

Television

1 Look at the TV. What types of programme can you see? Use the words in the box to help you.

> advert • cartoon • chat show
> comedy • cookery programme
> documentary • drama • film
> game show • reality show
> soap • sports programme
> the news

2 Think of one or two examples of each programme in 1.

cartoon – The Simpsons, Dragon Ball Z

3a PRONUNCIATION Where does the stress come in each noun or compound noun in 1?

ȧdvert   cartoȯn

3b ▶ 28 Listen, check and repeat.

4 SPEAKING Look at the words in bold in these questions. Check that you understand them. Then use the questions to interview your partner.

1 Do you ever watch any **live** programmes? What type?
2 What is your favourite **series**?
3 What **channel** is it on?
4 Who is your favourite TV **presenter**?
5 Who usually **turns** the TV **on** in your house?
6 What time do you usually **switch** the TV **off**?
7 Who is in charge of the **remote control** in your house?

Adjectives describing TV programmes

5 Look at these adjectives. Do they have a positive meaning (+) or a negative meaning (–)?

> awful • boring • cool • exciting • funny
> informative • interesting • moving
> popular • scary

6 Match some of the words in 5 with these sentences.

1 when something gives a lot of information *informative*
2 when something makes you feel frightened
   ....
3 when something is very bad ....
4 when many people like something ....
5 when something makes you laugh ....
6 when something makes you feel very emotional
   ....

7 LISTENING ▶ 29 Listen and decide what type of TV programmes these five people are talking about.

1 ....   4 ....
2 ....   5 ....
3 ....

8a Think of things or people for each adjective in 5 and make a note of them.

exciting – superhero films, live football

8b SPEAKING Work with a partner and compare ideas.

> *I think superhero films are really exciting.*

> *I don't. I think they're boring!*

SLOOOOOOOOOW TV

It's Friday night. What would you like to watch on TV? How about a reality show to find the best singer in the country? Or the funniest comedy programme on TV? Or how about watching a complete seven-and-a-half hour train journey from Oslo to Bergen in Norway?

One Friday night in 2009, against all predictions, a million people in Norway (20% of the population) decided to watch the programme about the longest railway in the country! This programme was the start of a new phenomenon called 'Slow TV'.

'It was the 100th anniversary of this route and we'd planned a couple of documentaries,' says Rune Møklebust, head of programming at the Norwegian public TV channel (NRK). 'Then someone said 'why not film the whole trip?'. We thought it would be something completely new … and cheap'. The programme went out at the same time as *The X Factor* and a popular comedy programme. It was the most popular programme that night. Many people said they only planned to watch for a few minutes, but they ended up watching for hours and hours.

Some Slow TV programmes are longer and slower than that first programme. There has been a nine-hour programme which showed the process of getting the wool from a sheep and turning it into a jumper. There has also been a 12-hour programme showing a wood fire burning. And an 18-hour programme showing somebody fishing (it took four hours to catch the first fish!). The longest programme so far was 134 hours, showing the coast of Norway from a ship. Møklebust used 11 cameras and filmed for five and a half days. Many people went to the coast to appear in the programme. 3.2 million people watched it. That's more than half the country!

08 Hours | **12** Hours

▶ Watch Now | ▶ Watch Now

So why is Slow TV so popular? Life is faster and more stressful than in the past. For many people, Slow TV is more relaxing than modern programmes where the pictures and sounds change rapidly. Also, more and more people live in big cities. Maybe Slow TV helps them to feel in contact with nature again. After all, this is real 'reality TV', with no editing, not like the programmes they call 'reality shows'.

Slow TV is getting bigger and bigger. And it isn't only Norwegians who are interested in it. A US company has started to show the programmes on over 100 channels. 1.1 million Americans watched the famous seven-and-a-half-hour train programme. But some Americans say that Slow TV was really an American invention. One of the most famous American artists, Andy Warhol, made a film in 1963. It was called *Sleep*. In the film, a poet called John Giorno sleeps for six hours!

1a Work with a partner. What can you see in the TV screens? Each one is of a TV programme. Which programme would you prefer to watch? Why?

1b You are going to read a magazine article about Slow TV. Before you read, what do you think Slow TV might be?

2 Read the text and check your prediction in 1b.

3 Choose the best answers.

1 When a lot of people watched the train programme in 2009, it was …
   a because there was nothing good on the other channels.
   b a surprise.
   c because Norwegians are interested in their railway.

2 Originally, Rune Møklebust didn't …
   a have a reason to make a programme about the train journey.
   b want to make a programme about the train journey.
   c plan to make a long programme of the train journey.

3 In Norway …
   a there are approximately 5 million people.
   b people generally live on the coast.
   c they are only really interested in nature programmes.

4 Slow TV is 'real' because …
   a they only use one or two cameras.
   b what they film is what you see.
   c they only film nature and animals, not people.

5 On American TV …
   a there are channels that are starting to show Norwegian programmes.
   b they are saying that an American artist invented Slow TV.
   c there are channels which now only show Slow TV.

4 Answer these questions.

1 Why did Rune Møklebust and his team decide to make their first long programme?
2 What reasons can explain the popularity of Slow TV?
3 What are the similarities between the film *Sleep* and Slow TV?

5 ⚙ CRITICAL THINKING

Think! Then compare ideas with your class.

■ 'Reality shows do not show the real world'. Do you agree? Why/Why not?

6 What do the underlined words in the text mean? Guess and then check in your dictionary.

7 SPEAKING What about *you*?

Would you like to watch any of the Slow TV shows mentioned in the text? Why/Why not?

Grammar in context

Flipped classroom: watch the grammar presentation video.

Comparatives and superlatives

1a Look at the comparative and superlative form of these adjectives.

Adjective	Comparative	Superlative
1 long	longer	the longest
2 big	bigger	the biggest
3 funny	funnier	the funniest
4 popular	more popular	the most popular
5 good	better	the best

Now match the adjectives with the correct rule.

a   adjectives with two syllables or more, use *more/most* + the adjective ....4........

b   one-syllable adjectives which end in one vowel + one consonant, double the last consonant and add *er* ....

c   two-syllable adjectives ending in *y*, omit *y* and add *ier* ....

d   one-syllable adjectives, add *er* ....

e   irregular adjectives have no set rule ....

1b Use the rules in 1a to write the comparative and superlative form of these adjectives.

1   crazy   ....

2   bad   ....

3   boring   ....

4   short   ....

5   sad   ....

1c Complete the sentences with the correct words.

1   The new series is more popular .... the old one.

2   It's the most popular series .... the US at the moment.

> GRAMMAR REFERENCE ➤ PAGE 68

2a PRONUNCIATION ▶ 30 Look at these sentences and listen. Then answer questions 1–3.

a   Films are longer than game shows.

b   Books are more interesting than films.

c   This programme was better than that one.

d   Soaps are more popular than reading.

1   Which colour represents the stress in the sentences: red or blue?

2   Which types of word receive the stress: nouns, main or auxiliary verbs, adjectives or articles?

3   What sound does the other colour represent?

2b ▶ 30 Listen again and repeat the sentences.

3a Complete these sentences with the comparative form of the adjectives given and *than*.

1   Cookery programmes are .... documentaries. (interesting)

2   Adverts can sometimes be .... the programmes. (good)

3   Reality shows are .... chat shows. (bad)

4   Watching films at the cinema is .... watching them on TV. (exciting)

5   Ben Stiller is .... Will Smith. (funny)

3b Work with a partner. Which of the sentences in 3a do you agree with?

4   Check that you understand the words in the box. They are words which we frequently use with comparative adjectives to modify them. Then choose the correct alternative.

> a bit • a lot • far • much • slightly

1   Watching TV is *far/a bit* more popular as a hobby than writing poetry.

2   Jack Black (1m 68cm) is *much/slightly* taller than Daniel Radcliffe (1m 65cm).

3   For most people, watching football on TV is *a lot/a bit* more exciting than watching yoga.

4   The programme lasted 60 minutes. It was *far/a bit* longer than normal, because it usually lasts 55 minutes.

5   SPEAKING Complete the sentences with a logical opinion. Then work with a partner and compare your sentences.

1   *Slow TV programmes are* a lot longer than *normal TV programmes*.

2   .... a lot younger than ....

3   .... slightly more popular than ....

4   .... far funnier than ....

5   .... much more informative than ....

6   .... a bit scarier than ....

6a Justin Timberlake has been a singer since 1995 and he is now one of the most famous people in the world. He started singing in a boy band and he looked very different. Look at him in these two photos. Make notes comparing his appearance. Use the words in the box for ideas.

> attractive • bad • dark • funny • good • curly • long old • serious • short • strong • young

6b SPEAKING Work with a partner. Take it in turns to compare the two photos.

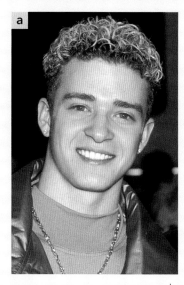

a

b

He's older in photo b.

Yes, and his hair is much darker.

6c SPEAKING Talk about *you*. Have you changed since you were seven?

7 Complete the questions with the superlative form of the adjectives given.

1 What is *the most interesting* (interesting) way to spend free time in your opinion?

2 What is .... (difficult) day of the week for you?

3 Who is .... (funny) person in the class?

4 Who is .... (happy) person you know?

5 What is .... (good) part of your day?

8a SPEAKING Interview different people in the class using the questions in 7.

8b SPEAKING Tell the class some interesting answers that people gave you.

Lucy thinks Sunday is the most difficult day of the week!

Adjectives ending in *-ing* and *-ed*

1 Choose the correct alternative in the examples and the rule.

1 When a film is *exciting/excited*, we feel *exciting/excited*.

2 When a documentary is *interesting/interested*, you feel *interesting/interested*.

To describe how somebody feels, we use the *-ing/-ed* ending.

2 Write the *-ing* or *-ed* forms of the words in the box. Check that you understand the words.

> boring • confusing • disappointing embarrassed • exciting • frightened interesting • moving • relaxed surprised • tired

3 Complete the sentences with the *-ing* or *-ed* form of the words given.

1 I was .... (surprise) to hear that they've stopped the series.

2 It was so .... (embarrass) when the presenter forgot what to say.

3 That new game show is really .... (confuse). I don't know what they have to do.

4 That film made me feel really emotional. I was .... (move).

5 The directors of the new show were very .... (disappoint) because not many people watched it.

6 Some people think that classical music is .... (bore).

7 I think classical music is really .... (relax).

4a Look at these things. Then make notes with your opinions of them.

> exams • pop music • reading • spiders sport • theme parks • watching documentaries

exams – tiring, make me feel frightened

4b SPEAKING Compare your ideas with a partner.

I think exams are really tiring.

Yes, and they sometimes make me a bit frightened.

Thinking about fame

LIFE SKILLS OBJECTIVES	KEY CONCEPTS
■ To think about the consequences of wanting to be famous. ■ To consider different opinions and attitudes to fame. ■ To give advice to somebody who wants to become famous.	**celebrity [n]:** (1) *A lot of celebrities stay at this hotel.* (2) *Some famous actors don't really enjoy their celebrity and don't want to be recognised.* **qualifications [n]:** *He didn't do any exams and left school with no qualifications.* **miss/cut class [phrase]:** *Did he miss class because he was ill or did he just cut class because he didn't want to come?* **bright [adj]:** *She's a very bright student. She understands new concepts very quickly.*

1 SPEAKING **Work with a partner and discuss these questions.**

1 Do you have an ambition in life? If so, what is it?

2 Would you like to be famous one day? Why/Why not?

3 If you would like to be famous, what would you like to be famous for?

2 READING **Read the text quickly and write one or two sentences to summarise what you think the message of the text is.**

3 **Read the text again and answer these questions.**

1 What does Murat Ucar want to be famous for?

2 In the documentary, where does Murat go instead of going to school?

3 How easy is it to become famous thanks to a reality show?

4 What two reasons do most 16 to 19-year-olds give for wanting to be famous?

5 What is the problem with some of the celebrities that young people admire?

6 What do we know about Michelle Obama when she was at school?

I just want to BE FAMOUS!

Murat Ucar is a bright 16-year-old from Tottenham, London, but he isn't doing very well at school. His teachers are worried because he doesn't go to many classes. Murat isn't worried because he believes that one day he will be famous. He doesn't mind if he becomes a famous model, actor or singer. The important thing is to be famous.

Murat appears in a documentary about young people today. In the documentary, we see Murat miss school for two weeks. Instead of going to school, he goes to Turkey to have an operation on his nose. After the operation, he tries to appear on The X Factor, to join a modelling agency and then a theatre company.

He isn't the only student like this in the UK. A survey says that more than one in ten young people would leave school to try to be famous. Sixteen percent of teenagers think that they can become famous one day by appearing in a reality show. In fact, the chances of becoming famous through a reality show are 30 million to one, worse than the chances of winning the lottery. Most of the 16- to 19-year-olds in the survey said that they want to be famous to have money and feel successful. Nineteen percent of the 777 young people who answered said fame was a way to 'let everyone know who

they were'. Seven percent said it would 'make them appear more attractive'. But experts say that the important thing is to do something because you enjoy it, not because you want to become a celebrity.

Young people need inspiration. Some teachers are worried because today's students admire celebrities with money but no qualifications. Some students now believe that they don't need to study because they can make lots of money by becoming famous.

Luckily, some famous people are trying to correct this idea. Michelle Obama visited a secondary school in London on one visit to the UK. She told the students about her own school days. 'I never cut class. I liked being smart. I loved being on time. I thought being smart was cooler than anything in the world.' Studying hard can lead to future success. Dreaming of fame is just that – dreams.

4a **Work with a partner. Look at these statements from the text on page 62. Complete them with the correct word(s).**

1   16% of teenagers think that they can become famous one day by appearing in a ....

2   7% said fame would 'make them appear more ....' .

3   Experts say that the important thing is to do something because you .... doing it, not because you want to become a ....

4   Young people admire celebrities who have .... but no ....

5   Some students now believe that they don't need to .... because they can make lots of money by becoming famous.

4b **What is your opinion of the statements? Do you agree/disagree/think they are surprising, scary …?**

4c SPEAKING **Discuss your opinions as a class. Do you have similar opinions? Why/Why not?**

5 LISTENING ▶ 31 **Watch or listen to four teenagers talking about fame. Is fame important for them? What do they want to do in life?**

Molly: _Yes/No_   _Wants to be:_ ....

Kieran: _Yes/No_   _Wants to be:_ ....

George: _Yes/No_   _Wants to be:_ ....

Amelia: _Yes/No_   _Wants to be:_ ....

6a ▶ 31 **Watch or listen again. What do you think of each person's attitude to fame? Do you think it is a sensible attitude or not? Why?**

6b **Work in a small group and compare your ideas. Give reasons.**

7 **Read about Eddie. What do you think about his plans for the future?**

Eddie

I like school and I get good marks, but I love playing football. I play four times a week and I'd love to be a professional. You don't need exams and qualifications – they're not important. All you need is skill. Footballers get loads of money and have a great lifestyle. Everyone knows who you are when you are a footballer. I know I want to leave school before my final exams, but I don't really know how to become a professional footballer.

LIFE TASK 👤

You want to prepare a video message or write an email to tell Eddie what you think about his plans. Work in a group.

Follow this plan:

1   *Say hello.*

2   *Give constructive comments about his idea to become a football player.*

3   *Give opinions and suggestions about his idea to leave school before doing his exams.*

4   *Make any other suggestions and comments that can help him.*

Listening

1 **SPEAKING** Do you ever watch British or American TV shows? Which ones? What do you think of them?

Downton Abbey – a popular British TV show.

2 **LISTENING** ▶ 32 Listen to a radio programme. The people are calling to say what they think of TV in the UK and what type of programmes they usually watch. Match the speakers and their answer. There are two options you don't need.

a game shows   d they don't watch TV
b sports programmes   e documentaries
c drama series   f comedy programmes

Tyler	**1**	....
Olivia	**2**	....
Harry	**3**	....
Lily	**4**	....

✔ **EXAM SUCCESS**

In the next activity you need to identify the statements that a speaker makes. Do you think the speaker will say exactly the same words as in the statements you read?

➤ EXAM SUCCESS page 145

3 ▶ 32 **Listen again. Which speaker …**

1 thinks having lots of different channels isn't always a good thing? ....

2 finds that TV makes it difficult for them to communicate with others? ....

3 thinks TV today is the same as always? ....

4 just watches TV to be happy and relaxed? ....

5 watches TV to have fun <u>and</u> to learn things? ....

6 thinks some types of programmes are better in the UK than anywhere else? ....

7 wants people to be more active? ....

8 thinks Americans make more exciting programmes. ....

4 **SPEAKING** What about *you*?

In general, what do you think of TV in your country?

Grammar in context

less … than, (not) as … as

1a Look at these sentences.

1 British TV is as good as TV in the US.
2 British series aren't as good as American series.
3 Their programmes are less informative than ours.

1b Are these statements *true* or *false*?

1 We use as … as to say that two things, people or situations are similar.
2 Not as … as and less … than have a similar meaning.
3 Not as … as and less … than are the opposite of more … than.

GRAMMAR REFERENCE ➤ PAGE 68

2 **Rewrite these sentences but keep the same meaning. Use *as … as, not as … as, less … than.* Use each expression twice.**

1 American TV series are more violent than European series.

European series *aren't as violent as American TV series.*

2 Soaps are interesting, but game shows are equally exciting.

Game shows ....
....

3 Computer games are more popular with today's teenagers than TV programmes.

TV programmes ....
....

4 Football programmes on TV are exciting. Football programmes on the radio are equally exciting.

Football programmes on the radio ....
....

5 Watching horror films in the cinema is scarier than watching them at home.

Watching horror films at home ....
....

6 Books are more informative than TV documentaries.

TV documentaries ....
....

3 **SPEAKING** **Work with a partner. Do you agree with the opinions in 2?**

What do you think about the first sentence?

I agree. I think American TV series are often very violent.

too and (not) enough

4a Look at the sentences.

1 People here are **too** lazy to switch the TV off.
2 The programmes aren't good **enough**.
3 People say they haven't got **enough** free time.
4 I'm happy **enough** with TV today.

4b Match the first and second halves of the rules.

1 We use **too**   **a** to say a person, thing or situation is insufficient.

2 We use **not … enough**   **b** to say a person, thing or situation is sufficient.

3 We use **enough**   **c** to say a person, thing or situation is excessive.

4c Look at the word order in the sentences in 4a.

1 Does **too** come before or after the adjective?
2 Does **enough** come before or after the adjective?
3 Does **enough** come before or after the noun?

GRAMMAR REFERENCE ➤ PAGE 68

5 Complete the text with the words in the box.

Matt Smith as Doctor Who.

> as • as • enough • not
> serious • than • too • young

Doctor Who is a world-famous science-fiction drama series made by the BBC. It's a British series, but it's as popular (a) .... many big American series. In most episodes there are scary moments. But the writers need to be careful. It can't be (b) .... frightening because it's a series for children. The great thing about the series is that children love it but it's exciting (c) .... for adults to enjoy, too. Doctor Who travels in space and in time. He travels in a blue police telephone box called the TARDIS. From the outside, it seems that there is (d) .... enough space for two or three people to be inside the TARDIS. But, luckily, the inside of the TARDIS isn't (e) .... small as the outside. In fact, it's enormous!

The series is already over 50 years old! Twelve actors have played the Doctor so far. Some of the actors have been less successful (f) .... others. But one of the most popular was Matt Smith. At first, some people thought he was too (g) .... to be Doctor Who, because he was only 26. And some people thought he wasn't (h) .... enough because he was always saying funny things. But he was such a great Doctor that, in the end, some people cried when he left the series!

6 Complete the sentences with the verb *to be* and *too* or *not … enough* plus the adjective given.

1 This film is for adults, and Aisha is only fifteen.
She *isn't old enough* .... (old) to see it.

2 This game show .... (easy). Everybody always wins.

3 This cartoon .... (original). It's exactly the same as all the others.

4 Owen needs to improve. He .... (good) to be in the first team.

5 It .... (hot) in here. Can you open the window?

6 I can't understand this film. The story .... (confusing)!

7 That horror film was awful. It .... (scary). I was so bored I fell asleep!

7a Look at the questions. Make notes with ideas. Use the adjectives in the box with *too* and *enough*.

> clever • fast • fit • good • healthy • lazy
> long • old • serious • short • slow • young

1 Could you be a newsreader on national TV at the moment?

2 Could you win a gold medal running 100 metres at the Olympic games next week?

3 Could you win a Nobel Prize next year?

7b SPEAKING Tell your partner your answers.

We aren't old enough to read the news.

And my hair's too long! The men who read the news always have short hair!

Negotiating

1 SPEAKING **Work with a partner. Imagine these programmes are on TV tonight. Which one(s) would you like to watch? Why?**

8 pm	8.00	**PICK Earthwatch** David Kent explores the wonders of the Amazon rainforest.	**You're Nicked!** An insight into the life of Britain's police force.	**Who Wants to be Incredibly Rich?** James Kay hosts the big money quiz.
	8.30			
9 pm	9.00	**Space 2112** First in a spectacular new Sci-Fi drama series.	**Catastrophes** Experts predict how the world will end.	**Food Nation** Three chefs remain in the competition and there's another event to cook for.
	9.30			
10 pm	10.00	**News**	**FILM Three's a Crowd (2009) ***** A young woman's life is turned upside down when her mother-in-law moves into the marital home.	**PICK Patterson's People** Interviews with the rich and famous.
	10.30	**Sports Roundup** Highlights from this afternoon's match between Liverpool and Barcelona.		

2a LISTENING ▶ 33 **Listen to two friends deciding what to watch on TV tonight.**

1 Tick (✓) the types of TV programme you hear.
2 Put two ticks (✓✓) for the programme they decide to watch.

chat show	☐☐	comedy	☐☐
drama series	☐☐	documentary	☐☐
game show	☐☐	cookery programme	☐☐

2b What do the two girls think about different types of programme?

1 drama
2 science fiction
3 documentaries
4 cookery programmes

3 ▶ 33 **Listen to the dialogue again. Tick (✓) the expressions that you hear.**

💬 **SPEAKING BANK**

Making suggestions
- Shall we (do something)?
- Why don't we (do something)?
- Let's (do something).
- How about (doing something)?

Responding to suggestions
- Great!
- OK.
- Fine.
- Yes, let's …
- I know what you mean, but …
- No, I prefer …
- But what about …?
- Good idea.
- Me too./Me neither.
- Yes, but …
- I'm not sure.

4 SPEAKING **Work with a partner. Take it in turns to suggest watching a programme from 1 and responding to the suggestion.**

> Shall we watch the cookery programme?

> I'm not sure. I don't think it's very exciting. What about …?

5 Look at these different ways of spending the evening. Work with a partner. Think of good and bad things about each activity.

a

b

c

d

e

f

PRACTICE MAKES PERFECT

6 SPEAKING **Work with a partner. Do this role-play using your ideas from 5 and the Speaking bank to help you.**

You and your partner want to spend the evening together.
- Suggest an activity and explain why you think it is a good idea.
- Listen to your partner's suggestion and explain why you don't want to do this activity.
- Talk about different activities until you come to a decision about what to do.

✔ **EXAM SUCCESS**

In this type of activity, what can you do if you can't think of anything to say?

▶ EXAM SUCCESS page 145

Developing writing

A review

1 Read this review of a British TV programme. Do you know the programme? If so, do you like it? If not, would you like to see it? Why/Why not?

Today	Sun	Mon	Tue

Review
The Voice | Saturday 7 pm
● ● ● ● ●

My favourite programme is *The Voice*. It's on BBC1. It's on Saturdays at about 7 o'clock in the evening and they repeat the programme on BBC3 on Sundays.

In *The Voice*, four famous singers listen to members of the public sing. Each star decides if they like the person's voice and if they want the person to be part of their team. Then the teams compete to see who has the best voice.

Personally, I love this programme because I love music and I also like game shows and reality shows. In my opinion, *The Voice* is really cool because the stars can't see the person who is singing. They can only listen. I think that's much fairer than on other singing shows where they choose the winners because of their appearance, not because of their voice.

I would recommend *The Voice* to anybody who likes pop music and reality shows. As far as I'm concerned, it's the best combination of those two types of programme that I've ever seen.

2a In which paragraphs does the information come?

Paragraph 1: ....

Paragraph 2: ....

Paragraph 3: ....

Paragraph 4: ....

- title, channel, time and day
- why the writer likes the programme
- a recommendation to watch/not to watch the programme
- a description of the programme

2b Make notes with the basic information that the writer gives.

1 Title: *The Voice*

2 Channel: ....

3 Day and time it's on: ....

4 Description of the programme: ....

5 Reasons why the writer likes it: ....

3 Read the review again and complete the expressions in the Writing bank.

✎ WRITING BANK

Useful expressions in a review

- *Personally* ...., I love this programme …
- ...., *The Voice* is really cool because …
- I .... that's much fairer than …
- I .... *The Voice* to anybody who …
- As .... concerned, it's the best …

4a Work with a partner. Make a list of TV programmes that are popular in your country at the moment.

4b SPEAKING Tell your partner your opinion of the programmes. Use the expressions in the Writing bank.

5 Make notes about your favourite TV programme. Think about the information in 2a.

PRACTICE MAKES PERFECT

6 Look at this task and write your review. Use the paragraph plan in 2a and the expressions in the Writing bank to help you.

Write a review of your favourite TV programme. Include:
- basic information about the programme (title, channel, time, day)
- a description of the programme
- reasons why you like it
- a recommendation (who is the programme good for?).

WRITING BANK ➤ PAGE 150

Grammar reference

Comparatives and superlatives

FORM			
	Adjective	Comparative	Superlative
One syllable	long short	longer shorter	the longest the shortest
One syllable ending in one vowel and one consonant	big fat	bigger fatter	the biggest the fattest
Two syllables ending in -y	lazy funny	lazier funnier	the laziest the funniest
Two or more syllables	important boring	more important more boring	the most important the most boring
Irregular	bad good far	worse better farther/further	the worst the best the farthest/furthest

USE
- We use the comparative to compare two people, places or things.
- We use the superlative to compare more than two people, places or things.
- We use *than* in sentences that compare two people, places or things.
  *Some adverts are worse **than** others.*
- We use *the* before the superlative form of the adjective and we often use *in*.
  *He's **the** nicest person **in** the class.*

less ... than, (not) as ... as

USE

Less is the opposite of *more*.
*Watching tennis is **less** popular **than** watching football.*
(= Watching football is more popular than watching tennis.)

- We use *as ... as* to say two things are the same.
*European films are **as** good **as** American films.*

- We use *not as ... as* to say that the second person or thing is more ... than the first one.
*Watching tennis isn't **as** popular **as** watching football.*
(= Watching football is more popular than watching tennis.)

too

FORM

The word *too* comes before the adjective.
*This story is **too** confusing. People can't understand it.*

USE
- We use *too* to say that something is excessive. It is not the same as *very* because it has a negative meaning.
  *He's **very** clever. (= positive)*
  *Yes, but sometimes he's **too** clever. (= negative)*

enough, (not) ... enough

FORM

The word *enough* comes after adjectives and before nouns.
*He's old **enough**.*
*He isn't old **enough**.*
*I haven't got **enough** money.*

USE
- We use *enough* to say that something is sufficient.
- We use *not enough* to say that something is insufficient.
  *He's old **enough** to learn to drive.*
  *I'm **not** good **enough** to win the competition.*

Vocabulary

1 Television advert (ad/advertisement) • cartoon • channel • chat show • comedy • cookery programme • documentary • drama • film • game show • live (adj) • presenter • reality show • remote control • series • soap • sports programme • switch on/off • the news • turn on/off

2 Adjectives describing TV programmes awful • boring • cool • exciting • funny • informative • interesting • moving • popular • scary

3 Adjectives ending in -ing and -ed bored • boring • confused • confusing • disappointed • disappointing • embarrassed • embarrassing • excited • exciting • frightened • frightening • interested • interesting • moved • moving • relaxed • relaxing • surprised • surprising • tired • tiring

4 Other words and phrases ➤ page 139

Grammar revision

Comparatives and superlatives — / 7 points

1 Correct the mistakes in these sentences.

1 My school is more bigger than this school.
2 You look thiner than the last time I saw you.
3 Some people think that watching sport is more boring that playing it.
4 The Volga is longest river in Europe.
5 Ethan is much worst at German than Jake.
6 Do you think this exercise is the most difficult of the book?
7 That's the sillyest thing you've said today.

less … than, (not) as … as — / 6 points

2 Make true sentences using the words and as … as, not as … as or less … than.

1 Spain/big/the US
2 A kilo of sugar/heavy/a kilo of iron
3 To become a doctor, philosophy/important/ anatomy
4 Jamie (born 2001)/old/Brad (born 2000)
5 I/good at maths/my best friend
6 Playing tennis/dangerous/parachuting

too, (not) enough — / 7 points

3 Write sentences with too, (not) enough and the words given.

1 Why is it difficult for people to climb Mt. Everest?

It .... (high)

2 Why can't your brother see that horror film?

He's only 15. He .... (old)

3 Why can't you run a marathon?

My legs .... (strong)

4 Why can't you buy a sports car?

I .... (money)

5 Why can't Amy drive?

She's only 16. She .... (young)

6 Why can't palm trees grow in the Arctic?

It .... (warm)

7 Why don't you like that song?

It's boring! It .... (slow)

Vocabulary revision

TELEVISION — / 6 points

1 Name these types of TV programme.

1 It tells you information about today's events.

....

2 They interview famous people. ....

3 It's based on a competition. ....

4 It looks at facts or historical events.

....

5 It goes between programmes to persuade you to buy something. ....

6 It follows the lives of real people living in a particular situation. ....

ADJECTIVES DESCRIBING TV PROGRAMMES — / 8 points

2 Complete the adjectives with vowels. Is each word positive (+) or negative (–)?

1 ... w f ... l ☐
2 b ... r ... n g ☐
3 c ... ... l ☐
4 ... n f ... r m ... t ... v ☐
5 m ... v ... n g ☐
6 p ... p ... l ... r ☐
7 r ... l ... x ... n g ☐
8 s c ... r y ☐

ADJECTIVES ENDING IN -ING AND -ED — / 6 points

3 Complete the sentences with the words in the box. There are twelve words but only six sentences.

> disappointed • disappointing • embarrassed
> embarrassing • frightened • frightening • relaxed
> relaxing • surprised • surprising • tired • tiring

1 I thought I was going to get ten in the exam, but I only got five. I was ....

2 It's .... to see you because I thought you were on holiday.

3 I went out with one black shoe and one brown shoe. It was really ....

4 I hate high places. Yesterday we went up a really big tower. I was very ....

5 The examiner was so nice. She made me feel .... before the exam.

6 I'm very .... after running. I can't move my legs!

6 Planet Earth

Vocabulary

Geographical features

1 **SPEAKING** Work with a partner. Name one famous example for each of the words in the box. Use a dictionary if necessary.

> beach • desert • forest • ice cap • island
> jungle/rainforest • lake • mountain
> mountain range • ocean/sea • river • valley

beach – Copacabana

2 ▶ 34 **Listen and repeat.**

3 **Play a game. Draw a word from 1 on the board. Can the class guess the word?**

The environment

4 **Work with a partner. Match the definitions with some of the words in the box.**

> drought • flood • global warming
> ~~greenhouse effect~~ • melt • nuclear disaster • oil spill
> ozone layer • pollution • recycle • save • waste

1 when heat cannot escape from the atmosphere and the temperature on Earth goes up ..... *greenhouse effect*

2 when ice turns to water ....

3 a long period of time when there is no rain
....

4 the part of the Earth's atmosphere which protects the earth from the sun ....

5 the process of making the air, water or land worse, with chemicals, for example ....

6 a large quantity of water that suddenly covers an area
....

7 the increase in the temperature on Earth
....

8 an accident with nuclear power, usually causing radioactivity ....

9 an accident when oil comes out of its container, for example at sea ....

5 **SPEAKING** Work with a partner. Use words from 4 to talk about the photos.

> *You can recycle bottles here. That can reduce pollution.*

a
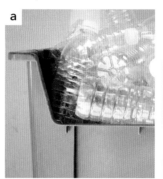

b

c
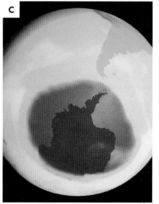

d

6 **LISTENING** ▶ 35 **Listen to four descriptions of environmental problems. Match each description to a photo in 5.**

1 ....   2 ....   3 ....   4 ....

7 **SPEAKING** Work with a partner. Ask and answer these questions.

1 How is global warming affecting your country?

2 Where and when do you have floods or droughts in your country?

3 How do people waste water or electricity in your country?

4 What do you do to save water or electricity?

5 What products or materials do you recycle?

1a
Work with a partner. Look at the two photos on the right. Talk about what you can see. What do you think is the connection between them?

1b
Look at the title of the article and the photos. What could 'the most important building in the world' be and why?

2
You have three minutes to read the text and check your prediction.

3
Choose the correct alternative. Write the letter of the paragraph where you found the answer.

1 Countries *pay/don't pay* to keep their seeds there.
Paragraph ....

2 If there is an electrical problem at the Seed Vault, the temperature *will/won't* be a problem.
Paragraph ....

3 The most important thing about the location of the Seed Vault is that *it is easy to protect from attacks/the altitude will keep the seeds dry*.
Paragraph ....

4 In the case of a future catastrophe, the important thing is to have a *lot/wide variety* of seeds.
Paragraph ....

5 The Svalbard Global Seed Vault *has/doesn't have* millions of types of seeds.
Paragraph ....

6 Norway built the Svalbard Global Seed Vault because of *global warming/possible environmental disasters*.
Paragraph ....

7 People believe droughts and floods *might/will never* make it difficult to find food in the future.
Paragraph ....

4
⚙ **CRITICAL THINKING**

Think! Then compare ideas with your class.

- Do you agree that this is the most important building in the world? Why?
- What plants from your country do you think are important to protect?

5
What do the underlined words in the text mean? Guess and then check in your dictionary.

6
SPEAKING **What about *you*?**

Are you generally optimistic or pessimistic about the future of the planet? Why?

Is this the most important building in
THE WORLD?

A Future problems
Each year, people are becoming more and more worried about the future of our planet. People are now starting to agree – global warming will definitely make a difference to the world's weather. On the one hand, some parts of the world may have more floods. But some other parts might suffer terrible droughts. All of this will have a serious impact on the world's agriculture. And that could make it difficult for us to get enough food to survive.

B A possible solution
This explains the idea behind the Svalbard Global Seed Vault. The Seed Vault is built into a mountain on an island near the North Pole. The aim of the building is to protect the world's agriculture from future catastrophes. This may not just be a question of global warming. Perhaps there will be a major nuclear disaster or war one day. These things definitely won't be a problem for Svalbard. Thanks to careful planning, experts say that it is going to survive any catastrophe.

C Protecting our plants
Some experts think that the population of the earth will probably go up by 50% in the next 40 years. Because of climate change, it probably won't be easy for some plants to survive. Having many different types of plants will be essential for agriculture to adapt to changes in the environment. In the Svalbard Global Seed Vault, there is space for 4.5 million types of seed. That's 2.5 billion individual seeds! At the moment there are over 770,000 different types there.

D Helping worldwide
Any country in the world can leave seeds in Svalbard. And the service is free. There are 1,500 potatoes from Peru, bananas from the Pacific Islands, and rice from more than a hundred different countries. The seeds of some plants, such as peas, only survive for 20 to 30 years. But others will last for hundreds of years.

E The most important building?
In 2028, the Svalbard Vault will celebrate its 20th anniversary. 200 years in the future, it's possible that the ice caps will melt. Even if this happens, Svalbard will be safe. That's because it is on a mountain and will be above the water level. And because it is so close to the North Pole, even if their electricity stops working, the ice will maintain a cool temperature of -3.5°C to keep the seeds safe. But the best protection is the fact that it is in such a remote place. After all, maybe one day this will be the most important building in the whole world.

Grammar in context

be going to and will

1a Look at the sentences.

a They think the population **will** go up by 50%.

b In 2028 the Svalbard Vault **will** celebrate its 20th anniversary.

c Where can I find more information? I know! I**'ll** look on the Internet.

d Yesterday the US decided what to do. They**'re going to** send more seeds.

e It's warm today. The ice **is going to** melt.

1b Match these explanations of the use of *will* and *be going to* with example sentences a–e in 1a.

We use **will** ...

1 for decisions that we take at the moment of speaking.   *c*

2 to talk about an objective truth.

3 to make a general prediction. We often use think, hope, expect with this use.

We use **be going to** ...

4 to make predictions based on some sort of evidence.

5 to talk about plans or intentions.

GRAMMAR REFERENCE ➤ PAGE 80

2a PRONUNCIATION Look at these sentences. Why do you think some words are marked in bold?

1 The situation is going to get worse.

2 Temperatures are going to go up.

3 It's going to be a hot summer.

4 We're all going to have problems.

5 I'm going to do something to help.

2b PRONUNCIATION ▶ 36 Listen. What happens to the words in bold? What is the pronunciation of *be going to*?

2c ▶ 36 Listen again and repeat.

3 Complete the sentences with the correct form of the verbs given using *will* or *be going to*.

1 Experts expect that the ice cap .... (disappear) one day.

2 It's only 10 am but the sun is already strong. It .... (be) a hot day.

3 A: I'm really hot.
   B: I .... (open) the window.

4 Next week .... (be) the anniversary of the world's worst oil spill.

5 My friends have decided they .... (write) a letter about the environment to the local newspaper.

6 People think that global warming .... (cause) lots of problems in the future.

7 A: I'm going to see a documentary about the environment.
   B: I .... (come) with you.

4 Write down six plans or intentions you have. Write about these areas:

1 school   4 sport/hobbies

2 home   5 family

3 work   6 friends

I'm going to do a school project next week.

5 Now write down six predictions for the future. Write about these areas:

1 the environment   4 fashion

2 TV   5 sport

3 politics   6 medicine

I think the planet will get hotter.

6 SPEAKING Work with a partner. Compare your plans and predictions from 4 and 5.

will, may, might

7a Look at the sentences and give an approximate percentage of certainty for each expression in bold.

1 The population will **probably** go up.
   70-80% certain

2 Global warming will **definitely** make a difference.

3 **Perhaps** there will be a nuclear disaster.

4 **It's possible that** the ice caps will melt.

5 We **may** have more and more floods.

6 Parts of the world **might** suffer droughts.

7 It **probably** won't be easy.

8 It **definitely** won't be a problem.

7b Look at the position of the adverbs *definitely* and *probably* in 7a. What do you notice?

GRAMMAR REFERENCE ➤ PAGE 80

✔ **EXAM SUCCESS**

You are going to do a sentence transformation activity. Read the instructions carefully. What things are important to check when you finish an activity like this?

➤ EXAM SUCCESS page 145

8 Rewrite the sentences keeping the same meaning. Use between two and five words, including the word given.

1 It's possible that the sea level will go up in the next 50 years.   **may**
The sea level _may go up_ in the next 50 years.

2 It's certain that parts of the earth will become deserts.   **definitely**
Some parts of the earth _____ deserts.

3 There's a possibility that the consequences will be catastrophic.   **perhaps**
_____ catastrophic.

4 It's certain life on the planet won't end in the next 20 years.   **definitely**
Life on the planet _____ in the next 20 years.

5 It's probable that people won't change their habits.   **won't**
People _____ habits.

6 The situation might get worse.   **possible**
_____ will get worse.

9 How certain do you think these predictions are? Write sentences with the expressions in 8.

1 Summers will get hotter.
2 Polar bears will become extinct.
3 Cars of the future won't use petrol.
4 We will have another ice age.
5 Natural disasters will become more common.
6 The south of Europe will become a desert

10 SPEAKING Work with a partner. Compare your answers in 9.

I think summers will definitely get hotter.

I think they may get hotter. I'm not sure.

Different uses of *get*

1 Look at *get* in these sentences and match each one with the correct meaning (a–e).

1 Summers are *getting* very hot.   ....
2 I *got* your email yesterday.   ....
3 Last week she *got* a book about pollution.   ....
4 What time will you *get* to the meeting?   ....
5 Can you *get* me the pen that's on the desk?   ....

a arrive   **c** become   **e** receive
b bring   **d** obtain or buy

2 Complete the sentences with the words in the box. What is the meaning of *get* in each sentence?

dark • late • ready • red • thin • worse

1 You look hot. Your face is getting _____.
2 My brother needs to eat more. He's getting _____.
3 Come on! You need to get _____ for school.
4 Scientists are very worried because they say the situation is getting _____.
5 Look at the time! It's getting _____. Time for bed.
6 I'll switch the light on. It's got very _____ in here.

3 What usually happens in these situations? Write sentences with *get* and the words in the box.

an email with news • ~~angry~~ • bread
home late • presents • tired

1 Somebody is saying horrible things to you.
You get angry.
2 You run for an hour or more.
_____ .
3 It's your birthday tomorrow.
_____ .
4 You're out at 11 pm and there are no buses.
_____ .
5 You're in a supermarket and you want to make a sandwich.
_____ .
6 Your friend in the US writes to tell you about what happened last week.

4a Work with a partner. Write a story where you use *get* as many times as possible.

4b SPEAKING Tell your story to the class. Who uses *get* the most?

Yesterday I got up at 7 am and I got ready for school.

Reducing our ecological footprint

LIFE SKILLS OBJECTIVES	KEY CONCEPTS
■ To learn about carbon footprints and water footprints. ■ To consider positive action we can take to reduce our ecological footprints. ■ To make an action plan to reduce our impact on the environment.	**climate change [n]:** *People are worried about climate change. We are having hotter summers and colder winters.* **carbon dioxide emissions [phrase]:** *The carbon dioxide emissions from old cars are worse than from new cars.* **greenhouse gases [phrase]:** *If we burn fossil fuels, the greenhouse gases in the atmosphere increase.* **fuel-efficient [adj]:** *Modern cars are more fuel-efficient and use less petrol than before.* **charge/recharge (a mobile phone) [v]:** *My mobile phone has no power, I need to charge it.*

1 **Work with a partner. Look at these things. Are they bad for the environment? Why/Why not?**

2 READING **Work with a partner. Student A: Read text A. Student B: Read text B. Answer the 4 questions about your text. Make notes with your answers.**

Text A: Questions

1 What is a carbon footprint?

2 What is the difference between the primary and secondary footprint? Give examples.

3 Does the text mention any of the things in 1? Does it say that each one is good or bad?

4 What does the text say people can do to reduce their carbon footprint?

Text B: Questions

1 What is a water footprint?

2 What is the difference between the primary and secondary footprint? Give examples.

3 Does the text mention any of the things in 1? Does it say that each one is good or bad?

4 What does the text say people can do to reduce their water footprint?

A carbon footprint

Everyone leaves a carbon footprint. It is the impact each person has on the environment through the emission of greenhouse gases.

Your carbon footprint has two parts: the primary footprint and the secondary footprint. The primary footprint shows the emissions of carbon dioxide and other greenhouse gases that you are directly responsible for. Examples are the emissions produced by travelling and using electricity. The secondary footprint shows the emissions that you are indirectly responsible for. These include things like the emissions produced when factories make the things that you buy. All of these carbon dioxide emissions contribute to global warming.

The size of your carbon footprint depends on many things. How you spend your free time is one of the most important. Do you watch TV and play video games or do you read or do sport outdoors? Do you fly when you go on holiday? If you do, your footprint will be much larger than if you go by train. Rail travel is three times more fuel-efficient than air travel. Where your food comes from will also affect your secondary footprint. Processed and packaged meat has a bigger impact on the environment.

You may think that you are not responsible for any emissions because your parents do all the shopping and decide a lot of things at home. And it's true that your school is responsible for the things you do there. But you can suggest ways to change their habits. You can also watch less TV, switch off the light when you leave a room and unplug your mobile phone when it has finished charging. Each small action will help make your footprint smaller.

B Water footprint

Water is essential in our daily lives. But sometimes the size of our water footprint is shocking. It shows the amount of water a person uses, directly or indirectly, every day.

All day we use water directly. This is our primary footprint. This includes the water we drink, the water we need for a shower or the water we use to wash the dishes. But what about the water that we use indirectly; the water used to produce, grow or make the things we buy? This is our secondary footprint, and sometimes it is much bigger than we think. After all, 70% of the world's fresh water is used for agriculture so the things we eat can make a big difference. And, to make almost anything, from a computer to a T-shirt, you need water. Here are some facts that may make you think about how much water we use in a day:

- Brushing your teeth uses about seven and a half litres of water.
- It takes approximately 1,286 litres of water to produce a loaf of bread. But it takes about 2,310 litres to produce a 150g steak!
- An automatic dishwasher uses approximately 40 litres of water. Washing dishes by hand can use up to 75 litres.
- A typical individual in the United States uses 500 litres of water each day. But over 1 billion people in the world use less than 6 litres of water per day.
- The average toilet uses 8 litres of clean water each time you use it.

3 SPEAKING **Use your notes in 2 to explain to your partner what carbon/water footprints are.**

4 **Work in a small group. Make a list of ideas about how your school could reduce its carbon and water footprints.**

   reduce the paper we use – recycle it

5   LISTENING ▶ 37 **Watch the video or listen to students talking about their ideas for reducing carbon and water footprints at their school. Do they mention any of your ideas in 4?**

6 ▶ 37 **Complete each sentence with one or two words. Watch or listen again if necessary.**

   1 At the school they have a box for .... and one for reusing all their old paper.

   2 You need .... litres of water to make a sheet of paper.

   3 They also recycle .... and .... at the school now.

   4 People were wasting water and .... towels in the washrooms.

   5 They wrote 'Every .... thing helps!' on their posters.

   6 In the past, everybody .... to switch the lights off at the end of the day.

   7 You need 10,000 litres of water to make a light bulb shine for .... hours.

7 **How many of the things in 5 and 6 do you already do at your school?**

LIFE TASK 🏃

You want to let other teenagers know about ecological footprints and what changes they can make to reduce their footprint at school. In groups prepare a poster or video with ideas about how to do this.

Follow this plan:

1 *Make a list of ideas for things you can do in your school life to reduce your footprints. Use the ideas in the texts and in the video. Add your own ideas and search for others on the Internet.*

2 *Decide if you are going to make a video or a poster.*

3 *Organise your ideas in a logical way. Think about how you are going to persuade other students to make changes.*

4 *Make your video/poster.*

5 *Show it to the class.*

Listening

1a SPEAKING **Work with a partner. Look at the photo. What can you see?**

1b Look at the words in the box. Check that you understand what they mean. What do you think could be the connection between them?

> charge a mobile phone • corridor
> dance floor • run • sustainable energy

2 LISTENING ▶ 38 **Listen to a science programme on the radio. Why do the words in 1b appear?**

3 ▶ 38 **Listen again. Are the sentences True (T) or False (F)?**

1 Simon Langton is the name of the school involved in this project. **T / F**

2 The idea came from a boy who is studying at the school. **T / F**

3 They think they can produce enough electricity to make hundreds of mobiles work for two and a half years. **T / F**

4 The students walk on the special floor when they go to technology lessons. **T / F**

5 Laurence first had the idea for this project when he was watching busy people moving around his university. **T / F**

6 The school is the first place to use this technology. **T / F**

7 You can use the technology to produce electricity by dancing. **T / F**

4 Look again at the false sentences. Why are they false?

5 SPEAKING **What about *you*?**

1 Do you like this idea to produce sustainable energy? Why/Why not?

2 Can you think of any other ideas at school or at home to produce sustainable energy?

Grammar in context

Zero conditional

1a Look at the sentences in the zero conditional. Then choose the correct alternative.

1 If you **run** in the corridors, you **get** into trouble.

2 You **produce** more energy if you **walk** fast.

We use the zero conditional to talk about *specific situations/things that are generally true*.

1b Look again at the sentences in 1a.

1 What tenses do we use in the zero conditional?

If + ... , ...

2 Does the half of the sentences with *if* always come first?

3 When do we use a comma in conditional sentences?

> GRAMMAR REFERENCE ▶ PAGE 80

2 Complete these sentences with the correct form of the verbs given.

1 If it's sunny, people often .... (go) to the beach.

2 If it .... (not rain) for months, the result is usually a drought.

3 If it rains a lot for months, there .... (be) often floods.

4 If you don't water plants, they .... (die).

5 If it .... (be) very sunny, it's bad for your eyes.

6 If the sun .... (shine) all day, the temperature goes up.

3a Write sentences to make general statements using the zero conditional.

1 If I'm late for school, *my teacher gets angry with me.*

2 If you sit too close to the TV, ...

3 If you go to bed late, ...

4 I feel sad if ....

5 I enjoy English classes if ....

6 My parents are happy if ....

3b SPEAKING **Work with a partner. Compare your sentences from 3a. Are any sentences the same?**

First conditional

4a Look at these sentences in the first conditional. Then choose the correct alternative.

1 If you **run** in the corridors at this school, the teachers **will be** really happy.

2 The school **will save** money if they **produce** extra electricity.

We use the first conditional to talk about _possible/ impossible_ situations and their consequences.

4b Look at the sentences again and choose the correct alternative.

1 In the part of the sentence with _if_ we use _the present simple/will or won't_.

2 In the other part of the sentence we use _the present simple/will or won't_.

GRAMMAR REFERENCE ➤ PAGE 80

5 Choose the correct alternative.

1 If we _don't/won't_ recycle paper now, we _need/will need_ to cut down more trees in the future.

2 If we _cut/will cut_ down more trees, the forests _disappear/will disappear_.

3 There _are/will be_ more deserts if the forests _disappear/will disappear_.

4 If there _are/will be_ more deserts, the planet _becomes/will become_ hotter.

5 Many plants and animals _die/will die_ if the planet _becomes/will become_ hotter.

6 Put the verbs in the correct tenses using the first conditional.

'If we **(a)** .... (not do) something soon, electronic products **(b)** .... (create) serious problems for the environment. We use more and more energy because we buy more and more electronic gadgets. If this situation **(c)** .... (continue), each house **(d)** .... (need) an incredible quantity of energy. The popularity of computers, tablets and mobile phones has created an enormous need for more power. In the 1970s homes contained, on average, just 17 electronic products. But now some people think that they **(e)** .... (not be) able to brush their teeth if they **(f)** .... (not have) an electric toothbrush. If we **(g)** .... (forget) to switch off all these electronic gadgets, we **(h)** .... (use) up all of our electricity for nothing.'

7 SPEAKING Work in groups. Begin with this sentence.

If I pass all my exams this year, I'll have a special holiday in the summer.

Take it in turns to add conditional sentences. How many sentences can you make?

> If I pass all my exams this year, I'll have a special holiday in the summer.

> If I have a special holiday in the summer, I'll go with my friends.

> If I go with my friends, I'll ...

Developing speaking

Making arrangements

1 SPEAKING Work with a partner and answer these questions.

Where do you like going at the weekend when it's …
1 sunny? 2 raining? 3 cold and snowing?

2 LISTENING ▶ 39 Listen to two people making arrangements for this weekend and answer these questions.

1 Where are they going?
2 When and where are they going to meet?
3 What are they going to take?
4 What will they do if it rains?

3 ▶ 39 Complete the dialogue. Listen again if necessary.

Jamie: Listen. Are you up to anything this weekend?
Danny: Not really. What about you?
Jamie: If the weather's **(a)** ...., Alex and I are going to go to the **(b)** .... Do you fancy coming?
Danny: Sure. What time shall we meet?
Jamie: How about **(c)** ....?
Danny: OK. Why don't we meet at the **(d)** ....?
Jamie: Fine. I'll bring some **(e)** .... and we can **(f)** ....
Danny: What will we do if it **(g)** ....?
Jamie: I'll give you a **(h)** .... and we'll go somewhere else.
Danny: OK. Listen. I'll ring **(i)** .... and ask her to come.
Jamie: Good idea. See you tomorrow at **(j)** ....

4 Tick (✓) the expressions in the Speaking bank that appear in the dialogue.

💬 **SPEAKING BANK**

Useful expressions for making arrangements
Asking about somebody's plans
- What are you up to at the weekend?
- Are you up to anything this weekend? ✓
- Do you fancy verb +-ing?

Arranging to meet
- What time shall we meet?
- Where shall we meet?
- Why don't we meet at ....?

Responding to plans and arrangements
- Sure./Fine./OK./Great./Good idea.
- Not really./Sorry, I can't./I prefer ....

Present continuous for future
Remember that we can use the present continuous as well as **be going to** to talk about future arrangements.
Where are we meeting tomorrow?

5a PRONUNCIATION ▶ 39 Listen to the start of the dialogue again. How do the speakers use their voices to show enthusiasm?

5b SPEAKING Work with a partner. Practise the first six sentences of the dialogue. Remember to show enthusiasm.

6 SPEAKING Work with a partner. Look at the places to go at the weekend in the box. Say if you like them. When is it best to go to them?

> beach • bowling alley • cinema
> the mountains • park • shopping centre
> sports centre • swimming pool

PRACTICE MAKES PERFECT ▮

7a SPEAKING Work with a partner. Use the dialogue in 3, the expressions in the Speaking bank and the diagram below to prepare a dialogue making arrangements.

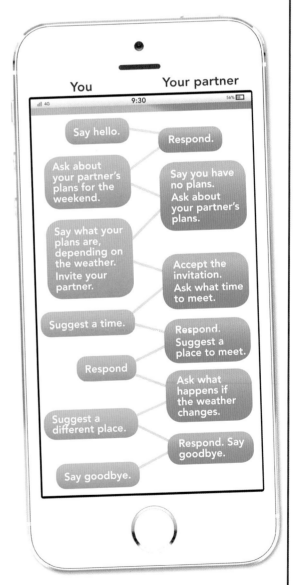

You / **Your partner**

Say hello. — Respond.
Ask about your partner's plans for the weekend. — Say you have no plans. Ask about your partner's plans.
Say what your plans are, depending on the weather. Invite your partner. — Accept the invitation. Ask what time to meet.
Suggest a time. — Respond. Suggest a place to meet.
Respond — Ask what happens if the weather changes.
Suggest a different place. — Respond. Say goodbye.
Say goodbye.

7b SPEAKING Practise your dialogue. Then change roles.

A formal letter

1 Read this newspaper article about climate change. What does the writer think about climate change and why?

HARRY MACDONALD'S VIEWPOINT

THIS WEEK: CLIMATE CHANGE IS REAL!

Why do some people continue saying that climate change isn't real? Haven't they looked out of their windows recently? Winters are colder and summers are hotter. And humans keep producing more and more carbon dioxide emissions. Just a coincidence?
I don't think so!

2 SPEAKING Work with a partner. What do you think about climate change? Do you agree or disagree with Harry Macdonald? Why?

3 Here is a letter to the editor of the newspaper. Does the reader agree or disagree with Harry Macdonald? Are any of your ideas from 2 here?

Dear Editor,

I am writing in response to Harry Macdonald's comments about climate change which appeared in your newspaper last week. Personally I agree with many of the things that Mr Macdonald says.

Firstly, it is clear that our weather is becoming more extreme each year. **Furthermore**, it appears that these changes are affecting the whole world, not just one or two areas.

Next, some people say that climate change is just a natural process. **Nevertheless**, there is evidence that man-made pollution is making climate change worse.

Finally, many people say it is too late to do anything about climate change. **However**, I think that governments and multinational companies use this as an excuse to continue polluting the atmosphere. **What is more**, I believe that if it is a question of the future of our planet, it is never too late to take action.

I will be interested in hearing other readers' opinions on this subject.

Yours faithfully,

Max Turner

4 The words in bold are all linkers. Put them in the correct place in the Writing bank below.

Linkers of sequence, addition and contrast

- Sequence: *Firstly,* .... ,
  ....

- Addition: *Furthermore,* ....

- Contrast: *However,* ....

5 Complete the sentences with linkers from the Writing bank.

1 I think climate change is a big problem.
.... , it is getting worse each year.

2 Let me explain what I think. .... , I want to explain my opinions about climate changes in the summer. Next, I want to tell you what I think about changes in the winter. .... , I want to talk about what we can do to stop the changes.

3 In general, I agree with the article.
.... , there are some things in it that I do not agree with.

PRACTICE MAKES PERFECT

6a Look at this topic and make notes.

A newspaper journalist writes:

'Young people don't really do anything to protect the environment. They don't believe that they can make a difference.'

Write a letter to the newspaper editor expressing your own opinion on this topic.
- Begin by explaining why you are writing.
- Express your opinion and explain your main reason for it.
- Give additional reasons for your opinion.
- End your letter.

WRITING BANK ➤ PAGE 150

6b Write your letter using the model in 3, your notes and the Writing bank to help you.

✔ EXAM SUCCESS

When you write in exam conditions, what can you do if you do not know a word or if you are not sure how to use a specific grammar structure?

➤ EXAM SUCCESS page 145

Language checkpoint: Unit 6

Grammar reference

be going to

USE

- We use *be going to* to talk about plans and intentions for the future. We use it for things that we have already decided to do in the future.
  I've decided that I'm going to study biology.

- We can also use *be going to* to make predictions about the future, particularly when we have evidence for the prediction.
  It's really cold. I think it's going to snow.

will

USE

- We use *will* and *won't* to make general predictions about the future. We often use *think*, *hope*, *expect*, *imagine*, etc. with *will* and *won't* to express our opinion about the future.
  I don't think the weather will be worse in the future.

- We also use *will* and *won't* when we decide to do something at the moment of speaking, for example when we suddenly offer to do something for someone.
  You look tired. I'll carry your bag.

- We use *will* and *won't* to talk about the future when we consider it to be an objective truth.
  It's my birthday next week. I'll be seventeen.

- We use *definitely*, *probably*, *perhaps*, *it's possible that* with *will* to say how certain we think something is. *Definitely* is when we are very certain, *probably* when we are quite certain, and *perhaps* and *it's possible that* when we are 50% certain.
  Definitely and *probably* come just after *will* but just before *won't*.
  I'll definitely be there. I definitely won't be there.

may, might

FORM

Affirmative	subject + may/might + verb in infinitive *The weather may get worse.*
Negative	subject + may not/might not (mightn't) + verb in infinitive *We may not be able to do anything.*

USE

- *May* and *might* are used in predictions when we are not sure about something. They express approximately 50% certainty.

Zero conditional

FORM

If + present simple, ... present simple.
If you go out in the rain, you get wet.
The teachers aren't happy if we don't do our homework.

USE

We use the zero conditional to talk about situations that are generally or always true.
If you take a fish out of water, it dies. (= This is not just a specific situation – it always happens.)

First conditional

FORM

If + present simple, ... *will* + infinitive
If the climate changes, food will be a problem.
If we don't do something soon, the situation will get worse.
The present simple comes in the part of the sentence with *if*. *Will* does not appear in this part of the sentence.
If it will be sunny, it will be hot today.

USE

We use the first conditional to talk about possible and probable situations in the future and their consequences.
If the sun comes out (possible future situation), *we'll go to the beach* (the consequence of this situation).

Vocabulary

1 Geographical features beach • desert • forest • ice cap • island • jungle/rainforest • lake • mountain mountain range • ocean/sea • river • valley

2 The environment drought • flood • global warming • greenhouse effect • melt • nuclear disaster • oil spill ozone layer • pollution • recycle • save • waste

3 Different uses of *get* arrive • bring • become (= a process or change of state) • obtain or buy • receive

4 Other words and phrases ➤ page 140

Grammar revision

be going to, will / 4 points

1 Correct the mistakes in these sentences.

1 The students going to go on an excursion.

2 What are your plans? What do you do tomorrow?

3 They say it's raining next week.

4 I can't meet you tomorrow because I'll do an exam.

will, may, might / 6 points

2 Complete the sentences with the words in the box.

perhaps • may • probably • definitely • will • won't

1 My team will .... win tonight. I'm sure.

2 I .... go next week but I don't know.

3 .... the problem will disappear.

4 They .... won't go out tonight because they have an exam tomorrow, but it's not impossible.

5 She definitely .... run tomorrow because she's got a broken leg.

6 It's possible that I .... see him tomorrow.

Zero conditional / 4 points

3 Answer these questions with complete sentences.

1 What happens if you mix blue and yellow?

....

2 What happens if you study hard for an exam?

....

3 What happens if you never brush your teeth?

....

4 What happens if you eat too much?

....

First conditional / 6 points

4 Complete the sentences with the correct form of the words given.

1 If the sun .... (shine), we'll be able to go out.

2 We'll go out if Mum .... (finish) work early.

3 If you do the exercise carefully, you .... (get) all the answers right.

4 It'll be great if she .... (come) tonight.

5 She'll leave hospital today if she .... (be) OK.

6 I .... (not bring) the dog if you don't want me to.

Vocabulary revision

GEOGRAPHICAL FEATURES / 7 points

1 Look at the names. What are the geographical features?

1 Sahara ....

2 around the Amazon ....

3 The Andes ....

4 Ipanema ....

5 Titicaca ....

6 The North Pole ....

7 Mallorca ....

THE ENVIRONMENT / 7 points

2 Complete the text with the words in the box.

droughts • floods • global warming
ozone layer • recycle • save • waste

(a) .... is getting worse – temperatures keep going up because of the hole in the (b) .... There have been (c) .... where water has destroyed towns. There are (d) .... where it hasn't rained for a long time. But many people (e) .... water – they use too much. It's important to (f) .... water and (g) .... things like bottles.

DIFFERENT USES OF GET / 6 points

3 Decide on a synonym for get in these sentences.

1 I got some juice from the shop. ....

2 Did you get home late last night? ....

3 I'll get you a glass of water. ....

4 I got my exam marks yesterday. ....

5 The book started well but it got boring. ....

6 She got an email from her friend. ....

Listening

1 SPEAKING **Work with a partner. The photos show different ways of finding out the news. Which do you prefer and why?**

2 LISTENING ▶ 40 **Listen to a radio programme where people are calling to say how they like to find out the news. Match the speakers and their preference. There is one option that you do not need.**

A the Internet

B the radio

C weekly news magazine

D newspaper

E TV

Amanda **1** ....

Jerry **2** ....

Sarah **3** ....

Dan **4** ....

3 ▶ 40 **Listen again. Which speaker …**

1 finds out the news at breakfast time?
Amanda/Jerry/Sarah/Dan

2 thinks that pictures and images are an important part of the news?
Amanda/Jerry/Sarah/Dan

3 thinks the news on TV isn't very informative?
Amanda/Jerry/Sarah/Dan

4 thinks the most important thing is to find out the news quickly?
Amanda/Jerry/Sarah/Dan

5 is tired of working with computers?
Amanda/Jerry/Sarah/Dan

Writing

4 SPEAKING **Work with a partner. Look at this topic and discuss your ideas.**

A newspaper journalist writes:

'I don't like it when famous people start talking about serious world problems like global warming. What do they know about it? I want actors to act and singers to sing. I don't want to listen to them telling me how to save the world.'

Some famous people, such as Angelina Jolie, do a lot of work to help charities.

5 **Write a letter to the newspaper editor expressing your own opinion on this topic.**

■ Begin by explaining why you are writing.

■ Express your opinion and explain your main reason for it.

■ Give additional reasons for your opinion.

■ End your letter.

Use of English

► TIP FOR USE OF ENGLISH

In sentence transformation activities, remember …
When you finish, check that you haven't changed the meaning of the original sentence and that you haven't used more than the maximum number of words permitted.

► EXAM SUCCESS page 145

6 **Rewrite the sentences keeping the same meaning. Use between two and five words, including the word given.**

1 Africa is hotter than India. **as**

India .... Africa.

2 Protecting the environment is more important than space exploration. **not**

Space exploration .... protecting the environment.

Speaking

► TIP FOR SPEAKING EXAMS

When negotiating, remember …
If you can't think of something to say, use fillers like *Well, Hmm* or *Let me think* to give you time to decide what you can say next. And don't be afraid to say something that is obvious.

► EXAM SUCCESS page 145

7 **Work with a partner. Make a list of different ways of making and responding to suggestions.**

8a **You want to watch TV with your partner. Look at what programmes are on tonight.**

No Place Like Home	Incredible Stories	Sports Night
A programme which shows you some of the best and biggest houses in the world. All the houses belong to famous people!	This series looks at normal people in extreme situations. This week we see the story of a teenager who rescued a surfer from a shark attack.	Tonight there's tennis, athletics, and of course all the best international football.
Family-Ville Yes, your favourite cartoon is back. Follow the lives of the most unusual family in the United States, and all their hilarious adventures.	**It's Only Natural** This nature documentary looks at the wildlife in one of the most beautiful places in the world – New Zealand.	

8b **SPEAKING Work with your partner. Make and respond to suggestions about what to watch. After two or three minutes, make a decision.**

3 Temperatures won't be warm enough for some types of animals. **too**

Temperatures .... for some types of animals.

4 The situation in Europe isn't as serious as in Africa. **more**

The situation in Africa .... in Europe.

5 It's possible that environmental problems will become more serious. **may**

Environmental problems .... more serious.

6 It's certain that some animals will die. **definitely**

Some animals ....

7 It's probable things won't get better. **probably**

I think that .... worse.

'CAN DO' PROGRESS CHECK UNITS 5–6   CEF

1 **How well can you do these things in English now? Give yourself a mark from 1 to 4.**

> 1 = I can do it very well.
> 2 = I can do it quite well.
> 3 = I have some problems.
> 4 = I can't do it.

a I can compare two or more things using different structures (*more/less than, as … as*). ☐

b I can name and describe different types of TV programme. ☐

c I can identify information in a radio programme about the news. ☐

d I can make and respond to suggestions about what to do in my free time. ☐

e I can write a basic review of a TV programme, expressing my opinions. ☐

f I can make predictions and talk about future plans and decisions using *will, may, might, be going to*. ☐

g I can talk about situations and their consequences using zero and first conditionals. ☐

h I can discuss the environment and pollution. ☐

i I can make arrangements for the weekend. ☐

j I can write a simple, formal letter to a newspaper, organising my ideas with linkers and in paragraphs. ☐

2 **Now decide what you need to do to improve.**

1 Look again at my book/notes.

2 Do more practice exercises.
   ► WORKBOOK Units 5 and 6

3 Ask for help.

4 Other: ....

7 Job hunting

Vocabulary

 a

 b

 c

 d

Jobs and work

1 SPEAKING **Work with a partner. What are the jobs in photos a–d? Use the words in the box to help you. Check that you understand all the words.**

> builder • fashion designer
> firefighter • journalist • librarian
> mechanic • nurse • plumber
> police officer • receptionist
> shop assistant • vet

2 ▶ 41 **Listen and repeat.**

3a **Work with a partner. For each letter of the alphabet, can you think of a job?**

A – architect, B – builder,
C – company director ...

3b **Is there a letter that you can't think of a word for? Ask other students.**

4 **Think of two or three jobs for these different categories. You can use words from 1 and your dictionary to help you.**

1 People who work with children:
teachers, au pairs, doctors

2 People who work outdoors:
....

3 People who do paperwork:
....

4 People who do manual work:
....

5 People who work with the public:
....

6 People who work in an office, with numbers or with computers:
....

Personal qualities

5 **Complete the sentences with the words in the box.**

> ambitious • calm • caring • clever/bright • confident
> creative • fit • hard-working • patient • reliable
> sensitive • sociable • strong • ~~well-organised~~

1 I'm a very *well-organised* person. I always plan very carefully and I know exactly what I'm doing.

2 You need to be .... and .... if you work with children because children need to know that you like them and will help them. You also need to be .... and .... because it's bad for the children if you get angry with them.

3 Police officers are usually .... and .... because in some situations they need to run fast and use force.

4 Top scientists are usually very .... They can find the answer to very complicated problems. They are also .... They need lots of imagination to think of new ideas.

5 Philip works in a bank. He's very .... – you know that he'll do his work well. He's .... too. He's often the first to start work and the last to leave.

6 Susan is very good at working in a team. She's very ...., she loves being with other people.

7 Firefighters need to be .... in difficult or dangerous situations in order to help people.

8 Charles is really .... He won't be happy until he's the company director!

6 LISTENING ▶ 42 **Listen to four people describing their jobs. What jobs do you think they are?**

1 ....   3 ....

2 ....   4 ....

7 SPEAKING **Work with a partner. Which words in 5 can you use to describe yourselves and why?**

> *I think I'm quite sociable because I'm friendly with people in class.*

Reading

DO YOU HAVE AN UNUSUAL JOB?
We want to hear from you!

1 Read a message board about three people who have unusual jobs. Match each person with the correct photo. What are their jobs? Write a name or simple explanation for each one.

✔ EXAM SUCCESS

You are going to do a True/False activity. What should you do after reading the text quickly for the first time to get a general idea?

➤ EXAM SUCCESS page 145

2 Read the texts again and decide if the statements are True (T) or False (F).

1 There are two different sides to Ryan's job. ....

2 Ryan's job suits any type of person. ....

3 Ryan believes that his job can have a positive influence on people. ....

4 Grace has to act in her job. ....

5 Shop assistants never know what Grace's real job is. ....

6 Grace sometimes writes articles in magazines. ....

7 Grace never writes bad things about the shop assistants because she feels sorry for them. ....

8 Some people are trying to get rickshaws off the roads. ....

9 All the personal qualities that a rickshaw driver needs are physical. ....

10 The worst time to find a customer is a week day in the winter. ....

3
⚙ CRITICAL THINKING

Think! Then compare ideas with your class.
- Do you think these jobs are important for society? Why/Why not?

4 What do the underlined words in the text mean? Guess and then check in your dictionary.

5 SPEAKING **What about _you_?**

1 What do you think of the different jobs?

2 Which of the three jobs in the text would you like to do the most? Why?

A In this photo I'm not the one who's going to jump. I'm getting that person ready. That's
5 my unusual job, and it's more difficult than it looks. You have to prepare people both physically and mentally. Some get really frightened so you have to make
10 them feel confident. And you must check all the equipment very carefully. If anything goes wrong, you're responsible. Of course, you mustn't be afraid of
15 heights! I like my job because I'm sociable and I can meet people from all over the world. All sorts of people come to do bungee-jumping. For some of them the
20 jump changes their life. It makes them feel more confident, like they can do anything! It's nice to know that by doing your job, you're making a difference. It can
25 be hard work though. At busy times we get 25 people jumping in an hour.

Ryan O'Connor, Wellington – 6th Mar 2.25 pm

B A lot of people like shopping. Me, I'm a professional 'mystery
30 shopper'. It's like being an actor, or a spy. For example, I go to a clothes shop and tell a shop assistant that I want to buy a coat. I pretend to be a normal
35 member of the public. I mustn't tell them who I really am. But when I finish, I have to do paperwork, answering questions about the service. Usually shops
40 pay me to do this. The boss wants to know if the shop assistants are doing a good job. Or sometimes magazines pay me because they want to write an article
45 comparing different shops. It's difficult because sometimes you have to say bad things about somebody who may lose their job because of your report. But I
50 suppose shop assistants should always treat their customers well.

Grace Simmons, Manchester – 6th Mar 3.02 pm

C I'm a rickshaw driver. Rickshaws are a mixture of a bike and a taxi. Two or three people
55 can sit at the back and you pull them by cycling. Nowadays there are a lot in London. Some taxi and bus drivers say we shouldn't be on the streets because we're
60 dangerous. It's important to stay calm in this job because those drivers often shout at us. But nearly all the work is late at night, when there isn't
65 much traffic. You don't have to have any qualifications to be a rickshaw driver, but you have to be fit and strong. You must be patient too because sometimes
70 you have to wait a very long time before finding a customer. Friday, Saturday and Sunday nights are the busiest. And rickshaws are much more popular in the
75 summer. In the winter you get cold and wet.

Gavin Henderson, London – 6th Mar 4.14 pm

Flipped classroom: watch the grammar presentation video.

 Modal verbs of obligation, prohibition and advice

1a Look at the sentences.

a You don't have to have any qualifications to be a rickshaw driver.

b But you have to be fit and strong.

c Shop assistants should treat their customers well.

d I mustn't tell them who I really am.

e You must check all the equipment very carefully.

f Some say that we shouldn't be on the streets because we're dangerous.

1b Which sentence(s) express:

1 obligation? *b/e*

2 no obligation? ....

3 prohibition? ....

4 advice or a recommendation? ....

1c What type of word comes after *must*, *mustn't*, *should*, *shouldn't*, *have to*, *don't have to*?

GRAMMAR REFERENCE ➤ PAGE 94

2a PRONUNCIATION **The letter 'l' is silent in the word 'should' – we do not pronounce it. Look at these sentences. Which letters do you think are silent in each sentence? Cross the letter(s) out.**

1 Firefighters should be calm.

2 You mustn't talk to the bus driver.

3 Discipline can be important.

4 My science teacher comes to school at half past eight.

5 Fashion designers shouldn't copy other people's designs.

6 He works as a guide at the castle on the island.

2b ▶ **43 Listen, check and repeat.**

3 Use *should* and *shouldn't* to give advice to these people. Use the pictures to help you. Then write one more sentence with *should* or *shouldn't* for each picture.

1 I want to be a tour guide.
   You should …

2 I want to be a chef.
   You should …

3 I want to be a doctor.
   You should …

4 I want to be a scientist.
   You shouldn't …

4 Choose the correct alternative. If you think both alternatives are correct, choose both.

1 You *must/have to* learn to play an instrument if you want to be a professional musician.

2 Builders *mustn't/don't have to* work in an office.

3 Doctors *mustn't/don't have to* tell secrets about their patients' health.

4 Do you *must/have to* wear a uniform in your job?

5 People who work in banks *must/have to* do a lot of paperwork.

6 A firefighter *has to/have to* work in a team.

7 An architect *mustn't/doesn't have to* be fit to do his or her job.

8 My sister must *deal/deals* with the public in her job.

5 Rewrite each sentence using a modal verb of obligation, prohibition or advice.

1 It is not necessary to have experience to do the job.

You *don't have to have experience to do the job* .

2 It is obligatory for builders to wear hard hats here.

Builders _____ .

3 It is a good idea for Frank to work in the summer.

Frank _____ .

4 In our school, teachers are not allowed to wear jeans.

In our school, _____ .

5 It isn't a good idea to wear very informal clothes for a job interview.

You _____ .

6 It is not obligatory for our receptionists to speak French.

Our receptionists _____ .

7 It is essential for Karen to be calm in her job.

Karen _____ .

6a SPEAKING **Look at the photos and choose a job. Make a note of things you *have to/don't have to/must/ mustn't/should/shouldn't* do in this job.**

a    b

c    d    e

6b Work with a partner. Describe the job. Can your partner guess what it is?

> You have to work at the weekend. You have to work in a team. You should learn other languages in case you go to play in a different country. You shouldn't eat fast food. You must be ambitious if you want to win competitions.

> Is it a football player?

> Yes, it is.

Compound adjectives

1 Look at these words. They are compound adjectives, adjectives made by joining two words. The two words are usually connected with a hyphen (–).

well-organised   hard-working

Complete the compound adjectives in the definitions with the words in the box.

> badly • blue/brown/green • easy
> full • good • part • right/left • well

1 when you don't work all day or all week in your job

_____-time

2 relaxed and calm

_____-going

3 when you don't get much money in your job

_____-paid

4 when you work all day and all week in your job

_____-time

5 when you get paid a lot of money in your job

_____-paid

6 with blue/brown/green eyes

_____-eyed

7 when you write with your right/left hand

_____-handed

8 attractive

_____-looking

9 famous

_____-known

10 rich

_____-off

2 ▶ 44 **Listen and check your answers.**

3a PRONUNCIATION ▶ 44 **Listen again and repeat. Where is the stress in the compound adjectives? Is it on the first word, the second word or on both?**

3b Practise saying the words with the correct stress.

4 Which of the compound adjectives on this page can you use to describe:

1 yourself?

2 your mother/father?

3 Rafael Nadal?

Rafael Nadal

Assessing your TRANSFERABLE SKILLS

LIFE SKILLS OBJECTIVES	KEY CONCEPTS
■ To learn about transferable skills and their importance in finding a job. ■ To consider practical examples of transferable skills in daily life. ■ To assess and express your own transferable skills.	**(un-)employed [adj]:** *When his company closed, he became unemployed and had to look for a new job.* **employer, employee [n]:** *Employers usually look for ambitious people to become their employees.* **problem solving [n]:** *She's good at problem solving, finding solutions in difficult situations.* **leadership [n]:** *People with good leadership can motivate and organise a group of people.*

1 **Work with a partner. What skills or qualities do both mechanics and chefs need?**

They both need to be reliable.
They both need to work with their hands.

2 READING **Read the article. What are 'transferable skills' and why are they important?**

TRANSFERABLE SKILLS

In the past, people left school, found a job and then continued to do that job for the rest of their lives. So, they only learned the skills for one specific job. But nowadays, most people do a number of jobs during their lifetime. This might be because they want to change jobs or perhaps they have to change jobs because they become unemployed. Today it is still important to learn skills for a particular job, but it is also important to learn 'transferable skills'. These are skills that we can use in not just one job but in almost any job.

So, what are the most important transferable skills for the 21st century? Of course, in just about any job you need IT skills. Computers and new technology are everywhere. If you're a shop assistant, an architect or a mechanic, you must be comfortable using new technology.

But even a highly-skilled user of new technologies needs other skills. Very few people work completely alone. So in order to be successful you have to be able to communicate well with others. Good communication is an interpersonal skill. Other interpersonal skills include leadership and teamwork. These are highly valued by employers. Can you motivate others and direct them if necessary? On the other hand, are you able to listen to and take orders from others? Can you work together as part of a bigger team? That's important if you work for a top international bank or

3 **Read the text again and answer these questions.**

1 Why were transferable skills less important in the past?

2 Who needs IT skills and why?

3 What are examples of 'interpersonal' skills and why are they necessary?

4 Who is maths important for?

5 What skill is important when there are situations we did not expect?

6 Do employers usually want ambitious or unambitious people? Why?

if you work in a local café. Creating a good impression on customers and colleagues is essential in almost all jobs, too.

Other general skills are important too. Maths is one of them. A waiter needs to be able to count money and give correct change. Bankers work with numbers and so do shop assistants. Using your hands can be useful in a number of jobs, too. And then there's problem solving. In any job there are situations that we are not ready for. It's important that you can react to those situations in a positive way and find solutions.

Finally, employers are interested in your personal qualities. Are you well-organised? Are you reliable and responsible? Most employers will also look for people who are ambitious and want to continue learning and improving in their job, so that the company moves forward too. In the end, perhaps this is the most important transferable skill of all – the desire to keep learning new things. As Albert Einstein said, 'Once you stop learning, you start dying!'

4 **Look back at your lists in 1. Did you write down any transferable skills? What important transferable skills from the text could be useful in the two jobs?**

5a LISTENING ▶ 45 **Watch or listen to three young people talking about things they do or did in their free time. Tick (✓) the transferable skills that are part of what they do or did.**

		Amelia	Kieran	Molly
1	Friendly and caring			
2	Good communication skills			
3	Good at motivating others			
4	Good at organising others			
5	ICT skills			
6	Leadership			
7	Maths and money			
8	Patience			
9	Problem solving			
10	Teamwork			

5b ▶ 45 **Listen again and make a note of examples to justify your answers in 5a.**

6 **Work in a small group and compare your answers in 5.**

LIFE TASK

You want to consider your own transferable skills.

Follow this plan:

1 Look at a list of transferable skills on page 147. Give yourself a mark from 5 (brilliant) to 1 (poor) for each skill. Add any other skills which you have which are not on the list.

2 For all of the skills where you have 3 or more, think of an example to justify your answer. It could be based on things you do at school, in your free time or to help out at home and/or in a job, if you have one

3 Use the list and your examples to write a description of your transferable skills. You could use this when you apply for a course or a job.

1 **SPEAKING** Extras are the people who appear in the background, behind the main actors in films and TV series. **What do you think are the good and bad things about working as an extra? Make two lists with a partner.**

2 **LISTENING** ▶ 46 **Listen to someone talking about being an extra. Tick the ideas in your lists which they mention.**

✔ EXAM SUCCESS

You are going to do a multiple-choice listening task. In this type of exercise you have to choose one of a number of statements which corresponds to the information in the listening text. What should you do if you don't hear the answer to one of the questions?

➤ EXAM SUCCESS page 145

---

3 ▶ 46 **Listen again and choose the correct answers.**

1 Sarah doesn't know what to do because …
   a they haven't offered her the job.
   b she isn't a professional actress.
   c she doesn't know if she likes the job they've offered.

2 Sarah probably won't get a famous actor's autograph because …
   a you can't say hello to the actors.
   b they don't allow you to ask for autographs.
   c all of the actors there are just normal people.

3 Extras …
   a spend more time waiting than acting.
   b only work five or ten minutes a day.
   c always have to repeat the same scene many times.

4 The main reason why Sarah may decide to take the job is because …
   a it is quite well-paid.
   b she has a cousin who works as an extra.
   c she really likes historical films.

5 Evan convinces Sarah to take the job by suggesting that she should …
   a speak to the director.
   b make good use of the time when she isn't actually filming.
   c become a film director one day.

4 **SPEAKING** **What about *you*?**

Would you like to work as an extra in a film or TV series? Why/Why not?

Grammar in context

Second conditional

1a **Look at these sentences. Then choose the correct alternative in sentences a–c.**

1 If I went, I'd meet some famous actors.

2 If I were you, I'd do it.

3 I would earn a hundred pounds if I worked all weekend.

a We use the second conditional for *possible and probable/improbable and imaginary* situations and their consequences.

b We use the second conditional to talk about *the past/the present or future*.

c We can use the expression If I were/was you, I'd … to *give advice/express obligation*.

1b **Choose the correct alternative.**

1 In the part of the sentence with *if* we use *the past simple/would(n't) + infinitive*.

2 In the other part of the sentence we use *the past simple/would(n't) + infinitive*.

3 We *can/can't* use **was** or **were** with if I/he/she …

GRAMMAR REFERENCE ➤ PAGE 94

2 **Look at the situations and write sentences using the second conditional.**

1 I don't work because I'm still at school.

   If I wasn't still at school, I'd work.

2 He isn't a pilot because he can't see very well.

   ....

3 She doesn't repair computers because she doesn't know how to.

   ....

4 I'm not a professional athlete because I'm not fast enough.

   ....

5 I don't work as an interpreter because I only speak two languages.

   ....

6 We want to leave this company because we aren't happy here.

   ....

7 She can't take part in the concert because she doesn't sing very well.

   ....

3 Complete the text with the correct form of the verbs in the box.

> be • do • eat • look • play • put

There are some very unusual jobs!

If people (a) .... golf better, this first job wouldn't exist. Some golf clubs pay professional divers to go into lakes and collect all the golf balls that go into the water.

If you (b) .... like a famous person, you would be able to make money. You could pretend to be the famous person and appear at parties or in adverts or TV shows.

Believe it or not, some people taste dog food professionally to check that it tastes good. If I (c) .... dog food, I'd be ill!

One hotel in London had a professional bed warmer. They paid somebody to get into the bed for five minutes and make it warm. If I (d) .... that job, I'd fall asleep all the time!

Would you buy an orange if it (e) .... green or yellow? Most people wouldn't. But in some warm places the natural colour of oranges isn't actually orange. That's why some people's job is to make oranges orange – by suddenly making them cold or by exposing them to ethylene gas.

If people (f) .... their chewing gum in the bin, we wouldn't need 'Gum Busters'. These are people who use water at high pressure to take away chewing gum from any type of surface.

4a Look at these situations. Think of good advice to give somebody in these situations. Make notes.

1 I need money.
2 I want to work in the US one day.
3 I want to help to protect the environment.
4 I'm always tired in the morning.
5 I can't sleep at night.
6 I make a lot of spelling mistakes.

4b SPEAKING Work with a partner. Take it in turns to ask for and give advice using *If I were you …*

> I need money.

> If I were you, I'd look for a job.

5a SPEAKING Look at the situations and think about what you would do in each one and why. Make notes.

1 When you arrive at school, you see that you aren't wearing shoes. You're wearing your slippers! What would you do?

2 You tell your best friend that you are too busy to go out tonight. Later, another friend persuades you to go out. Suddenly, you see your best friend 50 metres away, but they haven't seen you yet. What would you do?

3 Your mother is trying on some very unusual clothes in a clothes shop. She obviously likes them. She asks what you think of them. What would you do?

4 You buy a pair of jeans. When you get home, you find a very nice jacket inside the bag with your jeans. You didn't buy the jacket. What would you do?

5 Somebody offers to buy you a tablet if you do a bungee-jump. You really need a tablet but you are afraid of heights. What would you do?

5b Work with a partner. Compare your ideas for each situation.

> I would go home again.

> I wouldn't. The teachers wouldn't be happy if you missed class.

Making polite requests

SUMMER
JOB OFFERS

Red Lemon Fashions

We are looking for shop assistants for the summer. If you love fashion, we want you to join our team. Good conditions. Perfect for students.
Phone 0151 897 6543 for information about how to apply.

CINERAMA CINEMAS

We need people to work evenings and at the weekend. Responsibilities include checking tickets and selling popcorn and soft drinks. Watch the latest films ... free! Join our young and dynamic team!

Phone 0181 754 6022 for more information about wages and conditions.

US Au pairs
Ever wanted to visit California? Are you patient, caring and good with kids? Work as an au pair in LA this summer. Free flights, food and accommodation!
Phone 0121 977 2001 for enquiries and application forms.

ARE YOU MAD ABOUT SPORT?
Would you like to spend all summer teaching sport to people from around the world? Then come and work at our international sports camp!
Phone **0191 121 5533** for information about where to send CVs, etc.

SPORTS STAR CAMP

1a SPEAKING Look at the adverts for summer jobs. If you were looking for a job, which would you be interested in and why? Work with a partner and compare your answers.

1b Work with a partner. Choose a job and make a list of questions that you would want to ask to find out more information about the job.

Is the job full-time or part-time? What are the wages?

2 LISTENING ▶ 47 Listen to a teenager calling about one of the adverts. Which advert is she calling about? Does she ask any of your questions from 1?

3 ▶ 47 All the expressions in the Speaking bank are polite ways of requesting information. Listen to the dialogue again and put the requests in the order that you hear them.

💬 SPEAKING BANK

Useful expressions for making polite requests

Can you tell me what the wages are? ....

Could I ask for some information first? ....

Could you tell me if the job is full-time or part-time? ....

4 SPEAKING Work with a partner. Take it in turns to use the table to make polite requests for information.

	if	the job starts?
Could you tell me	what	I can apply?
Could I ask	when	you are looking for?
Can you tell me	how	we have to do?
	how much	you need experience?
	what sort of person	the wages are?

PRACTICE MAKES PERFECT

5a SPEAKING Work with a partner. Do this role-play using the polite requests from the Speaking bank.

You are speaking to somebody about a summer job. Find out:
- the dates and wages
- if the job is full-time or part-time
- necessary personal qualities
- if experience is necessary or not

Student A: Prepare questions to ask for information about the job at Cinerama Cinemas.

Student B: You have information about the job at Cinerama Cinemas on page 148. Invent any extra information if necessary.

Good afternoon. I'm calling about your job offer in the newspaper yesterday.

Yes. What would you like to know?

5b Now change roles.

Student B: Prepare questions to ask about the job at Sports Star Camp.

Student A: You have information about the job at Sports Star Camp on page 148. Invent any extra information if necessary.

Developing writing

A letter of application and CV

1 Read this letter of application and CV. Which summer job offer on page 92 do you think this person is replying to? Why?

> 34 Norton Road
> Stoke
> S03 6HT
> 14th February
>
> Dear Ms Simpson,
>
> I am writing in response to your advertisement in *The Stoke Times*. I would like to apply for the job which you advertised in this newspaper on 10th February.
> I enclose a CV with information about myself, including education and work experience. As you can see, I have experience of working with children and I also think that I am caring, patient and very hard-working.
> I look forward to hearing from you.
>
> Yours sincerely,
>
> Diana Huxley

CURRICULUM VITAE

——— GENERAL INFORMATION ———
Address   34 Norton Road, Stoke, S03 6HT
Telephone (home)   0342 455 3212
Telephone (mobile)   632 12 34 56
Email   dhuxley@anynet.uk

——— EDUCATION AND QUALIFICATIONS ———
Green Coat School, Stoke
A levels in Economics (Grade A), Sociology (Grade B) and English (Grade B)

——— WORK EXPERIENCE ———
March 2013 – March 2015
Part-time teaching assistant at Sunnydale Kindergarten, Stoke
July – August 2012
Helper at Green Valley Summer Camp, Brighton

——— INTERESTS ———
Cookery, Surfing
Good knowledge of computers – MS Office, PowerPoint, Excel, Word

2 Read the letter and CV again. Where does Diana give the following information – in her letter, in her CV or in both?

1 where and when she saw the
   job offer   letter / CV / both
2 her personal qualities   letter / CV / both
3 her contact details   letter / CV / both
4 her hobbies   letter / CV / both
5 information about her experience letter / CV / both

3 Read the letter and CV again and find the information in 2.

1 *The Stoke Times newspaper on 10th February*

4 Write your own CV. Use the CV in 1 as a model.

5 Look again at the letter in 1 and complete the information in the Writing bank.

6 Work with a partner. Look at this job advert. What qualities, skills or experience would be useful for this job?

JOB OPPORTUNITY

We need waiters and waitresses to work in our new, 21st century fast-food restaurant. Are you friendly? Are you fun? You are? Come and work for us!

Email a letter and CV to Gary Daly gdaly@21stcenturyfood.co.uk

You need to be sociable. Experience in a fast food restaurant would be useful.

PRACTICE MAKES PERFECT

7a Write a letter of application. Use the letter in 1, your ideas from 6, and the Writing bank to help you.

Write a letter to apply for the job at the fast-food restaurant and:
- state which job you are applying for
- say what experience you have
- describe your personal qualities
- end your letter.

WRITING BANK ➤ PAGE 151

7b Read letters by other students. Who would you give the job to? Why?

Grammar reference

have to, don't have to

FORM

Affirmative	Police officers have to wear a uniform.
Negative	Teachers don't have to wear a uniform.
Question	Do police officers have to wear a uniform?
Short answers	Yes, they do./No, they don't.

USE

- We use *have to* to talk about things which are obligatory or necessary.
- We use *don't have to* to talk about things which are not obligatory or necessary.

must, mustn't

FORM

Affirmative	You must switch off your mobile phone in class.
Negative	You mustn't use your mobile phone when driving.

USE

- We use *must* to talk about rules, regulations, and obligations.
- We use *mustn't* to talk about prohibitions.
- *Must* is not very common in the question form. We usually use *have to*.

should, shouldn't

FORM

Affirmative	You should arrive on time.
Negative	You shouldn't be late.
Question	Should I wait outside?
Short answers	Yes, I should./No, I shouldn't.

USE

- We use *should* and *shouldn't* to give and ask for advice and recommendations.

Second conditional

FORM

If + past simple, … would/wouldn't + infinitive

If I **knew** about cars, I**'d become** a mechanic.

If we **didn't listen**, we **wouldn't understand** his explanations.

If I **was** a millionaire, I **wouldn't know** what to do with my money.

The past simple comes in the part of the sentence with *if*. *Would* does not appear in this part of the sentence.

~~If I would need help, I would call you.~~

The part of the sentence with *if* can go at the start of the sentence or at the end. There is no difference in meaning. However, if the part with *if* goes at the start of the sentence we must use a comma before the second half of the sentence.

If I had a bike, I'd cycle to school.

I'd cycle to school if I had a bike.

- We can use *were* instead of *was* with *if*.

  If I were/was a millionaire, I would give money to that charity.

USE

We use the second conditional to talk about imaginary or improbable situations and their consequences.

The imaginary or improbable sentences are in the present or future, NOT in the past.

If I **found** money in the street (imaginary present situation), I **would give** it to the police (the consequence of this situation).

We use *If I were you, I'd …*, to give advice and recommendations.

If I were you, I'd study more.

Vocabulary

1 Jobs and work architect • builder • company director • fashion designer • firefighter • journalist • librarian • mechanic • nurse • plumber • police officer • receptionist • shop assistant • vet

2 Personal qualities ambitious • calm • caring • clever/bright • confident • creative • fit • hard-working • patient • reliable • sensitive • sociable • strong • well-organised

3 Compound adjectives badly-paid • blue/brown/green-eyed • easy-going • full-time • good-looking • part-time • right/left-handed • well-known • well-off • well-paid

4 Other words and phrases ➤ page 140

Grammar revision

1 Choose the correct alternative. If two alternatives are correct, choose both.

1 People *must/mustn't/don't have to* make a lot of noise in a hospital.

2 You *must/mustn't/have to* study a lot to be an architect.

3 People who work in a bank *doesn't have to/don't have to/mustn't* wear a uniform.

4 You *has to/have to/must* know how to use a computer to work in a bank.

5 Visitors to the museum *mustn't/must/don't have to* take photos. It is prohibited.

6 A professional football player *mustn't/doesn't have to/don't have to* work in an office.

7 You *must/don't have to/mustn't* drink and drive.

2 Choose the correct alternative.

Sam: I want to work in the US. Can you give me some advice?

Tanya: You should (a) *look/to look* for job adverts on the Internet.

Sam: (b) *I should/Should I* send my CV?

Tanya: Yes, if I were you I (c) *sent/would send* a letter and a CV by email. But you (d) *should/shouldn't* worry if it takes a long time for an answer. They probably have hundreds of people sending CVs. If I were you, I (e) *would/should* be patient.

3 Write sentences in the second conditional.

1 I/see a bear ➤ take a photo of it

....

2 my brother/be angry ➤ shout

....

3 my parents/win the lottery ➤ give me a present

....

4 I/not have a pen ➤ ask my friend for one

....

5 we/not have a TV ➤ talk more

....

6 he/not be very good at football ➤ not play in the first division

....

7 I/live in Italy ➤ speak Italian

....

8 we/have wings ➤ be able to fly

....

Vocabulary revision

1 Complete the jobs with vowels.

1 j......r n...l...s t

2 b......l d...r

3 p l...m b...r

4 s h...p......s s...s t...n t

5 r...c...p t......n...s t

6 v...t

7 f...s h......n d...s...g n...r

8 m...c h...n...c

2 Complete the sentences in a logical way.

1 Alex is very ambitious because ....

2 He's very reliable. He ....

3 She's very caring. Do you remember when she .... ?

4 Dean is very sociable. He always ....

5 When you're creative, you ....

6 If you are very bright, you ....

3 Complete with the appropriate word.

1 a job which gives you a lot of money:
well-............

2 relaxed and calm: easy-............

3 famous: well-............

4 when you write with your right hand:
right-............

5 attractive: good-............

6 when you work all day in your job:
full-............

8 Best friends forever

Vocabulary

(Aa) (Bb)

Friendships

1 Look at the pictures. Read the story and match the pictures to an appropriate word or phrase (a–j).

Maybe it's because I'm shy, but I've got quite a small **(a)** circle of friends. I'm really good friends with a small group of **(b)** classmates. I often **(c)** hang out with them at my house after school and sometimes we play sports in the park near school or go to the cinema. Apart from my classmates, I've got one other **(d)** close friend. His name's Adrian and he's a friend of my cousin. In fact, I met him at my cousin's house. The first time I chatted to Adrian, we found that we **(e)** see eye to eye on lots of things. There are many things that we **(f)** have in common. We like the same sports, the same subjects at school, the same TV programmes … Maybe that's no surprise, because I **(g)** get on really well with my cousin, too. Adrian and I never **(h)** have arguments with each other and we've never **(i)** fallen out. But I know that even if we had an argument one day, we would **(j)** make it up very quickly. That's what true friendship is about.

1 _h_   2 _____   3 _____

2 Match the words and phrases in the story in 1 with their definitions.

1 to have a good relationship with somebody _____
2 to stop being friendly with someone because you have had a disagreement with them _____
3 to become friends again after a disagreement _____
4 to meet and spend time together _____
5 to have angry disagreements with somebody _____
6 to agree with somebody _____
7 to have the same interests or opinions as someone _____
8 a group of friends _____
9 people in your class at school _____
10 a good friend _____

3 Complete these questions with the correct preposition.

1 Have you got a big or small circle _____ friends?
2 Do you see eye _____ eye with your parents?
3 When you have an argument _____ somebody, do you find it easy to make it _____ with them afterwards?
4 Have you ever fallen _____ with your best friend?
5 Do you have a lot _____ common with the people in your close family?
6 Do you usually get _____ well _____ your classmates?
7 Do you hang _____ with your friends every day after school?

4 SPEAKING Use the completed questions in 3 to interview your partner.

> *Have you got a big or small circle of friends?*

> *It's quite big, I think. I've got a lot of friends outside school.*

Feelings

5 Write the words in two columns (adjectives and nouns) in your notebook.

> afraid • anger • angry • bored • boredom
> excited • excitement • fear • happiness • happy
> loneliness • lonely • sad • sadness

6 ▶ 48 Listen, check and repeat.

7 LISTENING ▶ 49 Listen. Write down the feeling expressed by each speaker.

1 _____   3 _____   5 _____
2 _____   4 _____

8 SPEAKING Work with a partner. Ask and answer questions about the feelings in 5.

> *When do you feel bored?*

> *When I'm waiting for my friends.*

A LESSON IN FRIENDSHIP

Zafar and Nadeem had been great friends since the age of five. They used to go to the same primary school. When they finished primary school, they both went to the same secondary school. That school was a 20-minute walk from their village in a town on the other side of the river. Every morning Zafar and Nadeem used to walk there and back together.

Zafar and Nadeem didn't always see eye to eye. They didn't use to argue much, but occasionally they had arguments about school. They were both <u>competitive</u> and wanted to get the best marks in their class. One <u>wet</u> Wednesday afternoon, they were walking back from school together,

as always. But on this occasion Zafar was angry with Nadeem. Nadeem had got the highest mark in a test that day and he <u>kept on</u> talking about it. Zafar thought Nadeem was only doing it to make him feel bad. Anger took control of him and finally, in a moment of madness, he turned and <u>slapped</u> Nadeem in the face. Nadeem was <u>shocked</u> at first, but then he picked up a stick, and wrote in the sand by the side of the road: 'Today my friend Zafar slapped me'.

The pair of friends carried on their way home in silence. The rain kept on falling. As they got closer to the river, a section of the <u>river bank</u> broke because of the rain and the

water carried both boys into the river. Nadeem couldn't swim but straight away Zafar was there by his side, pulling him to <u>safety</u>. After Nadeem had calmed down, he took a <u>sharp</u> stone and wrote on a big rock: 'Today my friend Zafar saved my life'.

Zafar said: 'Earlier, you wrote in the sand saying that I hit you. But now you've written on a rock. Why?' Nadeem replied: 'Writing in the sand disappears quickly. When our friends do something bad to us, we should forget it quickly. But when friends do good things and show us kindness, we should always remember it, just as the writing on a rock remains forever.' When Nadeem had finished speaking, Zafar put his arm round his shoulder and they continued on their way home.

● ● ●

1 **Read this story about two friends called Nadeem and Zafar. Are Nadeem and Zafar still friends at the end of the story?**

2 **Put these events in the story in the correct order.**

a Nadeem and Zafar started studying at secondary school. ....

b Zafar wanted Nadeem to explain his actions. ....

c Nadeem wrote a message on a rock. ....

d Nadeem did very well in a test one day at school. ....

e Nadeem gave Zafar a lesson in friendship. ....

f Zafar hit Nadeem. ....

g Nadeem and Zafar met for the first time. ....

h Nadeem wrote a message in the sand. ....

i Zafar saved Nadeem's life. ....

j Zafar got particularly angry with Nadeem. ....

3 **Read the story again and answer these questions.**

1 What was the only problem in Nadeem and Zafar's relationship?

2 Why did Zafar hit Nadeem?

3 What happened to the river on this particular day?

4 Why did Zafar need to help Nadeem?

5 What did Nadeem need to write his second message?

6 What was the lesson that Nadeem gave Zafar about friendship?

4 ⚙️ **CRITICAL THINKING**

Think! Then compare ideas with your class.

■ What do you think about the message in this story? Do you agree with it? Why/Why not?

5 **What do the <u>underlined</u> words in the text mean? Guess and then check in your dictionary.**

6 SPEAKING **What about *you*?**

1 What do you think is the secret of friendship?

2 What other stories about friends or friendship do you know?

Grammar in context

 *Past perfect*

1a Look at the sentences. Which actions happened first, the green or the red?

1 Zafar was angry with Nadeem because he had got the highest mark.

2 When Nadeem had finished speaking, they continued on their way home.

1b Choose the correct alternative.

We use the past perfect to talk about an activity in the past which happened *before/ after* another activity in the past.

1c Complete the rule.

To make the past perfect, we use the past of .... + the ....

GRAMMAR REFERENCE ➤ PAGE 106

2a PRONUNCIATION **The contracted form of had is 'd. Look at these sentences. Add 'd to the sentences that should be in the past perfect.**

1 He .... known him since he was five.

2 They .... went to live in another town.

3 She .... gone to the shops.

4 We .... seen him that morning.

5 She .... took her phone with her.

6 I .... given him my pen.

2b ▶ 50 **Listen and check your answers.**

2c ▶ 50 **Listen again and repeat the sentences with 'd.**

3a Match the sentences.

1 I put my pyjamas on.
2 She finished the shopping.
3 They finished their lunch.
4 He got out of the pool.
5 We finished the test.
6 I found my keys.

a They left the restaurant.
b I got into bed.
c I opened the door.
d She carried it home.
e We gave it to the teacher.
f He dried himself with a towel.

3b Rewrite the sentences in 3a as one sentence. Put one verb in the past perfect and the other in the past simple. Use *when* or *after*.

1 *When I had put my pyjamas on, I got into bed.*

2 ....

3 ....

4 ....

5 ....

6 ....

4 Complete these sentences in a logical way using the past perfect.

1 I was lonely because *everybody had left.*

2 I was feeling ill because ....

3 They were very happy because ....

4 She was bored because ....

5 We were angry because ....

6 He was feeling sad because ....

7 Yesterday I was excited because ....

8 They were afraid because ....

5 Complete the text with the past perfect form of the verbs given.

Ryan was always an amazing student. Before he was seven, he (a) .... (learn) to speak five languages. Before he was 16, he (b) .... (pass) all his university entrance exams. When he left school, he went to live in Cambridge because they (c) .... (give) him a place to study there. Ryan (d) .... (not make) many friends when he (e) .... (be) at school. But by the end of the first week at university, he (f) .... (meet) lots of people with similar interests to him. At school he (g) .... (not see) eye to eye with most of his classmates. It seemed to him that he had much more in common with his university friends. It (h) .... (take) him a long time, but finally he had a circle of friends to chat to about his studies.

6 **SPEAKING** Work with a partner. Find out which of these things your partner had done by the age of seven.

1   begin to learn English
2   travel to a different country
3   learn to read
4   swim in the sea
5   start to ride a bike
6   go on holiday without his/her parents
7   use a computer

> I'd begun to learn English by the age of seven. And you?

> Yes, me too. I think I'd started by the age of five!

used to

7 Look at the sentences and choose the correct alternative in the rules.

1   Every morning Zafar and Nadeem **used to** walk there and back together.
2   They **didn't use to** argue much.

a   We use **used to** to talk about *single actions/habits* in the past.
b   After **used to** we use the *infinitive/past simple*.

GRAMMAR REFERENCE ➤ PAGE 106

8 Isabel used to live in a small village on the Costa del Sol in Spain. Now she lives in New York. Complete the sentences with *used to* or *didn't use to*.

1   Isabel .... speak Spanish all the time.
2   She .... travel by Subway.
3   She .... swim in the sea.
4   She .... see thousands of people on the streets.
5   She .... know everybody who lived in her street.
6   She .... wear warm clothes in winter.

9a **SPEAKING** Complete these sentences about yourself when you were seven with *used to* or *didn't use to*.

1   I .... have lots of homework.
2   I .... like drawing and painting.
3   I .... play computer games.
4   I .... read books in English.
5   I .... spend a lot of time alone.
6   I .... spend a lot of time at home.

9b Work with a partner. Compare your answers.

Noun suffixes *-ness, -ship, -dom*

1 Look at the words. Which suffix, *-ness*, *-ship*, or *-dom*, can we add to them? Does the spelling of any of the words change?

> bored • free • friend • happy • ill • king
> leader • lonely • mad • relation • sad • weak

bored – boredom

2 ▶ 51 Listen, check and repeat.

3 Complete the sentences using the noun form of the appropriate word in 1.

1   That's a crazy idea. It's ....!
2   .... is being able to control and direct a group of people.
3   To beat the other team we need to find their .... There must be something that they aren't very good at.
4   He loves the .... of being able to do what he likes, when he likes.
5   What's the .... between Lucas and Hannah? Are they family or friends?
6   Flu is a very common ....
7   Money can't buy you ....
8   I think television is popular because of the .... that people feel when they have nothing to do.

4a Complete the questions with the correct noun suffix.

1   What is important for a good *friend*............................?
2   What is your biggest *weak*............................?
3   How much *free*............................ do you think you have?
4   What do you think is the secret of *happ(y)*............................?
5   How do you stop *bore*............................?
6   Would you like to go to the United *King*............................ one day?
7   Have you ever had a moment of *mad*............................?

4b **SPEAKING** Work with a partner. Ask and answer these questions.

Managing friendships

LIFE SKILLS OBJECTIVES	KEY CONCEPTS
■ To learn about friendship styles. ■ To think about situations when you need to make new friends. ■ To decide the best way for new students to make friends at school and locally.	**feel part of [phrase]:** *Now I feel part of the group – we're all close and get on well.* **share [v]:** *When I have food at break time, I share it with my friends so they all have some.* **isolated, disconnected [adj]:** *I don't have any friends here. I feel isolated/disconnected from the others.* **take part in [phrase]:** *Some people like taking part in sports events but others prefer to watch.*

1a Choose the best alternative for you.

1 I prefer spending my time *alone/with my family/with one good friend/with a small group of friends/with a big group of friends*.

2 I've known most of my friends *for a very long time/for a year or so/since only recently*.

3 I find it *very easy/easy/difficult* to chat to somebody I meet for the first time.

1b In what situations do we have to make new friends? Work with a partner. Make a list.

2 READING **Read this page from a website. How many of your ideas from 1b can you find?**

ADVICE ▮ CATEGORIES ▮ FACTFILE A–Z ▮ HELPLINES

Making new friends

We all need to make new friends sometimes. There are many reasons why, including:

▮ **You may have moved to a new town or even a new country!**

5 ▮ **Your close friend or friends may have changed school or moved away.**

▮ **You may have fallen out with your circle of friends or you may have less in common with them than you used to.**

▮ **You may be away from your friends and family on a**

10 **holiday camp or an educational trip.**

WHAT YOU CAN DO:

▮ When you don't have friends, you can feel lonely. Remember that loneliness is very common. Almost everyone feels it at some time. It does not mean that there is something wrong with you. It is a situation that you can change. Changing the situation may involve finding and developing a circle of friends. But it may also mean learning to enjoy your times alone; to use them more constructively and enjoyably.

15 ▮ Do not wait for other people to visit you or speak to you. Try to talk to people you sit next to in class or at meals or in breaks. Say hello or even just smile at people you pass in the building.

▮ Try to put yourself in new situations where you will meet people with similar interests to you. Join in with activities that you are genuinely interested in and enjoy – clubs, sports or voluntary work. But do not do too much – don't fill your time with too many things just so that you are not alone.

20 ▮ Try not to be critical of your efforts. Remind yourself that close friendships take time to develop.

▮ Build relationships by being a good friend to others.

▮ Respond to others and their interests (but do not pretend to be interested if you aren't really).

▮ Some people are more comfortable in groups and others in 'one-to-one' situations. Consider your own preferences and 'style'. Find others with similar preferences.

3 According to the information in the text, are these statements True (T) or False (F)? Put the number(s) of the line(s) where you found the answer.

1 The only way to change your loneliness is by being with other people.   **T / F**

2 It is important to take the first step when you are lonely.   **T / F**

3 To stop loneliness, go out at every possible moment.   **T / F**

4 If you're lonely, don't go alone to do your favourite activities.   **T / F**

5 You need to be patient when you are lonely.   **T / F**

6 It's always better to be in big groups of friends than just with one friend.   **T / F**

4 SPEAKING **Work with a partner. Discuss your answers to these questions.**

1 Imagine you are at a language school in the UK for three weeks. Do you think you will find it difficult to make new friends? Why/Why not?

2 What's the best idea to help you make friends in the article?

5a Look at the photos. Work with a partner. How do you think they could help people to make new friends at university?

5b LISTENING ▶ 52 **Listen and put the four pictures in the order in which the students mention them.**

5c ▶ 52 **Explain the significance of each picture and how they helped to make friends. Listen again if necessary.**

6 ▶ 52 **Which speaker (1–4) …**

a made friends thanks to a skill they had?
....

b made friends almost without moving?
....

c needed time to make friends? ....

d made friends by helping other people to relax from their studies? ....

e had other people offering to do the same as them? ....

f did an activity that they really enjoyed in order to make friends? ....

7 Whose idea do you think would work best for you? Why?

LIFE TASK

You want to help new students at your school or in the area where you live who find it difficult to make new friends.

Follow this plan:

1 *Think of ideas to make new friends at school. Are there any official or unofficial clubs, societies or sports teams? Does the school organise any special social events? Could you begin a club or event to help new students? Is there somebody to speak to for advice and help if somebody is very lonely? Make a list of ideas.*

2 *Now do the same for the area where you live. For example, where do people usually hang out at the weekend?*

3 *Decide if you want to create a leaflet or a web page with the information. Organise your information and ideas.*

4 *Create your leaflet or webpage.*

5 *Let other students see it and evaluate it. Make any necessary changes to improve it.*

1 [SPEAKING] **Do this questionnaire. When you finish, compare results with a partner.**

DISCOVER YOUR SECRET SELF!

Put a tick (✓) next to any statements which you think are true for you.

Section 1

- [ ] I feel I have to be right all the time.
- [ ] If I don't do my best, I get angry with myself.
- [ ] When I go shopping, I don't buy anything if I'm not 100% happy with it.
- [ ] I enjoy criticising other people but I hate people criticising me.
- [ ] Understanding other people's opinions isn't easy for me.

Section 2

- [ ] I love giving presents to my friends and family.
- [ ] I'm good at drawing, writing and acting.
- [ ] I find it easy to talk about how I feel.
- [ ] When I feel sad or lonely I feel very sad or lonely.
- [ ] I hate rules and obligations because my freedom is the most important thing.

Section 3

- [ ] My idea of excitement is doing sudokus and crosswords.
- [ ] I always think hard before making a decision.
- [ ] I'm usually very hard-working at school.
- [ ] I stay calm in difficult situations.
- [ ] I learn by watching and reading more than by doing.

Section 4

- [ ] In a group, I'm the one who makes decisions.
- [ ] I hate being with people who can't make decisions.
- [ ] I love having a good argument.
- [ ] I'm not afraid of telling people what I think.
- [ ] I find it hard to say sorry.

2 **Now turn to page 148 to discover what your results mean.**

3 [LISTENING] ▶ 53 **Listen to Jessica talking to Jack about the questionnaire. Answer these questions.**

1 Which section (1–4) do they talk about?
2 Do Jessica and Jack agree with the results?

4 ▶ 53 **Listen again and choose the correct alternative.**

1 Last week Jessica decided *where they went/what they saw*.
2 Jack thinks Jessica isn't very good at *waiting/listening*.
3 Jessica and Jack have an argument about *why/how long* he waited last week.
4 Jessica *agrees/doesn't agree* that she likes arguing.
5 Jessica didn't like the *service/quality of the food* last night.
6 Jessica *often/never* apologises.

Gerunds and infinitives

1a Look at the sentences.

1 When I go shopp**ing**, I don't buy anything.
2 I love giv**ing** presents.
3 Understand**ing** other people's opinions isn't easy.
4 I find it easy **to talk** about how I feel.
5 I learn by watch**ing**.
6 Nobody wanted **to make** the decision.
7 **A:** Why did you shout at the waiter?
  B: **To tell** him the food was no good.

1b Put the rules below in the correct column.

We use the gerund:	We use the infinitive:
5	

1 … as the subject of a sentence.
2 … to explain why somebody does something.
3 … immediately after adjectives.
4 … after certain verbs like *want*.
5 … with *go* to talk about physical activities.
6 … after prepositions.
7 … after verbs of liking or disliking.

GRAMMAR REFERENCE ➤ PAGE 106

2 **Look at these statements. Which rule in 1b explains why we use the gerund or infinitive in each one?**

Section 5

- [ ] I find it difficult to say no if someone asks me to do something. ....
- [ ] I love making other people feel good. ....
- [ ] People often come to me to get advice. ....
- [ ] I always want to help my friends and family. ....

- [ ] I'm interested in becoming a doctor or a nurse one day. ....

Section 6

- [ ] I hate having arguments. ....
- [ ] When I have a problem, I don't fight, I go running. ....

- [ ] I think it's stupid to disagree about small things. ....

- [ ] Shouting is horrible, in my opinion. ....
- [ ] I make problems disappear by not thinking about them. ....

3 **Tick (✓) the statements in 2 that are true for you. Where do you have more ticks, in Section 5 or Section 6? Now find out what each section means on the next page.**

4 Complete the texts with the gerund or infinitive form of the verbs with *to*.

MOSTLY SECTION 5: YOU'RE A HELPER

Personality: You're warm and caring and you think it's easy (a) .... (make) friends. You do many things (b) .... (make) your friends' lives better. But (c) .... (be) helpful can sometimes get you into trouble because you want (d) .... (know) what problems people are having.

Romance: You like (e) .... (show) your emotions but you can be possessive. Don't go (f) .... (fall) in love too fast!

Ideal jobs: Nurse, doctor, primary school teacher

Advice: Learn to say no and don't be afraid (g) .... (make) it clear what *you* want from life.

MOSTLY SECTION 6: YOU'RE A PACIFIST

Personality: You never want (h) .... (argue) about anything. You're calm and open-minded. You enjoy (i) .... (listen) to other people and you think it's important (j) .... (hear) different opinions. But (k) .... (do) what other people want all the time can be tiring.

Romance: By (l) .... (accept) your partner's ideas, you seem an ideal partner. But it's important (m) .... (spend) time doing what *you* want.

Ideal jobs: Social worker, receptionist, gardener

Advice: (n) .... (defend) your own opinions isn't the same as being aggressive. Do it more often. Why? (o) .... (get) the respect of other people is important.

5 Do you agree with the results? Why/Why not?

William Hanna and Joseph Barbera

6 Read this text and find eight mistakes with gerunds and infinitives.

William Hanna and Joseph Barbera were the creators of popular cartoons. They were responsible for create Tom and Jerry, The Flintstones, and Scooby-Doo. Hanna and Barbera had different skills. Hanna, for example, liked singing and play music. Barbera was very good at think of funny situations for the characters. Hanna used to go walk and he enjoyed to be outdoors. Barbera relaxed by go to the beach. Eat good food was another of his hobbies. They had different personalities but they got on really well. They were always excited about work together. They remained partners and friends for over 60 years.

7 Finish these questions using a gerund or an infinitive.

What type of person are you?

1 Are you interested in *meeting new people* .... ?
2 Do you enjoy .... ?
3 One day do you want .... ?
4 Do you ever go .... ?
5 Do you find it easy .... ?
6 Is it important for you .... ?
7 Do you hate .... ?
8 Why do you go .... ?
9 Do you think .... is a good idea?
10 Are you excited about .... ?

8a SPEAKING **Ask your partner your questions from 7.**

8b SPEAKING **Tell the class some things you discovered about your partner.**

> *I discovered that my partner is interested in watching old black-and-white films.*

Developing speaking

Reporting a past event

1a SPEAKING **Work with a partner. What types of things do you like doing with your friends? Make a list.**

1b Look at the photos. What can you see in each photo? Which event would you prefer to be at and why?

2 LISTENING ▶ 54 **Listen to a conversation about the barbecue in picture b and answer these questions.**

1   Why did Joe have a barbecue?
2   Where was the barbecue?
3   What was the music like and why?
4   How many people went?
5   Who had made all the food?
6   Who did Lee meet at the barbecue?

3 **Look at the sentences in the Speaking bank. Match the verb forms in bold with the correct name of the tense and the explanation of its use.**

💬 SPEAKING BANK

Using different past tenses

1   I **went** to a barbecue.
2   We **used to** go there a lot.
3   They**'d made** a lot of food.
4   When I **was getting** food, I met Oliver.

a   past continuous
b   past perfect
c   past simple
d   *used to*

i   an activity in progress at a moment in the past. We often use it to describe scenes in the past.
ii a completed action in the past.
iii a past habit
iv an activity that happened before another action in the past.

4 **Think of an event that you went to with your friends or family. Prepare to talk about it by looking at these questions. Make notes but do not write complete sentences.**

1   Where did you go?
2   Who did you go with?
3   What did you do there?
4   How many people were there?
5   Did you know everybody there?
6   Who did you meet or chat to?
7   Was there any food? What was it like?
8   What did you wear?
9   Did you enjoy yourself?
10 What time did the event end?

PRACTICE MAKES PERFECT

5 SPEAKING **Work with a partner. Take it in turns to do this task. Use your notes from 4 and the Speaking bank to help you.**

Tell your partner about an event that you went to with your friends or family. Tell them:

■   what the event was
■   what you did there
■   your opinion of the event, giving reasons.

✓ EXAM SUCCESS

What language is useful in tasks where you have to report past events?

➤ EXAM SUCCESS page 146

Developing writing

An email of advice

1 Read this email. What problem does the writer of the letter have?

Dear Sophie,
I'm writing to you because I need some advice. Do you remember Ellie? We've been best friends since primary school. But recently I've realised that I don't have anything in common with her any more. Maybe it's because I sing in a band now and I spend a lot of time hanging out with them. When I'm with my friends in the band, we always talk about music and Ellie isn't really interested in that. So when she asks if she can come with us, I always have to invent reasons why she can't. I feel bad about lying to her. I know she's having a hard time. What should I do?
Please write back soon,
Rachel

2 SPEAKING Work with a partner. What advice would you give Rachel?

3 Read Sophie's reply. Is her advice similar to yours? Do you think it's good advice? Why/Why not?

Dear Rachel,
It was good to hear from you, but I'm sorry to hear about your problem. Here's my advice.
First of all, I think you really should chat to Ellie. Tell her the truth, that you've got a new hobby and new friends. Next, explain that it's difficult because your new friends don't have much in common with her. So, suggest spending some time alone with Ellie but say that you also need time alone with your new friends. After that, tell her that this new situation isn't her fault or your fault. Who knows? Maybe one day in the future you'll both have more in common again. Lastly, tell Ellie that you're sure she'll find a new group of friends soon, just like you have.
Anyway, I hope you find this advice useful.
Good luck!
Sophie

4 Look at the email again. Find words to complete the Writing bank.

WRITING BANK

Useful words and expressions to order your ideas
- First,
- Firstly,
- ....
- Then,
- ....
- ....
- Finally,
- ....

WRITING BANK ➤ PAGE 151

5a Read this email. What problem does this writer have? What advice would you give? Think of at least three different ideas.

Dear Henry,
I hope you're well. I've got a bit of a problem at the moment and I wanted to ask you for help.
Do you remember my friend Jonathan? He used to be in the basketball team with me. Recently, he's stopped talking to me. About a month ago he started going out with a new circle of friends. At about the same time, he left the basketball team. And at school his marks are getting worse. I really like Jonathan, and I don't mind if he goes out with other friends. But I'm worried about him. I think his new friends are having a really bad influence on him. What should I do?
Please write back soon and tell me what you think.
All the best,
Dan

5b SPEAKING Work with a partner. Compare your ideas. Are they similar?

6 PRACTICE MAKES PERFECT Write an email giving advice to Dan. Use the email in 3, your ideas from 5, and the Writing bank to help you.

✔ EXAM SUCCESS

Why is it important to read the question carefully in writing exams?

➤ EXAM SUCCESS page 146

Grammar reference

Past perfect

FORM	
Affirmative	subject + had ('d) + past participle *She had left the classroom.*
Negative	subject + had not (hadn't) + past participle *They hadn't seen her.*
Question	had + subject + past participle *Had you finished the exercise?*
Short answers	Yes, subject + had. No, subject + hadn't. *Yes, I had. No, they hadn't.*

USE

We use the past perfect to talk about actions that happened before another action or actions in the past.

*I **had done** my homework when my mum **came** home.* (= First I did my homework and then my mum came home.)

We often use time expressions such as *when*, *after*, *by the time*, *as soon as* with the past perfect.

used to

FORM	
Affirmative	I used to play with dolls when I was small.
Negative	She didn't use to have so many exams when she was at primary school.

USE

- We use *used to* to talk about past habits, things we did regularly in the past but not now.

Gerunds and infinitives

USE

We use the gerund:	We use the infinitive:
as the subject of a sentence. *Running is good for you.*	to explain why somebody does something. *Why did he go to the shops? To buy milk.*
after prepositions. *I'm interested in learning languages.*	immediately after adjectives. *It's good to express your feelings.*
after verbs of liking or disliking, e.g. *like, love, enjoy, can't stand, don't mind, hate.* *I enjoy going out.*	after certain verbs, e.g. *want, learn, agree, decide, expect, hope, seem, try, would like.* *I want to work for a newspaper.*
with *go* to talk about physical activities. *go running, go swimming, go cycling, go shopping, go fishing*	

Vocabulary

1 Friendships circle of friends • classmates • close friend • to fall out with somebody • to get on well with somebody • to hang out with somebody • to have an argument with somebody • to have in common • to make it up with somebody • to see eye to eye

2 Feelings afraid (adj) • anger (n) • angry (adj) • bored (adj) • boredom (n) • excited (adj) • excitement (n) • fear (n) • happiness (n) • happy (adj) • loneliness (n) • lonely (adj) • sad (adj) • sadness (n)

3 Noun suffixes -*ness*, *-ship*, *-dom* boredom • freedom • friendship • happiness • illness • kingdom • leadership • loneliness • madness • relationship • sadness • weakness

4 Other words and phrases ➤ page 141

Grammar revision

1 Complete the sentences in a logical way. Put one verb in the past perfect and the other in the past simple.

1 When I .... (finish) my breakfast, I .... (brush) my teeth.

2 When the students .... (do) the exam, the teacher .... (say) they could go.

3 She .... (dry) her hair after she .... (wash) it.

4 They .... (take) her to the hospital because she .... (have) an accident.

5 They didn't see the start of the film because when they .... (arrive) at the cinema it .... (start).

6 When he .... (write) the email, he .... (send) it.

7 They .... (go) into the museum when they .... (buy) the tickets.

2 Andy was very unfit five years ago, but now he's changed. Write logical sentences using *used to* or *didn't use to*.

1 He .... eat a lot of fast food.

2 He .... do exercise.

3 He .... prepare healthy meals.

4 He .... sit watching TV all day.

3 Choose the correct alternative. Why do we use the gerund or infinitive in each case?

1 I went to the shops *buying/to buy* food.

2 Are you interested in *seeing/see* that film?

3 *Smoking/To smoke* is bad for your health.

4 Why don't we go *fishing/to fish* this weekend?

5 Sam can't stand *cycling/to cycle* to school.

6 I want *listening/to listen* to that new album.

7 The burglar got in by *opening/open* the window.

8 Are you ready *helping/to help* me?

Vocabulary revision

1 Match the words from each column to complete the phrases.

1 to get on   a in common

2 to have   b eye to eye

3 to have things   c with somebody

4 to see   d well with somebody

5 to fall out   e an argument with somebody

6 to hang   f up with somebody

7 to make it   g out with somebody

2 Write the nouns for these adjectives. Is each feeling generally positive (+), negative (–) or it depends (=)?

1 sad ➤ ....

2 afraid ➤ ....

3 lonely ➤ ....

4 bored ➤ ....

5 angry ➤ ....

6 excited ➤ ....

7 happy ➤ ....

3 Read the definitions and write words ending with *-ness*, *-ship* or *-dom*.

1 the opposite of strength: w ....

2 the feeling when nobody is with you and you feel bad: l ....

3 something that affects people and makes them do crazy things: m ....

4 the connection between two people: r ....

5 something which makes you feel bad or unhealthy: i ....

6 being able to do what you want, with no obligations: f ....

7 the ability to organise and lead others: l ....

Reading

➤ EXAM SUCCESS page 145

> **TIP FOR READING EXAMS**

In True/False activities, remember …
Read the sentences that you need to prove true or false and find the section of the text where the information comes. Read those sections again in more detail.

1 **You are going to read a text about a young man called Fraser Doherty. First, match the words to the pictures.**

jam   grapes   recipe   factory

2 **Read the text. How has Fraser Doherty become a millionaire?**

THE JAM MILLIONAIRE

Fraser Doherty is very hard-working and ambitious. In fact, he's so hard-working and ambitious that at the age of 24 he was already a millionaire! Fraser was 14 when he started making jam. There had been a special way of making jam for generations and generations in the Doherty family. One
5 day his grandmother told Fraser the secret and, with her help, he began to invent his own unusual jams, all called SuperJam.

The jam was obviously good because soon Fraser was making it and selling it to his friends and neighbours after school. Within four years he was producing 1,000 jars of jam a week from his parents' home in Edinburgh, Scotland. In
10 2007, when he was just 17, he won a contract to produce 120,000 jars of jam a week for a big British supermarket. That meant that he needed to start producing jam in a factory, not at home.

When Fraser was 18 he studied business at Strathclyde University in Glasgow. He hoped that his business would go well and grow and if it did he
15 could sell to other supermarkets. Things went really well. Today he sells jam to over 2,000 supermarkets around the world, from Australia to Russia!

Traditional jams are often 80 per cent sugar, but Mr Doherty, whose company is called SuperJam, has created a
20 healthy alternative. He uses grape juice, not sugar. His aim was to make jam as healthy as possible. He wanted to replace the traditionally unhealthy jam with a 'super jam'. 'It was quite frightening to change a product that
25 people have made the same way for hundreds of years, but I wanted to add a new dimension.' Fraser has also been creative with new ingredients like kiwi and lime. A food
30 expert said: 'Fraser has taken an old product and he has made it young, exciting and modern.'

Mr Doherty's father, Robert, said that he was sad when Fraser moved to a factory
35 because he used to like watching Fraser making the jams at their family home in Edinburgh. But now he can certainly be happy with his son's incredible international success, based on a grandmother's secret recipe!

'Fraser has taken an old product and he has made it young, exciting and modern.'

3 **Read the text again and decide if the statements are True (T) or False (F). Write down the number(s) of the line(s) where you found the answer.**

1 Fraser Doherty's jams are a mixture of tradition and new ideas. .... T / F

2 Fraser started by producing 1,000 jars of jam a week. .... T / F

3 At first, Fraser made and sold the jam in his free time. .... T / F

4 Fraser still makes jam at home. .... T / F

5 Fraser has a very positive opinion of typical, old jam. .... T / F

6 Fraser wanted to make a new type of jam but he didn't know what people would think. .... T / F

7 Fraser's dad was happy when Fraser used their home for business. .... T / F

8 Fraser's dreams at university came true. .... T / F

Writing

> **TIP FOR WRITING EXAMS**

In writing exams, remember …
You lose marks if you do not answer the question and include all the information that appears in it.

➤ EXAM SUCCESS page 146

4 **Work with a partner. Look at this advice for writing a letter to apply for a job. What other advice can you think of?**

1 Say which advertisement you are writing about.

2 Write expressions like *I look forward to hearing from you.*

3 Do not use contractions.

5 **You see an advertisement for a summer job at Fraser Doherty's jam factory. Write a letter to apply and include this information. You can invent it.**

- Why you are writing
- Personal qualities you have that could help to get the job
- What experience you have

Listening

➤ TIP FOR LISTENING EXAMS

In multiple-choice listening activities, remember …

If you don't hear the answer to one question, start listening immediately for the answer to the next question. Don't panic. You will probably be able to hear the dialogue again.

➤ EXAM SUCCESS page 145

6 LISTENING ▶ 55 **Listen to two teenagers talking about working in the summer. What job do they talk about and in which place?**

7 ▶ 55 **Listen again and choose the correct answers.**

1 Sarah doesn't know what to do because
 a nobody has offered her a job for the summer.
 b she doesn't want to go away.
 c she doesn't know if she likes the job they've offered.

2 Sarah is worried because
 a she doesn't have any experience of working with children.
 b the last time she worked with children it didn't go very well.
 c she doesn't like little children.

3 When Jim worked with kids he was
 a tired.
 b bored.
 c angry all the time.

4 The family will
 a pay Sarah something.
 b pay for Sarah to go to New York but not to return.
 c only give Sarah free food and a room.

5 Jim thinks Sarah should
 a think hard before she takes the job.
 b get experience of working with kids before taking the job.
 c accept the job now and worry later.

8 What about *you*?

Do you think that looking after little children is a difficult job? Why/Why not?

Speaking

➤ TIP FOR SPEAKING EXAMS

In activities where you report past events, remember …
Use a variety of past tenses and different expressions of time and sequence (*first, next, then, later*).

➤ EXAM SUCCESS page 146

9 Look at this exam task. You have a few minutes to make a note of things you are going to say or questions you are going to ask. Do not write complete sentences.

Tell your partner about a time when you made a new friend. Tell your partner:
■ when and where you met the person
■ how you became friends
■ information about the person and your relationship with them

10 SPEAKING **Student A, tell your partner about your experience. When you finish, change roles.**

'CAN DO' PROGRESS CHECK UNITS 7–8 CEF

1 How well can you do these things in English now? Give yourself a mark from 1 to 4.

> 1 = I can do it very well.
> 2 = I can do it quite well.
> 3 = I have some problems.
> 4 = I can't do it.

a I can express obligation, prohibition and advice using modal verbs like *must* and *should*. ☐
b I can talk about imaginary situations and their consequences using the second conditional. ☐
c I can describe jobs and the personal qualities you need to do them. ☐
d I can ask about jobs, making polite requests. ☐
e I can write a simple job application. ☐
f I can talk about the past using the past perfect and *used to*. ☐
g I can talk about friendships and feelings. ☐
h I can understand texts about different personalities and relationships. ☐
i I can make nouns using the suffixes –*ness*, -*ship*, and –*dom*. ☐
j I can write an email giving advice to a friend. ☐

2 Now decide what you need to do next to improve.

1 Look again at my book/notes.
2 Do more practice exercises.
 ➤ WORKBOOK Units 7 and 8
3 Ask for help.
4 Other: ....

9 Bestsellers

Fiction

1 Work with a partner and match some of these words with the book covers. Check that you understand all the words.

> comic • crime novel • fairy tale • fantasy
> graphic novel • historical fiction • horror
> play • romance • science fiction • thriller

2 ▶ 56 Listen and repeat.

3 SPEAKING Work with a partner. Ask and answer these questions.

1 Do you like reading fiction?
2 How often do you read fiction?
3 Which types of fiction do you enjoy reading the most? Why?
4 Are there any types of fiction which you dislike? Which? Why?

Non-fiction

4 Match the words with the book titles (1–10).

> atlas • autobiography • biography
> cookbook • encyclopaedia • ~~guidebook~~
> magazine • manual • newspaper
> textbook

1 *Explore New York* ...guidebook...
2 *How to get the most from your tablet*
   ....
3 *My life* by Bill Clinton ....
4 *Shakespeare* by Bill Bryson ....
5 *My Grandmother's Mexican Kitchen:*
   100 Family Recipes ....
6 *Asia (World in maps)* ....
7 *The Times* ....
8 *Gateway* ....
9 *National Geographic* ....
10 ....*Britannica*

a Hamlet — William Shakespeare

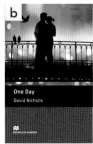

b One Day — David Nicholls

c L. A. Raid — Philip Prowse

d The Wizard of Oz — L. Frank Baum

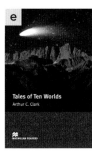

e Tales of Ten Worlds — Arthur C. Clark

f Viking Tales — Chris Rose

5a PRONUNCIATION Practise saying the words in 4 and put them in the correct column.

⬤•	⬤••	••⬤	•⬤••	•••⬤••
atlas				

5b ▶ 57 Listen, check and repeat.

5c Look again at the words in 1. Can you put any of them into these columns?

6 LISTENING ▶ 58 Listen to the conversations. What types of book or publication are the people talking about in each conversation? They can be fiction or non-fiction.

1 ....   4 ....
2 ....   5 ....
3 ....

7 SPEAKING Work with a partner. Compare how often, and in what situations, you read different non-fiction.

> I read cookbooks sometimes because I enjoy cooking. I read them to find new things to make.

> I never read cookbooks because I never cook. What about manuals?

1 Look at these photos and then read the article. Number the photos in the order that they appear in the article. Don't worry about the missing sentences at this stage.

a ☐   b ☐   c ☐   d ☐

THE LIFE OF A TOP CHILDREN'S AUTHOR

David Walliams is a top children's author. He loves writing fiction for kids, but he also does many other things!

1 .... Before, most people knew him as one of the two main actors in the British comedy series *Little Britain*. But now, especially with children, he is probably more famous as a bestselling author. In fact, some now say that he is the UK's most successful children's writer, having sold 2.8 million copies of his first six books in five years.

2 .... He started acting at school. Then he went to university and after that he joined the National Youth Theatre. That was where he met Matt Lucas who became his partner in creating the *Little Britain* series in 2003.

3 .... He showed that he could act in serious plays and films, not just comedies. He also worked as a judge on the popular reality show, *Britain's Got Talent*.

4 .... The second of these two books, *Mr Stink*, was for teenagers. It won the Children's Award in the People's Book Prize in 2010. The books were so popular that he continued writing.

5 .... It is about a boy who is the richest 12-year-old in the world. He has a Formula One racing car, a thousand pairs of trainers, a billion pounds, but there's just one thing he needs: a friend. The book came with a billion pound note that readers could use to enter a competition to win a day as a billionaire in London!

6 .... His sixth book, *Demon Dentist*, sold more than 220,000 copies in just the first two months of being on sale. Walliams said: '*Demon Dentist* is my very first horror story … I hope children of all ages will love the new book's combination of chills, action and of course comedy.'

7 .... He swims. But not just in his local swimming pool. In 2006, he swam from England to France. He made about one million pounds for charity. Since then he's also swum about 225 kilometres of the River Thames, this time raising two million pounds. When he finished, he told reporters: 'I think I've just swum the length of the Thames! I feel quite tired. I think a bath is the only water I want to see for quite a while.'

8 .... A boat was carrying copies of one of his books from China to the UK. A storm hit the boat and 30,000 copies of the book fell into the sea! His publisher said that they were making an extra 30,000 copies of the book in Europe to substitute the copies that the sea had destroyed.

✔ EXAM SUCCESS

You are going to do a missing sentences activity. In this type of activity you have to find the best place to put various sentences taken from a text. How can you check this activity when you finish?

➤ EXAM SUCCESS page 146

2 Read the article again and put sentences a–h into gaps 1–8 in the text.

a But it was in 2008 that he signed a contract to write two children's books.

b Walliams was born in 1971.

c His books have continued to sell well.

d When he isn't acting or writing, Walliams has an interesting hobby.

e He continued appearing on TV in different types of programmes.

f David Walliams is a man of many talents.

g However, he wasn't very lucky with water in 2013.

h His third book was called *Billionaire Boy*.

3 Look at the photos in 1 again. Explain the significance of each one.

4 ⚙ **CRITICAL THINKING**

Think! Then compare ideas with your class.

- How important is it for children to read? Why?

5 What do the underlined words in the text mean? Guess and then check in your dictionary.

6 SPEAKING What about *you*?

1 What were your favourite books or stories when you were younger?

2 Who is your favourite author now, and why?

Grammar in context

Flipped classroom: watch the grammar presentation video.

Reported speech – statements

1a **Look at what David Walliams said to journalists.**

1 *Demon Dentist* is my very first horror story.

2 I hope children of all ages will love the new book.

3 I think I've just swum the length of the Thames!

4 I feel quite tired.

Now look at what the journalist wrote.

a Mr Walliams said *Demon Dentist* was his very first horror story.

b He told us he hoped children of all ages would love the new book.

c He said that he thought he had just swum the length of the Thames.

d He told the interviewer that he felt quite tired.

1b **Answer these questions.**

1 What happens to the verbs when they go into reported speech?

2 What happens to most pronouns and possessive adjectives when they go into reported speech?

3 What is the difference between *say* and *tell*?

4 After *say* and *tell* do we always need to use *that*?

GRAMMAR REFERENCE ➤ PAGE 120

2 **Match these sentences in direct and reported speech. One of the reported speech sentences can go with more than one of the sentences in direct speech.**

1 I write novels. ....*f*....

2 I'm writing a novel. ....

3 I wrote a novel. ....

4 I've written a novel. ....

5 I'll write a novel. ....

6 I can write novels. ....

7 I may write a novel. ....

8 I have to write a novel. ....

a She said she could write novels.

b She said she was writing a novel.

c She said she had written a novel.

d She said she'd write a novel.

e She said she might write a novel.

f She said she wrote novels.

g She said she had to write a novel.

3 **Look at the examples in 2 and put the tenses and verbs in the correct places in the table.**

could • had to • might • past continuous
past perfect • past simple • would

Direct speech	Reported speech
1 present simple ➤	*past simple*
2 present continuous ➤	
3 past simple ➤	
4 present perfect ➤	
5 will ➤	
6 can ➤	
7 may ➤	
8 must/have to ➤	

4 **Complete the sentences with *said* or *told*. Which fictional character is 'he'?**

1 He .... he sometimes wore glasses.

2 He .... me he had come to Earth from a different planet.

3 He .... us that he could fly.

4 He .... that he was working as a journalist.

5 He .... he didn't like kryptonite.

6 He .... that he had an 'S' on the front of his costume.

5 **Rewrite the sentences in 4 as direct speech.**

1 *I sometimes wear glasses.*

6 **There are other words which we often change when we put statements into reported speech. Look at this example.**

'I read this book last week.'
She said she had read that book the previous week.

Use the words in the box to complete the table.

a (week/month/year) ago • here
last (week/month/year) • next (week/month/year)
this • today • tomorrow • tonight • yesterday

Direct speech	Reported speech
1 *this*	that
2	there
3	that day
4	the day before
5	the next/following day
6	that night
7	the following (week/month/year)
8	the previous (week/month/year)
9	a (week/month/year) before

7 **Report what this writer said in an interview. Use *say* and *tell*.**

   1 *She said that her name was Anna Caltabiano.*

   1 My name is Anna Caltabiano.
   2 I'm 17 years old.
   3 I've already written two novels.
   4 I started writing when I was 14.
   5 I live in California but I was born in Hong Kong.
   6 The first language I spoke was Japanese.
   7 Apart from writing, I'm just a regular teenage girl.
   8 My next novel will be out this summer.

8a **Write a true sentence about yourself and the summer. It can be about last summer, next summer, or the summer in general.**

I went to a sports camp last summer.
I always go to the beach in the summer.

8b **Read out your sentence to the other people in your class or group.**

8c **When everybody has read out their sentence, write down what different people said. Can you remember everyone's sentence?**

Mia said that she had gone to a sports camp the previous summer.

Jack told us that he always went to the beach in the summer.

8d SPEAKING **Work with a partner. Compare your answers. Do you have the same? If not, find out who is right by asking the person.**

Phrasal verbs connected with reading and writing

1 **Read these sentences. Can you guess the meaning of the phrasal verbs in *italics*?**

   1 I don't want to stop now. I want to **read on** to the end.
   2 Can you **read out** your answer to the next question so that we can all hear it?
   3 I don't understand some of these words. I'm going to **look** them **up** in my dictionary.
   4 I want you all to **turn over** the page and continue reading.
   5 Read the sentences and then **fill in** the gaps.
   6 He **flicked through** the book quickly to see if he liked it before he bought it.
   7 It doesn't look good when you make lots of mistakes and then you **cross** them **out**.

2 **Match the phrasal verbs in 1 with the definitions.**

   a Read so that other people can hear you.
   b Draw an X or a line through some writing to show that it's not correct.
   c Write information in empty spaces.
   d Try to find a particular piece of information in a book.
   e Continue reading.
   f Turn a page or piece of paper to see the other side.
   g Turn the pages of a book quickly, not looking carefully.

3 **Complete the text with the words in the box.**

> cross • flick • look • on • out • over

The other day I was in a bookshop. I picked up a novel by a new writer and began to (a) _____ through it. I didn't really read any of it, but I decided to buy it and took it home. When I started to read it carefully I didn't like the start much. But I decided to read (b) _____. There were lots of unusual words that I had to (c) _____ up in the dictionary. I turned (d) _____ another page and then another but I still didn't like it. I told my friend and he asked me to read (e) _____ a section so that he could hear. He said that the writer was using too many words to say something simple and that it was repetitive. He could (f) _____ out half the words because they were unnecessary. In the end, I stopped reading that book and picked up another one.

Enjoying FICTION

LIFE SKILLS OBJECTIVES

- To read and think about the start of a novel.
- To hear people recommending books to read.
- To read a book and discuss it in a 'book club'.

KEY CONCEPTS

browse [v]: *I was browsing an online bookshop because I wanted to buy a book but I wasn't looking for a specific title.* **blurb [n]:** *I read the blurb on the back of the book and it said that the book was 'a unique horror experience'.* **back cover [n]:** *Usually on the book's back cover it tells you about the book and the author.* **prologue [n]:** *Before the novel really began, there was a prologue.*

1 Look at the cover of this novel and answer these questions.

1 What can you see on the cover?
2 What type of novel do you think it is?
3 What do you think the novel is about? Guess.

2 READING **Read the prologue to the novel and answer these questions.**

1 What type of novel is it?
2 What does the prologue tell us about the 'angel experiment'?

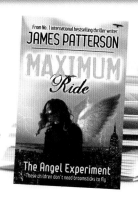

Prologue
ॐ

Congratulations. The fact that you're reading this means you've taken one giant step to surviving till your next birthday. Yes, you standing there, flicking through these pages. Do not put this book down. I'm really serious – your life could depend on it.

This is my story, the story of my family, but it could easily be your story too. We're all in this together, believe me.

I've never done anything like this, so I'm just going to jump in, and you try to keep up.

OK, I'm Max, I'm 14. I live with my family, who are five kids not related to me by blood, but still totally my family.

We're – well, we're kind of amazing. We're like nothing you've ever seen before.

Basically, we're pretty cool, nice, smart – and very special. The six of us – me, Fang, Iggy, Nudge, the Gasman and Angel – were made by the worst, most horrible 'scientists' you could possibly imagine. They created us as an experiment. An experiment where we ended up only 98% human. That other 2% has had a big impact, let me tell you.

We grew up in a science laboratory/prison called the School. It's pretty amazing that we can think or speak at all. But we can – and so much more.

There was one other School experiment that survived. Part human, part wolf – all predator: they're called Erasers. They're tough, smart and hard to control. They look human, but when they want to, they can change into wolf men. The School uses them as guards, police – and murderers. They want to kill us. And make sure the world never finds out about us.

But I'm not lying down just yet. I'm telling you, right?

This story could be about you – or your children. If not today, then soon. So please, please, take this seriously. I'm risking everything that matters by telling you – but you need to know.

Keep reading – don't let anyone stop you.

Max. And my family: Fang, Iggy, Nudge, the Gasman and Angel.

Welcome to our nightmare.

3 Read the text again and make notes about these characters.

1 Max
   14 years old, ...
2 Max's 'family'
3 the 'Erasers'

4 The author of this novel, James Patterson, is an expert at making people want to read on to find out what happens next in the story. He does this in different ways. Find a sentence from the text for each of these techniques.

1 The character talks directly to you, the reader.
   Yes, you standing there, flicking through these pages.
2 Generally, the sentences are short and direct.
3 Reading the text is like a dangerous adventure.
4 The reader is made to feel part of the adventure.
5 The writer introduces the characters in the story quickly and dramatically.
6 The language is informal and natural, like listening to a person talking.
7 There is intrigue – you want to know more information.

5 Would you like to continue reading the book? Why/Why not?

6a Work with a partner. Look at the books in the table. What do you know about them?

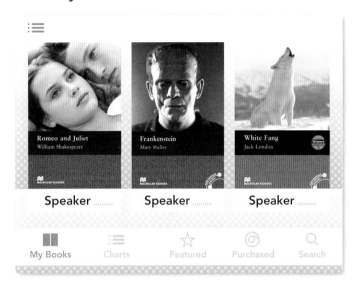

Speaker ....   Speaker ....   Speaker ....

6b LISTENING ▶ 59 Three students are going to read out a short section of the book that they have just finished reading. Then they are going to say what they think of the book. Listen or watch and in 6a match each speaker to a book.

6c ▶ 59 Watch or listen again. What did each speaker like about their book? Write the number of the speaker next to each item.

Romance	Interesting relationships ....
A serious message	Fascinating characters ....
Simple sentences	An unexpected story ....

7 Which of the three books would you most like to read and why?

LIFE TASK

You want to organise a book club.

Follow this plan:

1 *Each person should choose a book to read. Browse in a public or school library, or bookshop, ask friends or family for books or look on the Internet.*

2 *Read the book for homework. Decide how long you have to read the book and make sure you finish in that time.*

3 *Work in groups. Take it in turns to talk about your book. What did you like or dislike about it? Would you recommend this book to others? Why/Why not?*

1 SPEAKING **Work with a partner. Ask and answer these questions.**

1 Can you think of any books that have become films, like *The Hunger Games*?

2 Generally, do you prefer reading the book or watching the film adaptation? Why?

✓ EXAM SUCCESS

In the next activity you listen and complete gaps in some notes with the word(s) you hear. Is it possible to predict the *type* of words that are missing? How?

➤ EXAM SUCCESS page 146

2 LISTENING ▶ 60 **Listen and complete the notes. Use just one or two words for each space.**

Notepad

BOOK VS. FILM SURVEY

Comments

Reads one or two books a (a) ....

At the moment, reading a (b) ....
book.

Goes to the cinema two or three times a
(c) ....

(d) .... goes to see film adaptations.

Thinks that with books you know what the
characters (e) ....

The characters are almost like
(f) ....

Sometimes gets a shock watching films because
the characters (g) .... to the way she
imagined.

3 ▶ 60 **Are these statements True (T) or False (F)? Listen again if necessary.**

1 The interviewer asked her how often she bought books. T/F

2 He wanted to know how often she read science fiction. T/F

3 He asked her what she was reading at that moment. T/F

4 The man asked the girl how often she went to the cinema. T/F

5 He asked her if she had seen *The Hunger Games* films. T/F

6 He asked her whether she preferred reading fiction or non-fiction. T/F

Reported speech – questions

1a Look at these questions and statements. Which are direct questions (DQ) and which are reported questions (RQ)?

1 He asked her what she was reading at that moment. ....

2 He wanted to know if she had seen *The Hunger Games*. ....

3 How often do you go to the cinema? ....

4 Have you seen the *The Hunger Games*? ....

5 He asked her how often she went to the cinema. ....

6 What are you reading at the moment? ....

7 Do you prefer reading fiction or non-fiction? ....

8 He asked her whether she preferred reading fiction or non-fiction. ....

1b Choose the correct alternative.

1 We *change/don't change* tenses, pronouns and words like *this* and *here* in the same way in reported statements and reported questions.

2 We *use/don't use* question marks in reported questions.

3 We *use/don't use* the auxiliary verb *do* in reported questions.

4 We *put/don't put* the verb before the subject in reported questions.

5 We *use/don't use* if or *whether* in reported questions when there is no question word (*who, what, why*, etc.) in the original question.

GRAMMAR REFERENCE ➤ PAGE 120

2 Complete the sentences with a question word or *if/whether*.

1 They asked the novelist .... her favourite writer was. She said Tolkien.

2 Kate asked Jenny .... she wanted to do.

3 Paul wanted to know .... I had come by bus or by car.

4 Hannah asked me .... I wanted a coffee and I said yes.

5 They asked me .... I had brothers or sisters and I said no.

6 My teacher asked me .... I hadn't been at school the day before.

7 Karen's mum asked her .... she had had a good time.

3 Write what the people actually said in each situation.

1 The journalist asked the film director if he was making a film at that moment. He said that he wasn't but that he was going to start a new one soon.

Journalist: ....
....

Film director: ....
....

2 The writer asked the man if he had enjoyed her book. He said that he thought it was the most beautiful thing he'd ever read.

Writer: ....
....

Man: ....
....

3 The reporter asked the singer why she wouldn't answer any of his questions. She told him that she only wanted to talk about her new album and that she wasn't going to talk about anything else.

Reporter: ....
....

Singer: ....
....

4 The teacher asked the class whether they could write an essay for the next day, but they replied that they couldn't because they had to study for an exam and they wouldn't have enough time.

Teacher: ....
....

Students: ....
....

5 Julie wanted to know how many times I'd read my comic and I told her that I'd read it three times.

Julie: ....
....

Me: ....
....

4 Write this conversation in reported speech.

Keira: What did you do last night?
Matt: I didn't do much. I just watched TV with my parents.
Keira: Did you study for the literature exam?
Matt: When do we have the exam?
Keira: We're doing it today.
Matt: Why didn't you remind me?
Keira: I told you but you weren't listening. Why do you never pay attention to me?

5a As a class, choose a famous person who you would like to interview. It can be an actor, politician, singer, sports star …

5b Imagine that this person is coming to your school. With your partner, prepare five questions to ask them.

5c SPEAKING Choose a student to be the famous person. Interview them and make a note of their answers to your questions.

5d SPEAKING When you finish, work in pairs. Take it in turns to report back the interview.

First we asked him why he had decided to come to our school. He said that he'd been a student here.

Then we wanted to know …

A presentation

1 What is, in your opinion, the most enjoyable book you have ever read? Make notes about it using the 'You' column in this table.

	You	Speaker
Title		
Author		
Type of book		
Reasons why you like it – the story, descriptions, characters, style, etc.	1 .... 2 .... 3 .... …	1 .... 2 .... 3 .... …

2 LISTENING ▶ 61 Listen to a student giving a presentation about their favourite book. Complete the table with notes.

3 ▶ 61 Complete the expressions in the Speaking bank. Listen again if necessary.

💬 **SPEAKING BANK**

Useful expressions in presentations

Beginning a presentation
- I'm going to talk about …
- I'd .... to .... by saying …

Introducing arguments
- Firstly,
- First .... ,
- What's .... ,
- It's also .... that …
- Another thing is that …
- Last .... ,

Ending a presentation
- Finally,
- To sum .... ,

4 Join the sentence halves with advice about giving a presentation.

1 Write notes with your main ideas but …
2 Include an introduction and …
3 Put your ideas in …
4 Don't just read …
5 Look up at …
6 Speak in …

a a loud, clear voice.
b the audience.
c a logical order.
d a conclusion.
e not a complete text.
f aloud.

PRACTICE MAKES PERFECT

5a Prepare a presentation about the best book that you have ever read. Use your notes in 1 and the expressions in the Speaking bank. Do not write a complete text.

5b SPEAKING Give your presentation to the class or in groups. Remember to follow the advice in 4 and the advice about public speaking on pages 36 and 37.

A story

1 SPEAKING **Work with a partner. Put the pictures in order and tell the story.**

2 **Look at this sentence.**

A woman was writing.

Look at picture e and expand the sentence by adding words to describe the scene in more detail. How many words can you add?

3 **Look at this sentence. What types of words have been added to the sentence in 2? Is the sentence more interesting than the one in 2? Why?**

It was the middle of a cold winter and a bright young woman was sitting quietly at home writing her very first novel.

4 **Read these sentences and match each one to a picture from the story.**

1 *It was autumn and the golden leaves were falling softly and slowly from the trees.*

2 *Soon after, they started printing thousands of copies of the novel.*

3 *When the boss of the company had finished reading the book, he was extremely happy.*

5 **Look at the advice in the Writing bank. What examples of the advice can you find in the sentences in 4?**

✏ WRITING BANK

Useful advice for writing interesting stories
- Use adjectives and adverbs to make your writing more descriptive.
  *The **young** writer **immediately** took her novel to a **famous** publisher.*
- Use a variety of past tenses.
  *When she **had finished** the book, the young writer immediately **took** …*
- Use words and expressions of time and sequence.
  ***One day in spring**, a student went …*
  ***Suddenly** he saw …*
  ***Two months later,** the young man left …*

WRITING BANK ➤ PAGE 151

6 PRACTICE MAKES PERFECT **Write the story in 1. Use the sentences on this page and the advice in the Writing bank to help you.**

Grammar reference

Reported speech - statements

FORM

When the reporting verb (*say*, *tell*) is in the past, the tense of the verb in reported speech usually changes, going one tense 'back'.

Direct speech – tenses	Reported speech – tenses
'I work at home.' *Present simple*	She said she worked at home. Past simple
'I'm working.' *Present continuous*	She said she was working. Past continuous
'I have worked.' Present perfect	She said she had worked. Past perfect
'I worked.' Past simple	She said she had worked. Past perfect
'I had worked.' Past perfect	She said she had worked. Past perfect
'I will work.' will	She said she would work. would
'I can work.' can	She said she could work. could
'I may work.' may	She said she might work. might
'I must/have to work.' must/have to	She said she had to work. had to

Could, *would*, *should* and *might* do not change from direct to reported speech.

In reported speech, pronouns and possessive adjectives also change.

'I saw **your** brother.' ➤ Anna said **she** had seen **my** brother.

Here are some other words which change from direct to reported speech.

Direct speech	Reported speech
this/these	that/those
here	there
today	that day
yesterday	the day before
tomorrow	the next/following day
last night	the night before
next (week/month/year)	the following (week/month/year)
last (week/month/year)	the previous (week/month/year)
a (week/month/year) ago	a (week/month/year) before

With *say* you do not need to use a personal object to say who you are saying something to.

He said (...) he had been there.

~~He said John he had been there.~~

With *tell* you must use a personal object to say who you are saying something to.

He told John he had been there.

~~He told that he had been there.~~

USE

We use reported speech to report the words spoken by another person.

'There is nothing new in art except talent,' said Chekhov.

Chekhov said that there was nothing new in art except talent.

Reported speech – questions

FORM

The same changes occur with tenses, pronouns and other words as with reported statements. We do not use the auxiliary verb *do* in reported questions.

'Do you read novels?' ➤ She asked me if I read novels.

There is no inversion of subject and verb in reported questions.

'Who is she?' ➤ They asked me who she was.

Reported questions are not real questions so they do not need question marks.

When there is no question word (*who, what, how, why,* etc.), we use *if* or *whether*.

'Are you OK?' ➤ She asked me if I was OK.

Vocabulary

1 Fiction   comic • crime novel • fairy tale • fantasy • graphic novel • historical fiction • horror • play • romance science fiction • thriller

2 Non-fiction   atlas • autobiography • biography • cookbook • encyclopaedia • guidebook • magazine manual • newspaper • textbook

3 Phrasal verbs connected with reading and writing   cross out • fill in • flick through • look up • read on read out • turn over

4 Other words and phrases   ➤ page 142

Grammar revision

Reported speech – statements / 8 points

1 Write the sentences in reported speech.

1 'I'm going to a concert next week,' my sister said.
2 'I'll be late tomorrow,' Daniel told the teacher.
3 'This is my dictionary,' said Holly.
4 'I've always wanted to write stories,' said Sylvia.
5 'There is going to be a concert in this room,' they told us.
6 'The play will start at 7 pm tomorrow,' they said.
7 'We haven't read any of your books,' the students told the writer.
8 'I wrote the article yesterday,' said the journalist.

Reported speech – questions / 8 points

2 Write these questions in reported speech.

1 'Are you from Mexico?' she asked me.
2 'What time are you going to leave?' Jo asked Paul.
3 'Why were you crying?' I asked Katie.
4 'Have you ever read this book?' the teacher asked me.
5 'Will you help me tomorrow?' Tom asked her.
6 'Did the doctor see Sam yesterday?' Abigail asked her dad.
7 'Do you know the answer to this question?' our teacher asked us.
8 'How many pages does it have?' I asked Jo.

Vocabulary revision

FICTION / 8 points

1 Complete the sentences with the correct words.

1 A .... story is often about dragons, trolls or other imaginary creatures.
2 A .... is an exciting story about spies and assassinations.
3 You can read a .... or see it at a theatre.
4 A .... is a story about people who fall in love.
5 A .... is usually about a prince, a princess or a witch.
6 In .... fiction, the story takes place in the past.
7 A .... combines writing and art.
8 A .... story should be frightening.

NON-FICTION / 9 points

2 Which type of book or publication is best in these situations?

1 You want to find out about the geography of a country.
....
2 You want to read about the life of a person, in his/her own words. ....
3 You want to find new ideas for dinner. ....
4 You want to learn how to use your computer well.
....
5 You're going to Prague and want to know what to visit.
....
6 You want to know what's happening in the world today.
....
7 You want to revise maths for an exam. ....
8 You want to find out information about lots of different topics, to write a quiz. ....
9 Once a month you want to read new articles and texts with photographs and illustrations. ....

PHRASAL VERBS CONNECTED WITH READING AND WRITING / 7 points

3 Match the sentence halves.

1 I love this book, I want to read …
2 When you finish that page, turn …
3 You have to fill …
4 Because the text was difficult, I had to look …
5 I can't read what he wrote because he crossed …
6 I looked at the magazine quickly. I flicked …
7 I want to hear your answers so please read …

a them out to me in a loud voice.
b it out with a big X.
c over and read the next one.
d through it looking at the pictures.
e up lots of words.
f in the answers on your sheet.
g on tonight until I get to the end of it.

10 Log on

Vocabulary

Using a computer

1 Work with a partner. Match the words in the box with the technology in the picture.

> hard drive • headset (headphones/microphone)
> flashdrive/pendrive • keyboard
> monitor/screen • mouse • mouse mat
> printer • scanner • speaker • tablet
> USB cable • USB port • webcam

2 ▶ 62 **Listen, check and repeat.**

3 Match the sentence halves.

1 When you copy a document,
2 When you click on something with your mouse,
3 When you save something on a computer,
4 When you make a hardcopy of a document,
5 When you cut and paste something,
6 When you log on/off,

a you make it work.
b you start/finish using a computer by giving some information (e.g. a password).
c you keep the information that you put into it.
d you make another one that is the same as the original.
e you print it on paper.
f you take it from one document and put it in another place or document.

The Internet

4 LISTENING ▶ 63 **Read and listen to this description by a teenager of how she uses the Internet. Check that you understand the words in red. Use a dictionary if necessary.**

'I've got broadband so my connection to the Net is quite fast. I usually go online in the evenings, after I've finished my homework, but sometimes I use the Net for schoolwork, too. I surf the Net and look at my favourite websites (my homepage is a website about fashion). My favourite search engine is Google. I sometimes download music and films, but not often. I haven't got a blog but I chat online with my friends using a social networking website.'

5a PRONUNCIATION **Look at these two sentences. Is *download* a verb or a noun in each sentence?**

1 I want to *download* this song.
2 The *download* didn't work.

5b ▶ 64 **Listen to the two sentences. Is the pronunciation of *download* the same in each sentence?**

5c ▶ 64 **Listen again and choose the correct alternative.**

1 In two-syllable verbs the stress is usually on the *first/second* syllable.
2 In two-syllable nouns the stress is usually on the *first/second* syllable.

6a SPEAKING **Work with a partner. How often do you do these things (*never, sometimes, often, very often*)?**

1 print documents or photos
2 scan documents or photos
3 use a webcam
4 go online and surf the Net
5 download music or films
6 read or write blogs
7 chat online
8 use social networking sites

6b SPEAKING **Take it in turns to ask how often you do the different things. Are your answers similar?**

> *How often do you print documents or photos?*

> *Not often. I don't usually need to make hardcopies. I just make a copy on my flashdrive.*

1 Work with a partner. Answer the questions. If you don't know the answers, guess!

   1 Who invented the World Wide Web?

   2 When did they invent it?

   3 Approximately how many websites are there at the moment?

   4 When did the Web become freely available to the public?

2 Read the article and find the answers to the quiz in 1.

THE COMPUTER THAT BEGAN IT ALL

At the Science Museum in London, photographers try to get pictures of an old-fashioned black computer and keyboard. It doesn't look particularly special. But this computer was the machine that was used by British computer scientist Sir Tim Berners-Lee to create the World Wide Web back in 1989.

In the beginning, there was no big plan to change the world. The only idea was to improve communication between the thousands of scientists working for CERN (the European Organisation for Nuclear Research). Sir Tim was a 34-year-old physics graduate working as a software engineer at CERN in Switzerland in 1989. He saw the need for 'a universal linked information system', a way of using networks of computers to talk to each other. To do this, he created the first ever web browser. This web browser became the World Wide Web. Sir Tim thought of this name in 1990. Before that, probably not very seriously, he had considered the name The Information Mine, or T.I.M. for short.

In 1993, CERN allowed the technology to be freely used by all. And, within a few years, millions of people worldwide were using it. Now there are more than 600 million websites worldwide and the web has changed things forever. People are able to access information and share things in a way which was not possible before. It has provided a new dimension of communication. And it's enormous. Billions of people are online every day. Hundreds of millions of messages and pictures are sent and billions of dollars are spent every day by online shoppers.

Today, Sir Tim believes we need to defend the principles that have made the Web successful, and to continue expanding the possibilities of the Web. The main principle is that the Web should continue to be free for everybody to use and participate in. Sir Tim is optimistic about its future. He still believes that if you've got a bright idea for the Web, you can make it happen. You don't have to ask anyone. You should just do it.

But the Web is not perfect. Some people think that the Internet reflects the best and worst of people. But whatever people think, Sir Tim's old computer is going to be a star attraction at the Science Museum because the Web is so significant to people's lives. Many people will want to see the first Web server, the first machine in the world to ever deliver a webpage.

3 Read the article again and choose the best answers.

   1 People are taking photos of a computer at the Science Museum because …

     a it's very old.

     b a famous scientist uses it.

     c it has historic importance.

   2 The original idea of the World Wide Web was …

     a to allow communication between a group of computers.

     b to make information free all around the world.

     c to connect all the scientists in Switzerland.

   3 The World Wide Web has always …

     a been free.

     b been open for the whole world to use.

     c had billions of users.

   4 Sir Tim Berners-Lee believes that …

     a the future does not look good for the World Wide Web.

     b it is dangerous that everyone can use the World Wide Web.

     c everyone should be part of the future World Wide Web.

   5 The author thinks that …

     a the Web is nothing special because it belongs to everyone.

     b the Web is a perfect invention.

     c Sir Tim's computer will be a popular exhibit.

4 ⚙ **CRITICAL THINKING**

> **Think! Then compare ideas with your class.**
>
> ■ How important do you think the Internet is in today's world? Explain your answer.

5 What do the underlined words in the text mean? Guess and then check in your dictionary.

6 SPEAKING **What about _you_?**

How important is the Internet to you? Why?

The passive – present simple

1a Look at these sentences. Which are active and which are passive?

1 Hundreds of millions of messages are sent every day.
2 People send hundreds of millions of messages every day.
3 Online shoppers spend billions of dollars.
4 Billions of dollars are spent by online shoppers.

1b Are these statements *true* or *false*?

1 We use the passive when we are more interested in the action than in the person who does it.
2 We use the passive when we don't know who exactly does the action.
3 We use the passive when it is obvious who does the action.

1c Complete the rules.

1 To make the present simple passive we use .... + the past participle.

2 We use the preposition .... to introduce the agent, the person or thing which does the action.

> **GRAMMAR REFERENCE ➤ PAGE 132**

3 Are these sentences grammatically correct? If not, rewrite them.

What happens in an Internet minute?

- More than **204 million** emails are send.
- Around **20 million** photos is seen.
- More than **1.3 million** videos watched.
- About **47,000** apps are downloaded.
- Music are played by **hundreds of thousands** of people.
- More than **$83,000** spend in just one big Internet store.
- **Hundreds** of people open new social-networking accounts.

---

2 Complete the sentences with the correct form of the present simple passive.

BASIC GUIDE TO MAKING
SILICON CHIPS

1 Silicon .... (find) in sand.

2 The silicon .... (refine) to be 100% pure.

3 The pure silicon .... (heat) and .... (make) into small blocks called ingots.

4 The ingots .... (cut) into very small pieces and then later become thin chips.

5 Tiny components .... (add) to the chips.

6 Eight hundred transistors .... (put) onto an area with the diameter of a human hair!

7 Special clothes and masks .... (wear) by workers to protect the chips.

8 Finally, the chips .... (send) to computer factories.

4 Change these sentences from active to passive, or from passive to active. Include *by* plus the agent only when necessary.

1 They make a lot of silicon chips in India.
2 They employ many people in the computer industry.
3 They invent amazing new technology every day.
4 Most new games consoles are created by Sony, Nintendo and Microsoft.
5 Millions of kids play computer games every day.
6 Some governments control the use of the Internet.
7 You don't need a password to enter this site.

5a SPEAKING **Work with a partner. Look at the map of Italy and answer these questions.**

1 What things are made?
2 What fruit and vegetables are grown?
3 What fruit and vegetables are <u>not</u> grown?
4 What typical food is eaten?
5 What sports are played?
6 What things are exported?
7 What sport is <u>not</u> played?

5b SPEAKING **Work with a partner. Use the questions to talk about your country. Give as many details as possible (e.g. where exactly, how, when, who by …).**

Collocations with *email*

1 Read the text. The words in *italics* frequently go with the word *email*. Which of the words below in red match these icons?

1

....

2

....

3

....

The other day I tried to **(a)** *send* an email to my cousin but it **(b)** *bounced back*. The email **(c)** *address* wasn't correct. The problem was that my cousin had recently changed his email **(d)** *account*. He'd sent me a message with his new email address but I had accidentally **(e)** *deleted* it, so I didn't have it any more. I knew that one of my friends had my cousin's new email address so I sent my original email to my friend and asked her to **(f)** *forward* it to my cousin. The next day I was **(g)** *checking* my email and I saw that my cousin had **(h)** *replied to* my message.

2 Match five of the words in *italics* in 1 with these definitions.

1 an arrangement you have with an Internet company to use email ......*account*........

2 when an email doesn't go to the person you send it to and it comes back to you ....

3 the letters, numbers and symbols you need to write to send someone an email ....

4 to see if you have any emails ....

5 to send an email on to somebody ....

3 SPEAKING **Work with a partner. Ask and answer these questions.**

1 Have you got an email address? If so, how do you say it in English?
2 Do you have a free email account or do you pay?
3 When do you usually check your email?
4 How often do you delete the emails you receive?
5 Have any of your emails ever bounced back? Do you know why?
6 How much spam do you get via email?

Protecting yourself on the INTERNET

LIFE SKILLS OBJECTIVES	KEY CONCEPTS
■ To think about social media profiles. ■ To think about good advice for safe social networking. ■ To give advice to others about how to protect yourself online.	**social media [n]:** *She is an expert in social media, or the different ways people use new technologies to communicate.* **profile [n]:** *His personal profile gives the impression that he only likes sport and that he thinks he's better than everyone else.* **post [v, n]:** *I only post messages on the website when I have something important to say.* **share [v]:** *When you put a photo on a public website you share it with other people.* **privacy [n]:** *She's famous but her privacy is important to her. She doesn't talk about her private life in public.*

1a Work with a partner. What can you do on social networking websites? Make a list of ideas.

You can chat online.

1b SPEAKING What do you think are good and bad things about using social networking websites?

> *You can communicate with people all over the world.*

> *Yes, but you're probably giving information to people that you don't know.*

2 READING **Read this text and answer these questions.**

1 What main problem with social networking does the text talk about?

2 Does the text say that social networking is *always good/always bad/sometimes good and sometimes bad*? Explain your answer.

SOCIAL NETWORKING TODAY

Imagine you have applied for a job. Would you be happy for your future employer to look at your social networking profile? No? Well, be careful when you post online.

The things we say and show are public and usually remain online for a long time. So when we apply to university or for a job, it is usually very easy for the university or company to find out lots of information about us from our activity on social media. In some cases, this can be a positive thing. But in others it may go against us. It all depends on how we look after our online identity or profile.

A survey in the US discovered that 43% of all companies use social networking sites to investigate job candidates. In 51% of these cases, the company has found information that has made them decide not to give the person the job. There are a number of different reasons why companies decided to reject the candidate after looking at their social networking profile. Typical reasons were:

- The candidate posted inappropriate photos or information (46%)

- There was information about inappropriate behaviour (41%)

- The candidate said something bad or inappropriate about their previous employer (36%)

- The candidate had poor communication skills (32%)

- The candidate made discriminatory comments (28%)

- It became clear that the candidate had lied about their qualifications (25%)

NO JOB TOMORROW?

However, some employers (33%) also noted that they found information on social media sites that made a candidate more attractive or helped them to decide to offer the candidate the job. They mentioned these aspects as positive:

- The candidate gave a professional image (43%)

- Their online profile helped to get a good impression of their personality (46%)

- The candidate showed that they had a good variety of interests (40%)

- The information confirmed that they had the qualifications mentioned in their application (45%)

- The candidate was creative (36%)

- The candidate showed great communication skills (40%)

- Other people made very positive comments about the candidate (30%)

The research suggests that companies are using social media to get an idea of candidates' behaviour and personality outside of the interview. That means that your social media profile needs to send out the right message.

Article from *CareerBuilder*

3 Read the text again and answer these questions.

1 How many US companies investigate a candidate's social media profile?

2 Is it more common for this investigation to have a positive or negative consequence for the candidate?

3 What is the most common problem with a candidate's social media profile?

4 What can an employer discover about a person's qualifications by looking at social media?

5 In what different ways can your social media profile help you to get a job?

6 Why do companies look at social media to help them decide about a candidate?

7 What is the basic message of the text?

4 Look at these words or expressions. They appear in a video giving advice about using social networking sensibly. Work with a partner. What do you think the advice will be?

a Password 1234   d The right age

b Keep it private   e Kind words

c Think first!

5 LISTENING ▶ 65 Watch or listen. Put the words and phrases in 4 in the order that you hear them. Were your ideas in 4 right?

1 .... 3 .... 5 ....

2 .... 4 ....

6 ▶ 65 Watch or listen again. What advice do the speakers give about …

1 age limits?   4 good passwords?

2 photos and videos?   5 being cruel?

3 phone numbers?

7 Work with a partner. What do you think of the advice in 6?

LIFE TASK

You want to give a presentation about protecting yourself on the Internet.

Follow this plan:

1 *Work in a group. Think of more advice about safe use of social networking websites. Look for ideas on the Internet if necessary.*

2 *Organise your ideas in a logical way and decide what you are going to say for each point.*

3 *Decide what type of presentation you are going to give and create it. Include illustrations or graphics.*

4 *Give your presentation to the class.*

Listening

Main Page | Discussion

KIPEDIA
e Encyclopedia

Welcome to Wikipedia,
the free encyclopedia that anyone can edi
3,516,706 articles in English

Today's featured article

The Laplace–Runge–Lenz vector is a v
of the orbit of one astronomical body arou
two bodies interacting by Newtonian grav
it is the same no matter where it is calcu
More generally, the LRL v

1 SPEAKING **Work with a partner. What do you know about Wikipedia? Make notes. Use question words (who, what, why, etc.) for ideas.**

An encyclopaedia, free …

2 LISTENING ▶ 66 **Listen to a radio programme about Wikipedia. Did any of your ideas in 1 appear? Were they correct?**

3 ▶ 66 **Look at this text about Wikipedia. It contains seven mistakes. Find and correct the mistakes. Then listen again to check your answers.**

Wikipedia is the sixth most popular website in the world. It has about 365 million readers. It was started in 2001 by two Australians but it isn't written by them. Their original website became a 'wiki', a website that visitors can change and add information to. In 2007, approximately 170 articles were being added every day. 'Wiki Wiki' is an African expression which means 'quick'. Wikipedia articles can change quickly when things change in the world. Some people think this is a problem, because articles aren't always correct. Biographies are the most popular topic. 40% of articles on Wikipedia are about geography and places. There are more than 280 different language versions of Wikipedia. The English, German and French versions have a total of over four million articles.

4 What about *you*?

1 Do you ever use Wikipedia? When and what for?

2 Would you like to write an article for Wikipedia? What would you write about?

Grammar in context

The passive – other tenses

1a Look at these passive sentences. What tense is each one?

1 It was started in 2001.

2 In 2007, 1,700 articles were being added every day.

3 Over 24 million articles have been written.

4 Articles are being changed as we speak.

1b To change the tense in a passive sentence, do we change the verb *to be* or the past participle?

GRAMMAR REFERENCE ➤ PAGE 132

2 Change these sentences from active to passive.

1 Wikipedia has transformed traditional encyclopaedias.

2 Sir Tim Berners-Lee didn't start Wikipedia.

3 They are changing Wikipedia articles at this moment.

4 Ordinary people have written most of the articles for Wikipedia.

5 'Vandals' have ruined some Wikipedia articles.

6 They were creating a Wikipedia for children.

7 They have copied the article from Wikipedia.

8 A famous scientist wrote a Wikipedia article last year.

✔ EXAM SUCCESS

The next exercise is a cloze activity. You have a text with gaps, but they do not give you words to fill in the gaps. How do you decide which word is missing?
➤ EXAM SUCCESS page 146

3 Complete the text by filling in each space with one word.

Can technology help children learn?

In 2012, twenty tablets (a) .... given to some children in Wenchi, (b) .... is a poor village in Ethiopia. Nine months later, the children could say the alphabet in English and some could spell words. They weren't taught (c) .... a teacher because there are no teachers in the village. They (d) .... learned thanks to the tablets. The children's progress has (e) .... observed by experts from the Massachusetts Institute of Technology. It is part (f) .... a project to see if children (g) .... teach themselves to read with new technology. The project is for some of the poorest places (h) .... the world, places where (i) .... aren't any teachers or schools. One hundred million children around the world have no school or teacher. At this very moment, thanks to technology, something is (j) .... done to help some of those children.

4a SPEAKING **Work with a partner. Look at these trivia questions. Do you know the answers?**

1 How many *Iron Man* films have been made?
2 Where was the last World Cup played?
3 Who were *Firework* and *Roar* sung by?
4 Who is the Xbox made by?
5 In which century was the Colosseum built?

4b With your partner, write five trivia questions in the passive. You must know the answers to all your questions.

4c Join another pair and ask them your questions. Who got the most correct answers?

have something done

5 Look at these sentences and choose the correct alternative.

1 The writers get their work checked and edited by other readers.
2 They had the articles written by other people.

a We use the expression have something done when *we do an action ourselves/somebody does an action for us*.
b The structure is **have** + **object** + *gerund/past participle*.
c **Have** and **get** *are/aren't* similar in these sentences.
d We use *by/with* to introduce the person who does the activity for us.
e We *can/can't* use **have** and **get** in any tense.

GRAMMAR REFERENCE ➤ PAGE 132

6 Look at these pictures and the verb given. Write sentences about what the people had done last week.

1 fix ➤ *He had his computer fixed.*
....

2 cut ➤ ....
....

3 test ➤ ....
....

4 make ➤ ....
....

7a Are these questions correct? If not, rewrite them.

1 How often do you get your hair cut?
2 Have you ever had fixed your computer?
3 Do you like having your photo taken?
4 When was the last time you had tested your eyes?

7b Work with a partner. Ask and answer the correct questions.

Developing speaking

Comparing and contrasting photos

a

b

1 SPEAKING **Work with a partner. What similarities can you find between photos a and b? What differences are there?**

2 LISTENING ▶ 67 **Listen to a student comparing and contrasting photos a and b. Does she mention any of your ideas in 1?**

3 ▶ 67 **Put these expressions in the correct section in the Speaking bank. Which of the expressions did the student use? Listen again if necessary.**

1   In this photo … but/whereas in the other photo …

2   Both of the photos show …

💬 **SPEAKING BANK**

Useful expressions to compare and contrast photos
Comparing

■ _____

■ One/Another (big/important) similarity between the photos is …

■ Another thing they have in common is that …

Contrasting

■ _____

■ One/Another (big/important) difference between the photos is …

■ In this photo … However, in the other photo …

■ In contrast, …

4 **Complete the sentences with words from the Speaking bank.**

1   One important _____ is that the people in the photos are all using computers.

2   _____ photos show people working, either indoors or outdoors.

3   In the first photo the people seem serious, _____ in the second they seem happier.

4   In this photo they're using computers for fun. _____, in the other one they're using them for school work.

5   Another thing that they have in _____ is that they both show people in their free time.

6   This photo shows us an outdoor sport. In _____, the other photo shows us people doing sport indoors.

✔ **EXAM SUCCESS**

When you are describing photos, what can you do when you are not 100% sure of what you can see in the photo(s)?

➤ EXAM SUCCESS page 146

PRACTICE MAKES PERFECT

5a Work with a partner.

Student A: Look at the two photos at the bottom of page 148.
Student B: Look at the two photos at the top of page 148. Make notes about similarities and differences between the photos.

5b SPEAKING **Take it in turns to talk for about a minute about your two photos. Then say which photo you prefer and why. Use expressions from the Speaking bank to compare and contrast the photos.**

Developing writing

Text messages

1 Match the words with the abbreviations used in text messages.

1	are	**a**	2nite
2	at	**b**	2
3	before	**c**	YR
4	great	**d**	L8R
5	later	**e**	@
6	please	**f**	C
7	see	**g**	PLS
8	to/too	**h**	U
9	tonight	**i**	WOT
10	what	**j**	R
11	you	**k**	B4
12	your	**l**	GR8

2 Read these five text messages. What order were they sent in?

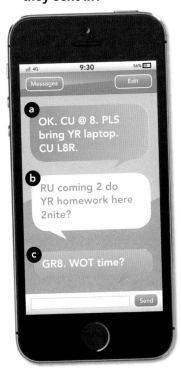

a OK. CU @ 8. PLS bring YR laptop. CU L8R.

b RU coming 2 do YR homework here 2nite?

c GR8. WOT time?

d We can't come B4 8.

e OK. Sarah n Matt R coming 2.

1 ..... *b* ..... **4** ....

2 .... **5** ....

3 ....

3 Write out the text messages in 2 as full sentences. Use the information in 1 to help you.

1 *Are you coming to do your homework here tonight?*

2 ....

3 ....

4 ....

5 ....

4 Read the information in the Writing bank. What do you think the complete words are?

> ### ✎ WRITING BANK
>
> **How to write text messages**
> - We often use abbreviations instead of writing the complete word.
> - To make abbreviations, we sometimes take away vowels from the word (e.g. PLS = please) or we replace words with symbols (e.g. @ = at) or numbers (e.g. L8R = later).
> - Here are some more common examples:
>   B BCZ HMWK L8 MSG SPK THX 2DAY 2MORO WKND XLNT
> - Remember! It is not correct to use these abbreviations in other types of writing like essays, formal letters, etc.
> - We can also use emoticons like ☺ or ☹ in text messages to show emotions.

5 Use abbreviations to make these text messages shorter.

1 What are you doing at the weekend?

WOT R U doing @ the WKND?

2 Thanks for helping me with my homework.

....

3 Can you come tomorrow to fix my computer?

....

4 You should be happy because your exam results are excellent.

....

5 Don't forget to send me a message later tonight.

....

6 I want to see you and Jo before I speak to the teacher tomorrow.

....

PRACTICE MAKES PERFECT

6a Look at the task and write a text message. Use abbreviations and the Writing bank to help you.

You need to use the Internet tomorrow to do a piece of work for school, but your connection at home doesn't work. Write a text message to a friend asking if you can go to their house tomorrow to use the Net.

WRITING BANK ➤ PAGE 151

6b Now give your message to your partner and write a reply to their message. Keep sending messages until you both know exactly when, where and why you are meeting and what you can do later.

Grammar reference

The passive

FORM

Subject + *be* + past participle (+ *by* + agent)

Computers are made in China. (present simple)

The Internet is being used by millions of people. (present continuous)

These computers have been used by NASA. (present perfect)

The Internet was created in 1989. (past simple)

The Internet will be transformed in the future. (will)

We make the passive with the appropriate tense and form of the verb *to be* and the past participle of the verb.

To make object questions in the passive, we put the first auxiliary verb before the subject.

Is the match being shown on TV?

Who was the World Wide Web invented by?

- We use the preposition *by* to introduce the agent, that is, the person or thing which does the action.

USE

We use the passive when:

- we are more interested in the action than the people who do the action.

  My computer has been fixed.

- we do not know who exactly does the action.

  Her laptop has been stolen.

- it is obvious or understood who did the action.

  The criminal was arrested at 5.30 pm.

have something done

FORM

Subject + *have* or *get* + object + past participle (*by* + agent)

I get my hair cut once every two months. (present simple)

He had cable TV installed. (past simple)

With this structure we make different tenses by changing the tense of *have* or *get*.

USE

- We use *have/get something done* to talk about actions which we don't do ourselves; somebody or something does them for us. We often pay them to do this action. **Get** is slightly more informal.

  I don't know anything about computers so when I have a problem I have my computer fixed by a friend who studied computers at university.

- We can use the preposition *by* to introduce the agent, that is, the person or thing which does the action. If it is not important who does the action, we do not put anything.

Vocabulary

1 Using a computer click on • copy • cut and paste • flashdrive • hardcopy • hard drive • headphones
headset • keyboard • log on/off • microphone • monitor • mouse • mouse mat • password • pendrive
printer • save • scanner • screen • speaker • tablet • USB cable and port • webcam

2 The Internet blog • broadband • chat online • download • homepage • online • search engine
social networking • surf the Net • website

3 Collocations with *email* bounce back • check email • delete an email • email account • email address
forward an email • reply to an email • send an email

4 Other words and phrases ➤ page 143

Grammar revision

The passive – present simple
/ 8 points

1 Write sentences in the present simple passive.

1 Computers/use/everywhere.

2 A lot of chocolate/eat/in the UK.

3 Shoes/not wear/in mosques.

4 Portuguese/speak/in Brazil.

5 Fish/not sell/at the butcher's.

6 Cars/make/by robots in this factory.

7 This programme/watch/by thousands of people.

8 The New Year/celebrate/in many countries.

The passive – other tenses
/ 8 points

2 Each sentence contains a mistake. Find the mistake and rewrite the sentence correctly.

1 The song 'Thriller' was sang by Michael Jackson.

2 The Champions League is won by Real Madrid in 2014.

3 London is visited for thousands of people.

4 The radio invented by Marconi.

5 Many products made in China nowadays.

6 The eclipse was saw by people around the world.

7 Oh no! His car has stolen.

8 The dog was been hit by a car yesterday.

have something done
/ 5 points

3 Write sentences with *have/get something done*.

1 My parents didn't paint the house. They …

2 He doesn't repair the car himself. He …

3 We didn't build the swimming pool ourselves. We …

4 I didn't correct the text myself. I …

5 She doesn't do her hair herself. She …

Vocabulary revision

USING A COMPUTER
/ 7 points

1 Match to make words or phrases.

1	pen	a	port
2	key	b	board
3	USB	c	copy
4	hard	d	cam
5	head	e	phones
6	web	f	drive
7	mouse	g	mat

THE INTERNET
/ 6 points

2 Read the definitions. Write the words.

1 look at various places on the Net ……… r ….

2 a computer program used for looking for information on the Internet ……… r ……… g ………

3 a type of diary on a website that changes regularly …. l ……..

4 connected to the Internet o ……………

5 move information to your computer from the Internet …… w ……………

6 the first place that you choose to appear on your screen when you connect to the Internet ………… p ……….

COLLOCATIONS WITH *EMAIL*
/ 6 points

3 Complete the sentences with six of the words in the box.

account • address • bounce • check
delete • forward • reply • send

1 When you get an email you should ……………… to it quickly.

2 When you get an email that you send to another person, you ……………… it.

3 When you don't want an email, you ……………… it.

4 When emails don't go to the correct address they ……………… back.

5 My email ……………… is fredbloggs@bloggs.co.uk.

6 When I go online, I ……………… my email.

Total: / 40 points

Reading

> **TIP FOR READING EXAMS**

In reading activities where you complete a text with missing sentences, remember …

When you finish, check the activity by reading the text with your answers in the correct place. Do the sentences go together logically? Do words like *this* or *it* make sense?

➤ EXAM SUCCESS page 146

1 **Read the text quickly. What is the connection between studying and the Internet in the text?**

1 .... There are tens of thousands of websites where you can buy essays. With most essay-writing companies, students pay per word. Sometimes they pay per page. Some companies offer to write a special, personalised essay, but at an extra cost. You can also pay extra for faster essays.

2 .... 3,500 specialists are employed by his company. They have written more than 15,000 essays for students. The company made £90,000 in just one week in May. Thanks to his company, Littlewood has a Ferrari and a Lamborghini in his garage. Universities say that the UK's academic reputation is suffering because of online essay companies, and education experts have predicted that schools will have to stop continuous assessment and start doing more exams again.

3 .... He says he simply offers them a guide. 'The essays are a starting point. Students use them to create their own work. Students analyse our answers and then they write their own. We're just showing them how to write a great essay.'

4 .... As one teacher replied: 'The suggestion that these essays are used by students as 'guides' is crazy and dishonest. We need to do something to stop it.' Many colleges and universities now have software which allows teachers to check if students are copying from five billion web pages. Many universities have somebody doing this full-time. 'It's not a question of catching people and punishing them. It's a question of helping students to understand what education really is. Education is research and investigation. In the end, the students who are using these services are just not learning the skills they need for their studies or for the rest of their lives.'

2 **Put these sentences in the correct place in the text. There is one extra sentence that you do not need.**

A Barclay Littlewood is the owner of one online essay-writing organisation.

B However, Internet cheating is now an enormous problem for schools and universities and it might make them go back to older, more traditional methods.

C Millions of pounds are spent each year on Internet cheating.

D But teachers are not convinced that students are using them in this way.

E Barclay Littlewood, on the other hand, says he doesn't help students to cheat.

3 **Read the text again and choose the best answers.**

1 The price of a basic online essay usually depends on …
  a who writes it.
  b what the subject is.
  c how long it is.

2 Barclay Littlewood is …
  a a businessman.
  b a writer of online essays.
  c an ex-teacher.

3 Educational specialists think that online cheating will …
  a change the way teachers teach.
  b change the way teachers assess students.
  c make it easier for students to pass exams.

4 Barclay Littlewood says …
  a students shouldn't just give teachers the essay that they buy.
  b he is helping students to copy work.
  c his objective is to help students get the best marks.

5 The text says that teachers …
  a have no way of knowing if students are copying essays.
  b are using technology to find people who are cheating.
  c want to make cheats suffer.

4 SPEAKING **What about *you*?**

What do you think about buying online essays?

Use of English

> **TIP FOR USE OF ENGLISH**

In activities where you have to complete gaps in a text, remember …
Look carefully at the words just before and after the gap. Do they need a special preposition or an article or an auxiliary verb, for example?

> ➤ EXAM SUCCESS page 146

5 **Complete the text about the magazine National Geographic. Use one word in each gap.**

The National Geographic Society began in 1888 with just a few members and now it is one of the largest scientific and educational organisations (1) .... the world. It was created (2) .... a group of 33 teachers, explorers and businessmen (3) .... 13ᵗʰ January 1888, in Washington, D.C. They met to talk about their interest in geography. Later that year, the first edition of the *National Geographic Magazine* was published. The articles and reports were (4) .... by professors but they weren't very interesting for people (5) .... weren't experts in geography. But then (6) .... magazine became easier to read. It started to have more photos. Some amazing photos have (7) .... printed in the magazine. When you flick (8) .... the magazine today you can still see many spectacular photos. So if one day you need to (9) .... up some information about geography for a school project, why not pick up a copy of *National Geographic*?

Speaking

> **TIP FOR SPEAKING EXAMS**

When comparing and contrasting photos, remember …
You can talk about similarities, not just differences.

> ➤ EXAM SUCCESS page 146

6a Look at the photos on page 148 for a few minutes. Think about similarities and differences between the photos. Make notes if you want but do not write complete sentences.

6b SPEAKING Work with a partner. Talk together and compare and contrast the photos. Which photo do you prefer and why?

Listening

> **TIP FOR LISTENING EXAMS**

In activities where you complete notes, remember …
Read the notes before you listen and predict what type of word goes in each space.

> ➤ EXAM SUCCESS page 146

7 LISTENING ▶ 68 **Listen and complete the notes. You can write a maximum of three words and/or numbers.**

The first SMS was sent in (1) .... SMS means (2) .... An SMS can only have (3) .... characters, or letters, from the Latin alphabet. The first SMS was sent by a man who was working for Vodafone. The first ever SMS was '(4) ....' At first, you couldn't send SMS to people who were with a (5) .... That stopped in (6) .... (7) .... made SMS popular because it was (8) .... to text than to make a phone call.

'CAN DO' PROGRESS CHECK UNITS 9–10 **CEF**

1 **How well can you do these things in English now? Give yourself a mark from 1 to 4.**

> **1** = I can do it very well.
> **2** = I can do it quite well.
> **3** = I have some problems.
> **4** = I can't do it.

a I can talk about what other people have said or asked using reported speech. ☐

b I can talk about books and reading. ☐

c I can identify information in an interview about books and films. ☐

d I can give a presentation about a book. ☐

e I can write a story and make it interesting. ☐

f I can describe actions using different forms of the passive and *have something done*. ☐

g I can talk about computers and the Internet. ☐

h I can identify information in a newspaper article about the Internet. ☐

i I can compare and contrast photos. ☐

j I can write a simple text message. ☐

2 **Now decide what you need to do next to improve.**

1 Look again at my book/notes.

2 Do more practice exercises.
> ➤ WORKBOOK Units 9 and 10

3 Ask for help.

4 Other: ....

(adj) = adjective
(adv) = adverb
(conj) = conjuction
(det) = determiner
(n/n pl) = noun/noun plural
(phr) = phrase
(prep) = preposition
(pron) = pronoun
(v) = verb

The most common and useful words in English are marked according to the Macmillan Dictionary 'star rating'. This is so you can easily recognise the vocabulary you need to know especially well.

★★★ = very common words   ★★ = common words   ★ = fairly common words

If there is no star next to the word, this means that it is not very common.

In the Macmillan Dictionary, (r) is used to indicate where the sound /r/ is pronounced in American English and some other regional varieties of English. In a standard British accent, (r) is only pronounced if it occurs at the end of a word which is followed by another word starting with a vowel sound, for example *far away* /fɑːr ə'weɪ/.

Unit 1

Ages and stages of life

adolescence (n) /ˌædə'les(ə)ns/
baby (n) ★★★ /'beɪbi/
birth (n) ★★★ /bɜː(r)θ/
child (n) ★★★ /tʃaɪld/
childhood (n) ★★ /'tʃaɪld,hʊd/
death (n) ★★★ /deθ/
middle age (n) /ˌmɪd(ə)l 'eɪdʒ/
middle-aged (adj) /ˌmɪd(ə)l 'eɪdʒd/
old age (n) ★ /ˌəʊld 'eɪdʒ/
senior citizen (n) /ˌsiːniə(r) 'sɪtɪz(ə)n/
teenager (n) ★★ /'tiːn,eɪdʒə(r)/
young adult (n) /ˌjʌŋ 'ædʌlt/

The family

aunt (n) ★★★ /ɑːnt/
born (adj) ★★★ /bɔː(r)n/
brother (n) ★★★ /'brʌðə(r)/
brother-in-law (n) /'brʌðər ɪn ˌlɔː/
cousin (n) ★★ /'kʌz(ə)n/
daughter (n) ★★★ /'dɔːtə(r)/
divorced (adj) /dɪ'vɔː(r)st/
father-in-law (n) /'fɑːðər ɪn ˌlɔː/
granddaughter (n) ★ /'ɡrand,dɔːtə(r)/
grandfather (n) ★★ /'ɡrand,fɑːðə(r)/
grandmother (n) ★★ /'ɡrand,mʌðə(r)/
grandson (n) ★ /'ɡrand,sʌn/
husband (n) ★★★ /'hʌzbənd/
mother-in-law (n) /'mʌðər ɪn ˌlɔː/
nephew (n) ★ /'nefjuː/
niece (n) ★ /niːs/
one-parent family (n) /ˌwʌn peərənt 'fam(ə)li/
only child (n) /ˌəʊnli 'tʃaɪld/
partner (n) ★★★ /'pɑː(r)tnə(r)/
single (adj) ★★★ /'sɪŋɡ(ə)l/
sister (n) ★★★ /'sɪstə(r)/
sister-in-law (n) /'sɪstər ɪn ˌlɔː/
son (n) ★★★ /sʌn/
stepfather (n) /'step,fɑːðə(r)/
stepmother (n) /'step,mʌðə(r)/
uncle (n) ★★ /'ʌŋk(ə)l/
wife (n) ★★★ /waɪf/

Noun suffixes -ment, -ion, -ence

argument (n) ★★★ /'ɑː(r)ɡjʊmənt/
concentration (n) ★★★ /ˌkɒns(ə)n'treɪʃ(ə)n/
confidence (n) ★★★ /'kɒnfɪd(ə)ns/
description (n) ★★★ /dɪ'skrɪpʃ(ə)n/
difference (n) ★★★ /'dɪfrəns/
discussion (n) ★★★ /dɪ'skʌʃ(ə)n/
improvement (n) ★★★ /ɪm'pruːvmənt/
independence (n) ★★★ /ˌɪndɪ'pendəns/
information (n) ★★★ /ˌɪnfə(r)'meɪʃ(ə)n/
movement (n) ★★★ /'muːvmənt/
retirement (n) ★ /rɪ'taɪə(r)mənt/

Other words and phrases

accept (v) ★★★ /ək'sept/
advice (n) ★★★ /əd'vaɪs/
alone (adj) ★★★ /ə'ləʊn/
approximately (adv) ★★ /ə'prɒksɪmətli/
argue (v) ★★★ /'ɑː(r)ɡju/
calmly (adv) /'kɑːmli/
chance (n) ★★★ /tʃɑːns/
communicate (v) ★★ /kə'mjuːnɪkeɪt/
completely (adv) ★★★ /kəm'pliːtli/
computer technician (n) /kəm'pjuːtə(r) tek,nɪʃ(ə)n/
contribute (v) ★★★ /kən'trɪbjuːt/
convenient (adj) ★★ /kən'viːniənt/
decision (n) ★★★ /dɪ'sɪʒ(ə)n/
demand (v) ★★★ /dɪ'mɑːnd/
disagreement (n) ★ /ˌdɪsə'ɡriːmənt/
discuss (v) ★★★ /dɪ'skʌs/
e-pal (n) /'iː ˌpæl/
exercise (n) ★★★ /'eksə(r)saɪz/
expert (n) ★★★ /'ekspɜː(r)t/
fridge (n) ★ /frɪdʒ/
government (n) ★★★ /'ɡʌvə(r)nmənt/
hard time (n) /ˌhɑː(r)d 'taɪm/
headphones (n pl) /'hed,fəʊnz/
impossible (adj) ★★★ /ɪm'pɒsəb(ə)l/
interrupt (v) ★★ /ˌɪntə'rʌpt/
knock (v) ★★★ /nɒk/
late (adj) ★★★ /leɪt/
limit (n) ★★★ /'lɪmɪt/
loud (adj) ★★ /laʊd/
make sure (phr) /ˌmeɪk 'ʃɔː(r)/
meal (n) ★★★ /miːl/
order (v) ★★★ /'ɔː(r)də(r)/
personal (adj) ★★★ /'pɜː(r)s(ə)nəl/
privacy (n) ★ /'prɪvəsi/, /'praɪvəsi/
private space (phr) /ˌpraɪvət 'speɪs/
provide (v) ★★★ /prə'vaɪd/
realise (v) /'rɪəlaɪz/
reasonable (adj) ★★★ /'riːz(ə)nəb(ə)l/
respect (n) ★★★ /rɪ'spekt/
responsibility (n) ★★★ /rɪ,spɒnsə'bɪləti/
right(s) (n pl) ★★★ /raɪt(z)/
shout (v) ★★★ /ʃaʊt/
special (adj) ★★★ /'speʃ(ə)l/
style (n) ★★★ /staɪl/
timetable (n) ★★ /'taɪm,teɪb(ə)l/
turn (music) down (v phr) /ˌtɜː(r)n 'daʊn/
unique (adj) ★★★ /juː'niːk/
untidy (adj) ★ /ʌn'taɪdi/
volume (n) ★★★ /'vɒljuːm/

Unit 2

Crimes

break into (v phr) /ˌbreɪk 'ɪntuː/
burglary (n) ★ /'bɜː(r)ɡləri/
damage (v) ★★★ /'dæmɪdʒ/
fraud (n) ★★ /frɔːd/
mugging (n) /'mʌɡɪŋ/
piracy (n) /'paɪrəsi/
robbery (n) ★ /'rɒbəri/
shoplifting (n) /'ʃɒp,lɪftɪŋ/

steal (v) ★★★ /stiːl/
theft (n) ★★ /θeft/
vandalism (n) /'vændə,lɪz(ə)m/

Criminals

burglar (n) ★ /'bɜː(r)glə(r)/
fraudster (n) /'frɔːdstə(r)/
mugger (n) /'mʌgə(r)/
pirate (n) /'paɪrət/
robber (n) ★ /'rɒbə(r)/
shoplifter (n) /'ʃɒp,lɪftə(r)/
thief (n) ★★ /θiːf/
vandal (n) /'vænd(ə)l/

Detective work

accuse a suspect (phr)
/ə,kjuːz ə 'sʌspekt/
analyse evidence (phr)
/,ænəlaɪz 'evɪd(ə)ns/
arrest (n & v) ★ /ə'rest/
arrest a suspect (phr)
/ə,rest ə 'sʌspekt/
charge (n & v) ★★★ /tʃɑː(r)dʒ/
charge a suspect (phr)
/,tʃɑː(r)dʒ ə 'sʌspekt/
collect evidence (phr)
/kə,lekt 'evɪd(ə)ns/
collection (n) ★★★ /kə'lekʃ(ə)n/
investigate a case (phr)
/ɪn,vestɪgeɪt ə 'keɪs/
investigation (n) ★★★
/ɪn,vestɪ'geɪʃ(ə)n/
proof (n) ★★ /pruːf/
prove (v) /pruːv/
question (n & v) ★★★ /'kwestʃ(ə)n/
question a suspect (phr)
/,kwestʃ(ə)n ə 'sʌspekt/

Phrasal verbs connected with investigating and finding

come across (v phr) /,kʌm ə'krɒs/
find out (v phr) /,faɪnd 'aʊt/
look for (v phr) /'lʊk fɔː(r)/
look into (v phr) /,lʊk 'ɪntuː/
turn up (v phr) /,tɜː(r)n 'ʌp/
work out (v phr) /,wɜː(r)k 'aʊt/

Other words and phrases

accessory (n) ★★ /ək'sesəri/
account (n) ★★★ /ə'kaʊnt/
afterwards (adv) ★★★
/'ɑːftə(r)wə(r)dz/
apologise (v) ★★ /ə'pɒlədʒaɪz/
behave (v) ★★ /bɪ'heɪv/

belief (n) ★★★ /bɪ'liːf/
blog post (n) /'blɒg ,pəʊst/
case (n) ★★★ /keɪs/
complicated (adj) ★★ /'kɒmplɪ,keɪtɪd/
detective (adj & n) ★★ /dɪ'tektɪv/
display (v) ★★★ /dɪ'spleɪ/
escape (v) ★★★ /ɪ'skeɪp/
experienced (adj) ★★ /ɪk'spɪəriənst/
festival (n) ★★★ /'festɪv(ə)l/
human (n & adj) ★★★ /'hjuːmən/
hurt (v) ★★★ /hɜː(r)t/
lie (v & n) ★★★ /laɪ/
lock (v) ★★★ /lɒk/
luxury (adj) ★ /'lʌkʃəri/
melted (adj) /'meltɪd/
newspaper (n) ★★★ /'njuːz,peɪpə(r)/
pair (n) ★★★ /peə(r)/
possession (n) ★★ /pə'zeʃ(ə)n/
pretend (v) ★★ /prɪ'tend/
property (n) ★★★ /'prɒpə(r)ti/
run away (v phr) /,rʌn ə'weɪ/
smart (adj) ★★ /smɑː(r)t/
stand up for (v phr) /,stænd 'ʌp fɔː(r)/
still (adv) ★★★ /stɪl/
suit (n) ★★★ /suːt/
tell the truth (phr) /,tel ðə 'truːθ/
theory (n) ★★★ /'θɪəri/
unprotected (adj) /,ʌnprə'tektɪd/
value (n) ★★★ /'væljuː/
violence (n) ★★★ /'vaɪələns/
work of art (n) /,wɜː(r)k əv 'ɑː(r)t/
worth (adj) ★★★ /wɜː(r)θ/

Gateway to exams: Units 1–2

bunker (n) /'bʌŋkə(r)/
complain (v) ★★★ /kəm'pleɪn/
delicatessen (n) /,delɪkə'tes(ə)n/
dish (n) ★★ /dɪʃ/
emergency (adj) ★ /ɪ'mɜː(r)dʒ(ə)nsi/
headquarters (n pl) ★★
/hed'kwɔː(r)tə(r)z/
manually (adv) /'mænjʊəli/
order (v & n) ★★★ /'ɔː(r)də(r)/
responsibly (adv) /rɪ'spɒnsəbli/

Unit 3

Countries, nationalities and languages

Arabic (adj & n) /'ærəbɪk/
Argentina (n) /,ɑː(r)dʒən'tiːnə/

Argentinian (adj & n)
/,ɑː(r)dʒən'tɪniən/
Austria (n) /'ɒstriə/
Austrian (adj & n) /'ɒstriən/
Brazil (n) /brə'zɪl/
Brazilian (adj & n) /brə'zɪliən/
Bulgaria (n) /bʌl'geəriə/
Bulgarian (adj & n) /bʌl'geəriən/
Egypt (n) /'iːdʒɪpt/
Egyptian (adj & n) /ɪ'dʒɪpʃ(ə)n/
German (adj & n) /'dʒɜː(r)mən/
Japan (n) /dʒə'pæn/
Japanese (adj & n) /,dʒæpə'niːz/
Mexican (adj & n) /'meksɪkən/
Mexico (n) /'meksɪkəʊ/
Poland (n) /'pəʊlənd/
Polish (adj & n) /'pəʊlɪʃ/
Portuguese (adj & n) /,pɔː(r)tʃə'giːz/
Russia (n) /'rʌʃə/
Russian (adj & n) /'rʌʃ(ə)n/
Spanish (adj & n) /'spænɪʃ/
Swiss (adj & n) /swɪs/
Switzerland (n) /'swɪtsə(r)lənd/
Thai (adj & n) /taɪ/
Thailand (n) /'taɪlænd/
Turkey (n) /'tɜː(r)ki/
Turkish (adj & n) /'tɜː(r)kɪʃ/

Learning a language

do an essay (phr) /,duː ən 'eseɪ/
do an exercise (phr)
/,duː ən 'eksə(r)saɪz/
do homework (phr)
/,duː 'həʊm,wɜː(r)k/
do/study English (phr)
/,duː/,stʌdi 'ɪŋglɪʃ/
do/take an exam (phr)
/,duː/,teɪk ən ɪg'zæm/
make a mistake (phr)
/,meɪk ə mɪs'teɪk/
memorise (v) ★ /'meməraɪz/
practice (n) ★★★ /'præktɪs/
practise (v) ★★ /'præktɪs/
revise (v) ★ /rɪ'vaɪz/
revision (n) ★★ /rɪ'vɪʒ(ə)n/
student (n) ★★★ /'stjuːd(ə)nt/
study (v) ★★★ /'stʌdi/
translate (v) ★★ /trans'leɪt/
translation (n) ★★ /trans'leɪʃ(ə)n/

Negative prefixes

illegal (adj) ★★ /ɪ'liːg(ə)l/
impossible (adj) ★★★ /ɪm'pɒsəb(ə)l/

incorrect (adj) ★ /ˌɪnkəˈrekt/
informal (adj) ★★ /ɪnˈfɔː(r)m(ə)l/
invisible (adj) ★★ /ɪnˈvɪzəb(ə)l/
irregular (adj) ★ /ɪˈregjʊlə(r)/
unhappy (adj) ★★ /ʌnˈhæpi/
unusual (adj) ★★★ /ʌnˈjuːʒʊəl/

Other words and phrases

accommodation (n) ★★
 /əˌkɒməˈdeɪʃ(ə)n/
area (n) ★★★ /ˈeəriə/
artificial (adj) ★★ /ˌɑː(r)tɪˈfɪʃ(ə)l/
audience (n) ★★★ /ˈɔːdiəns/
based (adj) /beɪst/
block (n) ★★★ /blɒk/
body language (n) /ˈbɒdi ˌlæŋgwɪdʒ/
character (n) ★★★ /ˈkærɪktə(r)/
closely (adv) ★★★ /ˈkləʊsli/
co-exist (v) /ˌkəʊɪgˈzɪst/
collect (v) ★★★ /kəˈlekt/
concentrated (adj) /ˈkɒns(ə)nˌtreɪtɪd/
confusion (n) ★★ /kənˈfjuːʒ(ə)n/
culture (n) ★★★ /ˈkʌltʃə(r)/
data (n) ★★★ /ˈdeɪtə/
detailed (adj) ★★★ /ˈdiːteɪld/
do business (phr) /ˌduː ˈbɪznəs/
experiment (n) ★★★ /ɪkˈsperɪmənt/
explanation (n) ★★★ /ˌekspləˈneɪʃ(ə)n/
fascinating (adj) ★★ /ˈfæsɪneɪtɪŋ/
fold (v) ★★ /fəʊld/
gesture (n) ★★ /ˈdʒestʃə(r)/
impolite (adj) ★ /ˌɪmpəˈlaɪt/
insecure (adj) /ˌɪnsɪˈkjʊə(r)/
interview (n) ★★★ /ˈɪntə(r)ˌvjuː/
main (adj) ★★★ /meɪn/
manga comic (n) /ˈmæŋgə ˌkɒmɪk/
map (n) ★★★ /mæp/
map (v) ★ /mæp/
multinational company (n)
 /ˌmʌltiˌnæʃ(ə)nəl ˈkʌmp(ə)ni/
nod (v) /nɒd/
non-verbal (adj) /ˌnɒn ˈvɜː(r)b(ə)l/
North America (n) /ˌnɔː(r)θ əˈmerɪkə/
origin (n) ★★★ /ˈɒrɪdʒɪn/
peace (n) ★★★ /piːs/
polite (adj) ★ /pəˈlaɪt/
prepare (v) ★★★ /prɪˈpeə(r)/
public (adj) ★★★ /ˈpʌblɪk/
rainbow (n) ★ /ˈreɪnˌbəʊ/
region (n) ★★★ /ˈriːdʒ(ə)n/
secure (adj) ★★ /sɪˈkjʊə(r)/
series (n) ★★★ /ˈsɪəriːz/

shake (v) ★★★ /ʃeɪk/
sincerity (n) /sɪnˈserəti/
social network (n)
 /ˌsəʊʃəl ˈnetwɜː(r)k/
soft (adj) ★★★ /sɒft/
straight (adj) ★★ /streɪt/
the Philippines (n) /ðə ˈfɪləˌpiːnz/
tourism (n) ★★ /ˈtʊərɪz(ə)m/
universal (adj) ★★ /ˌjuːnɪˈvɜː(r)s(ə)l/
verbal (adj) ★ /ˈvɜː(r)b(ə)l/
voice (n) ★★★ /vɔɪs/
war (n) ★★★ /wɔː(r)/

Unit 4

Parts of the body

ankle (n) ★★ /ˈæŋk(ə)l/
arm (n) ★★★ /ɑː(r)m/
back (n) ★★★ /bæk/
cheek (n) ★★ /tʃiːk/
chest (n) ★★★ /tʃest/
chin (n) ★★ /tʃɪn/
ear (n) ★★★ /ɪə(r)/
elbow (n) ★★★ /ˈelbəʊ/
face (n) ★★★ /feɪs/
finger (n) ★★★ /ˈfɪŋgə(r)/
foot (n) ★★★ /fʊt/
forehead (n) ★★ /ˈfɒrɪd/, /ˈfɔː(r)ˌhed/
hand (n) ★★★ /hænd/
head (n) ★★★ /hed/
heel (n) ★★ /hiːl/
hip (n) ★★ /hɪp/
knee (n) ★★★ /niː/
leg (n) ★★★ /leg/
mouth (n) ★★★ /maʊθ/
neck (n) ★★★ /nek/
nose (n) ★★★ /nəʊz/
shoulder (n) ★★★ /ˈʃəʊldə(r)/
stomach (n) ★★ /ˈstʌmək/
thigh (n) ★★ /θaɪ/
throat (n) ★★★ /θrəʊt/
thumb (n) ★★ /θʌm/
toe (n) ★★ /təʊ/
wrist (n) ★★ /rɪst/

Health problems and illnesses

broken (adj) ★★ /ˈbrəʊkən/
cold (n) ★★★ /kəʊld/
cough (n) ★ /kɒf/
earache (n) /ˈɪəreɪk/
flu (n) ★ /fluː/

headache (n) ★ /ˈhedeɪk/
hurt (v) ★★★ /hɜː(r)t/
injure (v) ★★ /ˈɪndʒə(r)/
pain (n) ★★★ /peɪn/
sore (adj) ★ /sɔː(r)/
stomach ache (n) /ˈstʌmək ˌeɪk/
temperature (n) ★★★ /ˈtemprɪtʃə(r)/
toothache (n) /ˈtuːθeɪk/
virus (n) ★★★ /ˈvaɪrəs/

Compound nouns connected with health and medicine

first aid (n) /ˌfɜː(r)st ˈeɪd/
food poisoning (n) /ˈfuːd ˌpɔɪz(ə)nɪŋ/
health centre (n) /ˈhelθ ˌsentə(r)/
heart attack (n) ★ /ˈhɑː(r)t əˌtæk/
painkiller (n) /ˈpeɪnˌkɪlə(r)/
waiting room (n) /ˈweɪtɪŋ ˌruːm/

Other words and phrases

action (n) ★★★ /ˈækʃ(ə)n/
airway (n) /ˈeə(r)weɪ/
ambulance (n) ★★ /ˈæmbjʊləns/
bandage (n) ★ /ˈbændɪdʒ/
bleed (v) ★ /bliːd/
blood (n) ★★★ /blʌd/
breathe (v) ★★ /briːð/
cancer (n) ★★★ /ˈkænsə(r)/
collapse (v) ★★ /kəˈlæps/
common (adj) ★★★ /ˈkɒmən/
compression (n) /kəmˈpreʃ(ə)n/
conscious (adj) ★★ /ˈkɒnʃəs/
cure (n) ★★ /kjʊə(r)/
cushion (n) ★ /ˈkʊʃ(ə)n/
double (n) ★ /ˈdʌb(ə)l/
elevation (n) /ˌeləˈveɪʃ(ə)n/
get rid of (v) /ˌget ˈrɪd ɒv/
ground (n) ★★★ /graʊnd/
healthy (adj) ★★★ /ˈhelθi/
hit (v) ★★★ /hɪt/
ice rink (n) /ˈaɪs ˌrɪŋk/
increase (n) ★★★ /ˈɪŋkriːs/
increase (v) ★★★ /ɪnˈkriːs/
injury (n) ★★★ /ˈɪndʒəri/
insufficient (adj) ★★ /ˌɪnsəˈfɪʃ(ə)nt/
law (n) ★★★ /lɔː/
lie down (v phr) ★★★ /ˌlaɪ ˈdaʊn/
list (n) ★★★ /lɪst/
medicine (n) ★★ /ˈmed(ə)s(ə)n/
moment (n) ★★★ /ˈməʊmənt/
note (n) ★★★ /nəʊt/

obsession (n) ★ /əb'seʃ(ə)n/

painful (adj) ★★ /'peɪnf(ə)l/

period (n) ★★★ /'pɪəriəd/

physical (adj) ★★★ /'fɪzɪk(ə)l/

promote (v) ★★★ /prə'məʊt/

pushchair (n) /'pʊʃˌtʃeə(r)/

recent (adj) ★★★ /'riːs(ə)nt/

recovery position (n)
/rɪ'kʌv(ə)ri pəˌzɪʃ(ə)n/

remedy (n) ★★ /'remədi/

right angle (n) /'raɪt ˌæŋg(ə)l/

scene (n) ★★★ /siːn/

scientific (adj) ★★★ /ˌsaɪən'tɪfɪk/

serious (adj) ★★★ /'sɪəriəs/

simple (adj) ★★★ /'sɪmp(ə)l/

skin (n) ★★★ /skɪn/

sore (adj) ★ /sɔː(r)/

suntan (n) /'sʌnˌtæn/

survey (n) ★★★ /'sɜː(r)veɪ/

tight (adj) ★★ /taɪt/

tip (n) ★★ /tɪp/

unconscious (adj) ★ /ʌn'kɒnʃəs/

well-being (n) /ˌwel 'biːɪŋ/

Gateway to exams: Units 3–4

active (adj) ★★★ /'æktɪv/

acupuncture (n) /'ækjʊˌpʌŋktʃə(r)/

at sea (phr) /æt 'siː/

bilingual (adj) /baɪ'lɪŋgwəl/

brain (n) ★★★ /breɪn/

case (n) ★★★ /keɪs/

drug (n) ★★★ /drʌg/

dry (adj) ★★★ /draɪ/

hygiene (n) ★ /'haɪdʒiːn/

land (n) ★★★ /lænd/

paracetamol (n) /ˌpærə'siːtəmɒl/,
/ˌpærə'setəmɒl/

recover (v) ★★★ /rɪ'kʌvə(r)/

regularly (adv) ★★★ /'regjʊlə(r)li/

seasick (n) /'siːˌsɪk/

seasickness (n) /'siːˌsɪknəs/

treatment (n) ★★★ /'triːtmənt/

Unit 5

TV programmes

advert (ad/advertisement) (n) ★
/'ædvɜː(r)t/

cartoon (n) ★ /kɑː(r)'tuːn/

channel (n) ★★★ /'tʃæn(ə)l/

chat show (n) ★ /'tʃæt ˌʃəʊ/

comedy (n) ★★ /'kɒmədi/

cookery programme (n)
/'kʊk(ə)ri ˌprəʊgræm/

documentary (n) ★ /ˌdɒkjʊ'ment(ə)ri/

drama (n) ★★★ /'drɑːmə/

film (n) ★★★ /fɪlm/

game show (n) /'geɪm ˌʃəʊ/

live (adj) ★★ /laɪv/

programme (n) ★★★ /'prəʊgræm/

reality show (n) /ri'æləti ˌʃəʊ/

remote control (n) ★ /rɪˌməʊt
kən'trəʊl/

series (n) ★★★ /'sɪəriːz/

soap (n) ★★ /səʊp/

sports programme (n)
/'spɔː(r)ts ˌprəʊgræm/

the news (n) ★★★ /ðə 'njuːz/

turn/switch on/off (v phr) ★★★
/ˌtɜː(r)n/swɪtʃ 'ɒn/'ɒf/

TV presenter (n) /ˌtiː 'viː prɪˌzentə(r)/

Adjectives describing TV programmes

awful (adj) ★★ /'ɔːf(ə)l/

boring (adj) ★★ /'bɔːrɪŋ/

cool (adj) ★★★ /kuːl/

exciting (adj) ★★ /ɪk'saɪtɪŋ/

funny (adj) ★★★ /'fʌni/

informative (adj) ★ /ɪn'fɔː(r)mətɪv/

interesting (adj) ★★★ /'ɪntrəstɪŋ/

moving (adj) ★★ /'muːvɪŋ/

popular (adj) ★★★ /'pɒpjʊlə(r)/

scary (adj) ★ /'skeəri/

Adjectives ending in *-ing* and *-ed*

boring/ed (adj) ★★/★★ /'bɔːrɪŋ/
bɔː(r)d/

confusing/ed (adj) ★★/★
/kən'fjuːzɪŋ/kən'fjuːzd/

disappointing/ed (adj) ★/★
/ˌdɪsə'pɔɪntɪŋ/ˌdɪsə'pɔɪntɪd/

embarrassing/ed (adj) ★/★
/ɪm'bærəsɪŋ/ɪm'bærəst/

exciting/ed (adj) ★★/★★
/ɪk'saɪtɪŋ/ɪk'saɪtɪd/

frightening/ed (adj) ★/★
/'fraɪt(ə)nɪŋ/'fraɪt(ə)nd/

interesting/ed (adj) ★★★/★★★
/'ɪntrəstɪŋ/'ɪntrəstɪd/

moving/ed (adj) ★★/★★ /'muːvɪŋ/
muːvd/

relaxing/ed (adj) ~/★ /rɪ'læksɪŋ/
rɪ'lækst/

surprising/ed (adj) ★★★/★★★
/sə(r)'praɪzɪŋ/sə(r)'praɪzd/

tiring/ed (adj) ~/★★★ /'taɪərɪŋ/
'taɪə(r)d/

Other words and phrases

a bit (adv) /ə 'bɪt/

addict (n) ★ /'ædɪkt/

admire (v) ★★ /əd'maɪə(r)/

anniversary (n) ★★ /ˌænɪ'vɜː(r)s(ə)ri/

appear (v) ★★★ /ə'pɪə(r)/

burn (v) ★★★ /bɜː(r)n/

celebrity (n) ★ /sə'lebrəti/

cheap (adj) ★★★ /tʃiːp/

coast (n) ★★★ /kəʊst/

complete (adj) ★★★ /kəm'pliːt/

edit (v) ★★ /'edɪt/

end up (v phr) /ˌend 'ʌp/

fame (n) ★★ /feɪm/

invent (v) ★★ /ɪn'vent/

invention (n) ★★ /ɪn'venʃ(ə)n/

journey (n) ★★★ /'dʒɜː(r)ni/

lazy (adj) ★★ /'leɪzi/

leave school (phr) /ˌliːv 'skuːl/

lifestyle (n) ★★ /'laɪfˌstaɪl/

lottery (n) ★ /'lɒtəri/

miss/cut class (phr) /ˌmɪs/ˌkʌt 'klɑːs/

model (n) ★★★ /'mɒd(ə)l/

modelling agency (n)
/'mɒd(ə)lɪŋ ˌeɪdʒ(ə)nsi/

nature programme (n) /'neɪtʃə(r)
ˌprəʊgræm/

negotiate (v) ★★ /nɪ'gəʊʃieɪt/

Norway (n) /'nɔː(r)weɪ/

operation (n) ★★★ /ˌɒpə'reɪʃ(ə)n/

Oslo (n) /'ɒzləʊ/

phenomenon (n) ★★ /fə'nɒmɪnən/

poet (n) ★★ /'pəʊɪt/

population (n) ★★★ /ˌpɒpjʊ'leɪʃ(ə)n/

professional (adj) ★★★ /prə'feʃ(ə)nəl/

qualification (n) ★★★
/ˌkwɒlɪfɪ'keɪʃ(ə)n/

rapidly (adv) /'ræpɪdli/

route (n) ★★★ /ruːt/

single (n) ★★ /'sɪŋg(ə)l/

slightly (adv) ★★★ /'slaɪtli/

smart (adj) ★★ /smɑː(r)t/

stressful (adj) /'stresf(ə)l/

theatre company (n)
/'θɪətə(r) ˌkʌmp(ə)ni/

trip (n) ★★★ /trɪp/

wool (n) ★★ /wʊl/

Wordlist: Units 6–7

Unit 6

Geographical features

beach (n) ★★★ /biːtʃ/

desert (n) ★★ /'dezə(r)t/

forest (n) ★★★ /'fɒrɪst/

ice cap (n) /'aɪs ˌkæp/

island (n) ★★★ /'aɪlənd/

jungle (n) ★ /'dʒʌŋg(ə)l/

lake (n) ★★ /leɪk/

mountain (n) ★★★ /'maʊntɪn/

mountain range (n) /'maʊntɪn ˌreɪndʒ/

ocean (n) ★★ /'əʊʃ(ə)n/

rainforest (n) ★ /'reɪnˌfɒrɪst/

river (n) ★★★ /'rɪvə(r)/

sea (n) ★★★ /siː/

valley (n) ★★★ /'væli/

The environment

drought (n) /draʊt/

environment (n) ★★★ /ɪn'vaɪrənmənt/

flood (n) ★★ /flʌd/

global warming (n) ★
/ˌgləʊb(ə)l 'wɔː(r)mɪŋ/

greenhouse effect (n) /'griːnhaʊs
ɪˌfekt/

melt (v) ★★ /melt/

nuclear disaster (n)
/ˌnjuːkliə(r) dɪ'zɑːstə(r)/

oil spill (n) /'ɔɪl ˌspɪl/

ozone layer (n) /'əʊzəʊn ˌleɪə(r)/

pollution (n) /pə'luːʃ(ə)n/

recycle (v) ★ /riː'saɪk(ə)l/

save (v) ★★★ /seɪv/

waste (n & v) ★★★/★★ /weɪst/

Different uses of get

arrive (v) ★★★ /ə'raɪv/

become (a process or change of
state) (v) ★★★ /bɪ'kʌm/

bring (v) ★★★ /brɪŋ/

obtain/buy (v) ★★★ /əb'teɪn/baɪ/

receive (v) ★★★ /rɪ'siːv/

Other words and phrases

altitude (n) ★ /'æltɪˌtjuːd/

asteroid (n) /'æstəˌrɔɪd/

atmosphere (n) ★★ /'ætməsˌfɪə(r)/

bulb (n) ★ /bʌlb/

carbon dioxide emissions (phr)
/ˌkɑː(r)bən daɪ'ɒksaɪd ɪˌmɪʃ(ə)nz/

carbon footprint (n)
/ˌkɑː(r)bən 'fʊtprɪnt/

catastrophe (n) /kə'tæstrəfi/

charge/recharge (a mobile phone) (v)
/tʃɑː(r)dʒ/riː'tʃɑː(r)dʒ/

climate (n) ★★ /'klaɪmət/

corridor (n) ★★ /'kɒrɪdɔː(r)/

definitely (adv) ★★ /'def(ə)nətli/

electrical (adj) ★★ /ɪ'lektrɪk(ə)l/

electricity (n) ★★★ /ɪˌlek'trɪsəti/

energy (n) ★★★ /'enə(r)dʒi/

extinct (adj) ★ /ɪk'stɪŋkt/

formal (adj) ★★★ /'fɔː(r)m(ə)l/

fuel-efficient (adj) /'fjuːəl ɪˌfɪʃ(ə)nt/

go up (v phr) /ˌgəʊ 'ʌp/

greenhouse gases (n pl)
/'griːnhaʊs ˌgæsɪz/

hole (n) ★★★ /həʊl/

impact (n) ★★★ /'ɪmpækt/

indirectly (adv) /ˌɪndə'rektli/

level (n) ★★★ /'lev(ə)l/

litre (n) ★ /'liːtə(r)/

peas (n pl) ★ /piːz/

petrol (n) ★★ /'petrəl/

planet (n) ★★ /'plænɪt/

plant (n) ★★★ /plɑːnt/

primary (adj) ★★★ /'praɪməri/

rail (n) ★★★ /reɪl/

reduce (v) ★★★ /rɪ'djuːs/

remote (adj) ★★ /rɪ'məʊt/

secondary (adj) ★★★ /'sekənd(ə)ri/

seed (n) ★★★ /siːd/

survive (v) ★★★ /sə(r)'vaɪv/

sustainable energy (phr)
/səˌsteɪnəb(ə)l 'enə(r)dʒi/

technology (n) ★★★ /tek'nɒlədʒi/

tile (n) /taɪl/

variety (n) ★★★ /və'raɪəti/

vault (n) /vɔːlt/

Gateway to exams: Units 5–6

extreme (adj) ★★ /ɪk'striːm/

informative (adj) ★ /ɪn'fɔː(r)mətɪv/

space exploration (n)
/'speɪs ekspləˌreɪʃ(ə)n/

Unit 7

Jobs and work

builder (n) ★★ /'bɪldə(r)/

fashion designer (n) /'fæʃ(ə)n
dɪˌzaɪnə(r)/

firefighter (n) /'faɪə(r)ˌfaɪtə(r)/

journalist (n) ★★ /'dʒɜː(r)nəlɪst/

librarian (n) ★ /laɪ'breəriən/

mechanic (n) ★ /mɪ'kænɪk/

nurse (n) ★★★ /nɜː(r)s/

plumber (n) ★ /'plʌmə(r)/

police officer (n) ★ /pə'liːs ˌɒfɪsə(r)/

receptionist (n) ★ /rɪ'sepʃ(ə)nɪst/

shop assistant (n) /'ʃɒp əˌsɪst(ə)nt/

vet (n) /vet/

Personal qualities

ambitious (adj) ★★ /æm'bɪʃəs/

bright (adj) ★★★ /braɪt/

calm (adj) ★★ /kɑːm/

caring (adj) /'keərɪŋ/

clever (adj) ★★ /'klevə(r)/

confident (adj) ★★ /'kɒnfɪd(ə)nt/

creative (adj) ★★ /kri'eɪtɪv/

fit (adj) ★★★ /fɪt/

hard-working (adj) ★
/ˌhɑː(r)d 'wɜː(r)kɪŋ/

patient (adj) ★★ /'peɪʃ(ə)nt/

reliable (adj) ★★ /rɪ'laɪəb(ə)l/

sensitive (adj) ★★★ /'sensətɪv/

sociable (adj) /'səʊʃəb(ə)l/

strong (adj) ★★★ /strɒŋ/

well-organised (adj)
/ˌwel 'ɔː(r)gənaɪzd/

Compound adjectives

badly-paid (adj) /ˌbædli 'peɪd/

blue/brown/green-eyed (adj)
/'bluː/'braʊn/'griːn ˌaɪd/

easy-going (adj) /ˌiːzi 'gəʊɪŋ/

full-time (adj) ★★ /'fʊl ˌtaɪm/

good-looking (adj) ★★ /ˌgʊd 'lʊkɪŋ/

part-time (adj) ★★ /'pɑː(r)t ˌtaɪm/

right/left-handed (adj)
/ˌraɪt/ˌleft 'hændɪd/

well-known (adj) ★★ /ˌwel 'nəʊn/

well-off (adj) /ˌwel 'ɒf/

well-paid (adj) /ˌwel 'peɪd/

Other words and phrases

application (n) ★★★ /ˌæplɪ'keɪʃ(ə)n/

autograph (n) /'ɔːtəˌgrɑːf/

background (n) ★★★ /'bækˌgraʊnd/

bungee jumping (n)
/'bʌndʒiː ˌdʒʌmpɪŋ/

contact details (n) /'kɒntækt ˌdiːteɪlz/

CV/Curriculum Vitae (n) ★ /ˌsiː 'viː/
kəˌrɪkjʊləm 'viːtaɪ/

director (n) ★★★ /dəˈrektə(r)/, /daɪˈrektə(r)/

diver (n) /ˈdaɪvə(r)/

employed (adj) /ɪmˈplɔɪd/

employee (n) ★★★ /ɪmˈplɔɪiː/, /ˌemplɔɪˈiː/

employer (n) ★★★ /ɪmˈplɔɪə(r)/

equipment (n) ★★★ /ɪˈkwɪpmənt/

extra (n) ★ /ˈekstrə/

gas (n) ★★★ /ɡæs/

get dressed up (phr) /ˌɡet drest ˈʌp/

heights (n pl) ★★★ /haɪts/

highly (adv) ★★★ /ˈhaɪli/

historical fiction (n) /hɪˌstɒrɪk(ə)l ˈfɪkʃ(ə)n/

hunt (v) ★★ /hʌnt/

impression (n) ★★★ /ɪmˈpreʃ(ə)n/

interpersonal (adj) /ˌɪntə(r)ˈpɜː(r)s(ə)nəl/

interpreter (n) ★ /ɪnˈtɜː(r)prɪtə(r)/

magazine (n) ★★★ /ˌmæɡəˈziːn/

manual (adj) ★ /ˈmænjʊəl/

member (n) ★★★ /ˈmembə(r)/

mentally (adv) /ˈment(ə)li/

mixture (n) ★★★ /ˈmɪkstʃə(r)/

motivate (v) ★★ /ˈməʊtɪveɪt/

obligation (n) ★★★ /ˌɒblɪˈɡeɪʃ(ə)n/

paperwork (n) ★ /ˈpeɪpə(r)ˌwɜː(r)k/

problem-solving (n) /ˈprɒbləm ˌsɒlvɪŋ/

prohibition (n) /ˌprəʊɪˈbɪʃ(ə)n/

qualifications (n pl) ★★★ /ˌkwɒlɪfɪˈkeɪʃ(ə)nz/

quality (n) ★★★ /ˈkwɒləti/

repair (v) ★★ /rɪˈpeə(r)/

rickshaw (n) /ˈrɪkˌʃɔː/

scene (n) ★★★ /siːn/

service (n) ★★★ /ˈsɜː(r)vɪs/

shout at (v phr) /ˈʃaʊt æt/

skill (n) ★★★ /skɪl/

society (n) ★★★ /səˈsaɪəti/

solution (n) ★★★ /səˈluːʃ(ə)n/

sorts (n pl) ★★★ /sɔː(r)ts/

spy (n) ★ /spaɪ/

suit (v) ★★★ /suːt/

take orders (phr) /ˌteɪk ˈɔː(r)də(r)z/

teamwork (n) /ˈtiːmˌwɜː(r)k/

train (v) ★★★ /treɪn/

transferable (adj) /trænsˈfɜːrəb(ə)l/

treat (v) ★★★ /triːt/

unambitious (adj) /ˌʌnæmˈbɪʃəs/

unemployed (adj) ★★★ /ˌʌnɪmˈplɔɪd/

Unit 8

Friendships

circle of friends (phr) /ˌsɜː(r)k(ə)l əv ˈfrendz/

classmate (n) /ˈklɑːsˌmeɪt/

close friend (phr) /ˌkləʊs ˈfrend/

fall out (with somebody) (v phr) /ˌfɔːl ˈaʊt/

get on well (with somebody) (phr) /ˌɡet ɒn ˈwel/

hang out (with) (v phr) /ˌhæŋ ˈaʊt/

have arguments (with somebody) (phr) /ˌhæv ˈɑː(r)ɡjʊmənts/

have in common (v phr) /ˌhæv ɪn ˈkɒmən/

make (it) up (v phr) /ˌmeɪk ˈʌp/

see eye to eye (phr) /siː ˌaɪ tuː ˈaɪ/

Feelings

anger (n) ★★ /ˈæŋɡə(r)/

boredom (n) ★ /ˈbɔː(r)dəm/

excitement (n) ★★ /ɪkˈsaɪtmənt/

fear (n) ★★★ /fɪə(r)/

happiness (n) ★★ /ˈhæpinəs/

loneliness (n) /ˈləʊnlinəs/

sadness (n) ★ /ˈsædnəs/

Adjectives

afraid (adj) ★★★ /əˈfreɪd/

angry (adj) ★★★ /ˈæŋɡri/

bored (adj) ★★ /bɔː(r)d/

excited (adj) ★★ /ɪkˈsaɪtɪd/

happy (adj) ★★★ /ˈhæpi/

lonely (adj) ★★ /ˈləʊnli/

sad (adj) ★★★ /sæd/

Noun suffixes

freedom (n) ★★★ /ˈfriːdəm/

friendship (n) ★★ /ˈfren(d)ʃɪp/

illness (n) ★★★ /ˈɪlnəs/

kingdom (n) ★★★ /ˈkɪŋdəm/

leadership (n) ★★★ /ˈliːdə(r)ʃɪp/

madness (n) ★ /ˈmædnəs/

relationship (n) ★★★ /rɪˈleɪʃ(ə)nʃɪp/

weakness (n) ★★ /ˈwiːknəs/

Other words and phrases

beat (v) ★★★ /biːt/

carry on (v phr) /ˌkæri ˈɒn/

club (n) ★★★ /klʌb/

competitive (adj) ★★ /kəmˈpetətɪv/

constructively (adv) /kənˈstrʌktɪvli/

critical (adj) ★★★ /ˈkrɪtɪk(ə)l/

criticise (v) ★★ /ˈkrɪtɪsaɪz/

disconnected (adj) /ˌdɪskəˈnektɪd/

expectation (n) ★★★ /ˌekspekˈteɪʃ(ə)n/

fall in love (phr) /ˌfɔːl ɪn ˈlʌv/

fault (n) ★★★ /fɔːlt/

feel part of (phr) /ˌfiːl ˈpɑː(r)t ɒv/

forever (adv) ★★ /fər'evə(r)/

ideal (adj) ★★★ /aɪˈdɪəl/

isolated (adj) ★ /ˈaɪsəˌleɪtɪd/

keep on (v phr) /ˌkiːp ˈɒn/

leaflet (n) ★★ /ˈliːflət/

locally (adv) ★★ /ˈləʊk(ə)li/

marks (n pl) ★★★ /mɑː(r)ks/

occasion (n) ★★★ /əˈkeɪʒ(ə)n/

official (adj) ★★★ /əˈfɪʃ(ə)l/

personality (n) ★★★ /ˌpɜː(r)səˈnæləti/

primary school (n) ★ /ˈpraɪməri ˌskuːl/

replace (v) ★★★ /rɪˈpleɪs/

river bank (n) /ˈrɪvə(r) ˌbæŋk/

romance (n) ★ /rəʊˈmæns/

safety (n) ★★★ /ˈseɪfti/

secondary school (n) /ˈsekənd(ə)ri ˌskuːl/

section (n) ★★★ /ˈsekʃ(ə)n/

share (v) ★★★ /ʃeə(r)/

sharp (adj) ★★★ /ʃɑː(r)p/

shocked (adj) ★ /ʃɒkt/

silence (n) ★★★ /ˈsaɪləns/

slap (v) ★ /slæp/

stick (n) ★★ /stɪk/

subway (n) /ˈsʌbˌweɪ/

sudoku (n) /suˈdəʊkuː/

take part in (phr) /ˌteɪk ˈpɑː(r)t ɪn/

unofficial (adj) /ˌʌnəˈfɪʃ(ə)l/

voluntary (adj) ★★ /ˈvɒlənt(ə)ri/

wet (adj) ★★★ /wet/

Gateway to exams: Units 7–8

alternative (n) ★★★ /ɔːlˈtɜː(r)nətɪv/

business (n) ★★★ /ˈbɪznəs/

generation (n) ★★★ /ˌdʒenəˈreɪʃ(ə)n/

Unit 9

Fiction
comic (n) /'kɒmɪk/
crime novel (n) /'kraɪm ˌnɒv(ə)l/
fairy tale (n) /'feəri ˌteɪl/
fantasy (n) ★★ /'fæntəsi/
graphic novel (n) /ˌgræfɪk 'nɒv(ə)l/
historical fiction (n)
  /hɪˌstɒrɪk(ə)l 'fɪkʃ(ə)n/
horror (n) ★★ /'hɒrə(r)/
play (n) ★★★ /pleɪ/
romance (n) ★ /rəʊ'mæns/
science fiction (n) ★ /ˌsaɪəns 'fɪkʃ(ə)n/
thriller (n) ★ /'θrɪlə(r)/

Non-fiction
atlas (n) /'ætləs/
autobiography (n) /ˌɔːtəʊbaɪ'ɒgrəfi/
biography (n) ★ /baɪ'ɒgrəfi/
cookbook (n) /'kʊk,bʊk/
encyclopaedia (n) ★ /ɪnˌsaɪklə'piːdiə/
guidebook (n) ★ /'gaɪd,bʊk/
magazine (n) ★★★ /ˌmægə'ziːn/
manual (n) ★★ /'mænjʊəl/
newspaper (n) ★★★ /'njuːz,peɪpə(r)/
textbook (n) /'teks(t),bʊk/

Phrasal verbs connected with reading and writing
cross out (v phr) /ˌkrɒs 'aʊt/
fill in (v phr) /ˌfɪl 'ɪn/
flick through (v phr) /ˌflɪk 'θruː/
look up (v phr) /ˌlʊk 'ʌp/
read on (v phr) /ˌriːd 'ɒn/
read out (v phr) /ˌriːd 'aʊt/
turn over (v phr) /ˌtɜː(r)n 'əʊvə(r)/

Other words and phrases
action (n) ★★★ /'ækʃ(ə)n/
adaptation (n) ★ /ˌædæp'teɪʃ(ə)n/
author (n) ★★★ /'ɔːθə(r)/
award (n) ★★★ /ə'wɔː(r)d/
back cover (n) /ˌbæk 'kʌvə(r)/
bestseller (n) /ˌbest 'selə(r)/
billionaire (n) /ˌbɪljə'neə(r)/
blurb (n) /blɜː(r)b/
browse (v) ★ /braʊz/

charity (n) ★★★ /'tʃærəti/
chills (n pl) ★ /tʃɪlz/
congratulations (n pl) ★
  /kənˌgrætʃʊ'leɪʃ(ə)nz/
contract (n) ★★★ /'kɒntrækt/
creature (n) ★★★ /'kriːtʃə(r)/
dramatically (adv) /drə'mætɪk(ə)li/
enter (a competition) (v) ★★★
  /'entə(r)/
evil (adj) ★★ /'iːv(ə)l/
frequently (adv) ★★★ /'friːkwəntli/
giant (adj) ★★ /'dʒaɪənt/
guard (n) ★★★ /gɑː(r)d/
intrigue (n) /'ɪntriːg/
judge (n) ★★★ /dʒʌdʒ/
main (adj) ★★★ /meɪn/
matter (v & n) ★★★ /'mætə(r)/
natural (adj) ★★★ /'nætʃ(ə)rəl/
nightmare (n) ★★ /'naɪt,meə(r)/
novel (n) ★★★ /'nɒv(ə)l/
on sale (phr) /ˌɒn 'seɪl/
pound note (n) /ˌpaʊnd 'nəʊt/
predator (n) ★★ /'predətə(r)/
presentation (n) ★★★
  /ˌprez(ə)n'teɪʃ(ə)n/
prison (n) ★★★ /'prɪz(ə)n/
prologue (n) /'prəʊlɒg/
publisher (n) ★★ /'pʌblɪʃə(r)/
racing car (n) /'reɪsɪŋ ˌkɑː(r)/
raise (v) ★★★ /reɪz/
recipe (n) ★★ /'resəpi/
related (adj) ★★ /rɪ'leɪtɪd/
repetitive (adj) /rɪ'petətɪv/
risk (v) ★★ /rɪsk/
science laboratory (n)
  /'saɪəns lə,bɒrət(ə)ri/
separate (v) ★★★ /'sepəreɪt/
serious (adj) ★★★ /'sɪəriəs/
significance (n) ★★ /sɪg'nɪfɪkəns/
step (n) ★★★ /step/
storm (n) ★★ /stɔː(r)m/
talent (n) ★★ /'tælənt/
technique (n) ★★★ /tek'niːk/
trilogy (n) /'trɪlədʒi/
visible (adj) ★★ /'vɪzəb(ə)l/
youth (n & adj) ★★★ /juːθ/

Unit 10

Using a computer
click on (v phr) /'klɪk ɒn/
copy (v) ★★ /'kɒpi/
cut and paste (v) /ˌkʌt ən(d) 'peɪst/
flashdrive (n) /'flæʃ,draɪv/
hard drive (n) /'hɑː(r)d ,draɪv/
headset (n) /'hed,set/
headphones (n pl) /'hed,fəʊnz/
keyboard (n) ★ /'kiː,bɔː(r)d/
log on/off (v phr) /ˌlɒg 'ɒn/'ɒf/
make a hardcopy (phr)
  /ˌmeɪk ə hɑː(r)d'kɒpi/
microphone (n) ★ /'maɪkrə,fəʊn/
monitor (n) ★ /'mɒnɪtə(r)/
mouse (n) ★★ /maʊs/
mouse mat (n) /'maʊs ,mæt/
password (n) ★ /'pɑːs,wɜː(r)d/
pendrive (n) /'pen,draɪv/
print (v) ★★★ /prɪnt/
printer (n) ★★ /'prɪntə(r)/
save (v) ★★★ /seɪv/
scanner (n) ★ /'skænə(r)/
screen (n) ★★★ /skriːn/
speaker (n) ★★★ /'spiːkə(r)/
tablet (n) ★★ /'tæblət/
USB cable (n) /ˌjuː es 'biː ,keɪb(ə)l/
USB port (n) /ˌjuː es 'biː ,pɔː(r)t/
webcam (n) /'web,kam/

The Internet
blog (n & v) /blɒg/
broadband (n) /'brɔːd,bænd/
chat/go online (phr) /ˌtʃæt/
  ˌgəʊ ɒn'laɪn/
download (n) /'daʊn,ləʊd/
download (v) /ˌdaʊn'ləʊd/
homepage (n) ★ /'həʊm,peɪdʒ/
search engine (n) ★ /'sɜː(r)tʃ ,endʒɪn/
social networking (n)
  /ˌsəʊʃəl 'netwɜː(r)kɪŋ/
surf the Net (phr) /ˌsɜː(r)f ðə 'net/
website (n) ★★ /'web,saɪt/

Collocations with email
bounce back (v phr) /ˌbaʊns 'bæk/
check email (phr) /ˌtʃek 'iːmeɪl/

delete an email (phr)
/də,liːt ən 'iːmeɪl/

email account (n) /'iːmeɪl ə,kaʊnt/

email address (n) /'iːmeɪl ə,dres/

forward an email (phr)
/,fɔː(r)wə(r)d ən 'iːmeɪl /

reply to an email (phr)
/rɪ,plaɪ tʊ ən 'iːmeɪl /

send an email (phr) /,send ən 'iːmeɪl/

Other words and phrases

abbreviation (n) ★ /ə,briːvi'eɪʃ(ə)n/

access (v) /'ækses/

apply (v) ★★★ /ə'plaɪ/

available (adj) ★★★ /ə'veɪləb(ə)l/

browser (n) /'braʊzə(r)/

candidate (n) ★★★ /'kændɪdeɪt/,
/'kændɪdət/

comment (n) ★★★ /'kɒment/

cruel (adj) ★★ /'kruːəl/

defend (v) ★★★ /dɪ'fend/

diameter (n) ★ /daɪ'æmɪtə(r)/

discriminatory (adj) /dɪ'skrɪmɪnət(ə)ri/

document (n) ★★★ /'dɒkjʊmənt/

expand (v) ★★★ /ɪk'spænd/

for short (phr) /fə(r) 'ʃɔː(r)t/

go against (v phr) /,gəʊ ə'genst/

graduate (n) ★★ /'grædʒuət/

graphic (n) /'græfɪk/

grow (v) ★★★ /grəʊ/

identity (n) ★★★ /aɪ'dentɪti/

image (n) ★★★ /'ɪmɪdʒ/

inappropriate (adj) ★★ /,ɪnə'prəʊpriət/

mask (n) ★★ /mɑːsk/

media (n) /'miːdiə/

network (n) ★★★ /'net,wɜː(r)k/

old-fashioned (adj) ★★
/,əʊld 'fæʃ(ə)nd/

original (n) ★ /ə'rɪdʒ(ə)nəl/

post (v & n) ★★/★★★ /pəʊst/

principle (n) ★★★ /'prɪnsəp(ə)l/

profile (n) ★★ /'prəʊfaɪl/

pure (adj) ★★★ /pjʊə(r)/

reference (n) ★★★ /'ref(ə)rəns/

remain (v) ★★★ /rɪ'meɪn/

server (n) ★★ /'sɜː(r)və(r)/

share (v) ★★★ /ʃeə(r)/

silicon chip (n) /,sɪlɪkən 'tʃɪp/

social media (n) ★ /,səʊʃəl 'miːdiə/

software engineer (n)
/'sɒf(t)weə(r) endʒɪ,nɪə(r)/

typical (adj) ★★★ /'tɪpɪk(ə)l/

version (n) ★★★ /'vɜː(r)ʃ(ə)n/

worldwide (adj) ★ /,wɜː(r)ld'waɪd/

Gateway to exams: Units 9–10

(alphabet) characters (n)
/('ælfə,bet) 'kærɪktə(r)z/

edition (n) ★★ /ɪ'dɪʃ(ə)n/

entertainment (n) ★★
/,entə(r)'teɪnmənt/

explorer (n) /ɪk'splɔːrə(r)/

Latin alphabet (n) /,lætɪn 'ælfəbet/

pick up (v phr) /,pɪk 'ʌp/

SMS (Short Message Service) (n)
/,es em 'es (,ʃɔː(r)t 'mesɪdʒ
'sɜː(r)vɪs)/

✔ Exam success

Unit 1

READING: MULTIPLE-CHOICE ACTIVITIES

Step 1: Read the text quickly to get a general understanding.

Step 2: Read all the answers carefully. Sometimes the difference between two answers is just one word.

Step 3: Find the section of the text where you think each answer comes and read it again slowly, in more detail.

Step 4: If you aren't 100% sure which answer is best, take away any answers which you know are not correct.

Step 5: When you finish, check that you have an answer for each question. Never leave answers blank in an exam.

SPEAKING: INFORMATION ROLE-PLAYS

- If you don't understand what the examiner or your partner says, ask them in English to repeat or to speak more slowly. Use expressions like: 'Sorry, can you say that again?' or, 'Sorry, could you speak more slowly?'
- Listen to your partner and the examiner. In a conversation we speak *and* listen.
- Show that you're interested in what the other person is saying. Use expressions like: 'Really?' 'That's interesting.' 'Do you?', 'Me too.'
- Use 'Well', 'Hmm' or 'Let me think' to give you time to think of what you want to say next.
- Use basic question words like *Who? What? When? Where? How? Why?* to help you think of more questions to keep the conversation going.

Unit 2

LISTENING: TRUE/FALSE/NOT MENTIONED ACTIVITIES

Step 1: Read the questions before you listen. They can give you ideas about the topic of the text and the vocabulary you are going to hear.

Step 2: You can usually hear the recording twice. Try not to panic if you do not understand information the first time. If you don't hear the answer to one question, start listening immediately for the answer to the next question.

Step 3: Use the second listening to find the answers you didn't hear the first time and to check the answers you already have.

Step 4: When you finish, check that you have an answer for each question. Never leave answers blank in an exam.

WRITING: KNOWING ABOUT EVALUATION

In exams it is important to know how many marks there are for different sections and to know what the examiners want. Usually examiners want to see if you:

- answer the question and include the information they ask for
- write clearly
- organise your ideas logically
- use accurate and varied grammar
- use accurate and varied vocabulary
- use punctuation and capital letters correctly

Unit 3

USE OF ENGLISH: MULTIPLE-CHOICE CLOZE ACTIVITIES

Step 1: Read the complete text without thinking about the gaps. This helps you to get a general understanding of the text.

Step 2: Before you look at the answers that they give you, think about the *type* of word you need (noun, verb, pronoun, article, etc.) and the general *meaning*.

Step 3: Read the answers that they give you. Choose the one which you think is best. Look very carefully at the words which come just before and after the gap. Do they help you to find the answer?

Step 4: If you aren't sure which answer is right, take away any answers which you know are not correct.

Step 5: Read the sentence again with your answer in the gap.

Step 6: When you finish, check that you have an answer for each question. Never leave answers blank in an exam.

SPEAKING: KNOWING ABOUT EVALUATION

In exams it is important to know how many marks there are for different sections and to know what the examiners want. Usually examiners in speaking exams want to see if you:

- communicate successfully
- speak fluently
- use accurate and varied grammar
- use accurate and varied vocabulary
- pronounce words clearly

Unit 4

READING: MATCHING ACTIVITIES

In this type of activity, you have to say which text or part of a text contains a piece of information.

Step 1: Read all the texts or parts of the text quickly to get a general understanding.

Step 2: Read the piece(s) of information that you need to find. Look for key words that help you to find the text or part of the text which contains the information.

Step 3: Read that specific text or part of the text again in more detail.

Step 4: If you are not sure that you have found the correct answer, read other sections again in more detail.

Step 5: When you finish, check that you have an answer for each question. Never leave answers blank in an exam.

WRITING: CONTENT AND STYLE

- When a question tells you to put information in your text, you lose marks if you do not include the information. You can use your imagination but you must remember to include all the information in the instructions.
- When you write letters, messages and notes it is essential to write in the correct style. When you write to a friend, use contractions and informal expressions. When you write a formal or semi-formal letter, message or note, do not use contractions or informal language. If your letter is grammatically correct but not in the correct style, you lose marks.

Unit 5

LISTENING: IDENTIFYING THE SPEAKER ACTIVITIES

In this type of activity you match different speakers with the things they say.

Step 1: Before you listen, think about the topic of what you are going to listen to. This will help you to predict ideas and words that could appear in the recording.

Step 2: Read the questions to know how many speakers there are and what they may say.

Step 3: When you listen, remember that in the listening text the speakers will probably express the same ideas using different words and expressions. Thinking of synonyms for the words in the statements can help you to identify the answers.

Step 4: Don't worry if you don't understand everything the first time you listen. Usually you listen twice. Use the second listening to find the answers you didn't hear the first time and to check the answers you already have.

SPEAKING: NEGOTIATING

In negotiating activities, you usually work with another person. The examiner explains a situation where you and the other speaker need to come to a decision.

In this type of exercise, remember that there isn't usually a right or wrong answer. Basically, the examiner wants to hear you speaking English. If you can't think of something to say:

- Ask your partner a question like *What do you think?* This gives you time to think of what you can say next.
- Use fillers like *Well, Hmm* or *Let me think* to give you time to think of what you want to say next.
- Don't be afraid to say something you think is obvious.
- Give full explanations for your opinions and ideas.
- Listen to what your partner or the examiner is saying. In a conversation we speak *and* listen.
- If you don't understand what the examiner or your partner is saying, ask them in English to repeat or to speak more slowly. Use expressions like: *Sorry, can you say that again?* or, *Sorry, could you speak more slowly?*

Unit 6

USE OF ENGLISH: SENTENCE TRANSFORMATION ACTIVITIES

In this type of activity you have a sentence and you must complete a second sentence so that it means the same as the original sentence. In some exercises you must use a word that they give. In this case, you cannot change the form of this word. Generally you can only use between two and five words, including the word they give you.

Step 1: Read the original sentence carefully. Think about the meaning of the sentence, the type of structure(s) used, the tense(s) used, etc.

Step 2: If they give you a word, think about its meaning. Think also about the grammatical function of the word. Does it always or usually go with another word or tense?

Step 3: Write your sentence.

Step 4: When you finish, check that you:

- have not changed the meaning of the original sentence.
- have not changed the form of the word they gave you.
- have not used more that the maximum number of words permitted.

WRITING: EXAM CONDITIONS

- When you write in exam conditions, you cannot usually use a dictionary or grammar book. If you do not know a word, think of a similar word or a more basic or general word. Do not leave a gap or write the word in your own language. If necessary, change what you were going to say.
- If you are not sure how to use a grammatical structure, think of a different way to say the same thing.
- Answer the question. You might not get any points if you don't answer the question properly.
- Pay attention to the maximum and minimum number of words in the instructions. Plan and organise your essay before you write and check it carefully for mistakes when you finish.

Unit 7

READING: TRUE-FALSE ACTIVITIES

Step 1: Read the text quickly to get a general understanding.

Step 2: Read the sentences that you need to prove true or false.

Step 3: Find the parts of the text where the information comes. Read them again in more detail.

Step 4: If there is no information to say if a sentence is true, mark the statement false.

Step 5: When you finish, check that you have an answer for each question. Never leave answers blank in an exam.

LISTENING: MULTIPLE-CHOICE

Step 1: Read the different answers before you listen. They can give you ideas about the topic of the text and the vocabulary you are going to hear in it. Remember that sometimes the difference between two answers is just one word.

Step 2: You usually hear the recording twice. Try not to panic if you do not understand information the first time. If you don't hear the answer to one question, start listening immediately for the answer to the next question.

Step 3: Use the second listening to find the answers you didn't hear the first time and to check the answers you already have.

Step 4: When you finish, check that you have an answer for each question. Never leave answers blank in an exam.

Unit 8

SPEAKING: REPORTING ACTIVITIES

In this type of activity you have to talk about something (real or imaginary) that happened in the past. You may need to speak alone or have a conversation with the examiner or another student.

- Remember to use past tenses correctly. We use the past simple for completed activities in the past. The past continuous is for activities in progress at a moment in the past. We can use it to describe scenes in the past. The past perfect is for activities that happened before other activities in the past. *Used to* is for past habits.
- Use expressions of time and sequence (*first, next, then, later,* etc.) to make the order of events clear.
- Use basic question words like *Who? What? When? Where? How? Why?* to help you think of more things to say.
- Use fillers like *Well, Hmm* or *Let me think* to give you time to think of what you want to say next.
- Listen to what your partner or the examiner is saying. In a conversation we speak *and* listen.
- If you don't understand what the examiner or your partner is saying, ask them in English to repeat or to speak more slowly. Use expressions like: *Sorry, can you say that again?* or, *Sorry, could you speak more slowly?*

WRITING: ANSWERING THE QUESTION

- Remember that in writing exams you lose marks if you do not answer the question. It is not enough to write a composition with no grammatical mistakes and with a wide variety of vocabulary. You must also include all the information that appears in the question.
- Reading the question carefully can also help you to decide which tenses and vocabulary you need to use.

Unit 9

READING: MISSING SENTENCES ACTIVITIES

In this type of activity you have to fill gaps in a text with sentences taken out of the text. There are sometimes more sentences than spaces.

Step 1: Read the text quickly to get a general idea of what it is about. To do this type of exercise you do not usually have to understand every word, so don't panic if you don't understand everything.

Step 2: Read the sentences which go in the text. What does each sentence talk about?

Step 3: Find the sections of the text which correspond to the information in the sentences and read them again slowly, in more detail. Put each sentence in the most probable space.

Step 4: When you finish, check by reading the text with your answers in the correct place. Do the sentences go together logically? Do words like *this* or *it* make sense? Check also that you have one answer for each question. Never leave answers blank in an exam.

LISTENING: COMPLETING NOTES

- Always read the incomplete notes *before* you listen. This helps you to know what to listen for. Look carefully at the words that come just before or after each space and think about what *type* of word is missing (noun, verb, adjective, adverb, etc.).
- It is not usually necessary to understand every word that you hear. Listen out for the sections which correspond to the information in the notes. Pay special attention to these sections.
- Usually you only need to write one or two words in each space. Be careful with spelling and your handwriting.
- Don't worry if you don't understand everything the first time you listen. Usually you listen twice. Use the second listening to find the answers you didn't hear the first time and to check the answers you already have.

Unit 10

USE OF ENGLISH: CLOZE ACTIVITIES

Step 1: Read the complete text without thinking about the gaps. This is to get a general understanding of the text.

Step 2: Look again at the gaps and especially the words which come just before and after the gap. Do those words need a special preposition? Is an article or auxiliary verb missing? Think about the type of word you need (noun, verb, pronoun, article, etc.) and the general meaning.

Step 3: Fill in the gap with the word that you think is best. Read the sentence again with your answer in the gap to check it. Check that the meaning is logical, but check also that the word fits in grammatically. Sometimes there may be more than one possible answer but you only need to put one.

Step 4: When you finish, check that you have one answer for each question. Never leave answers blank in an exam.

SPEAKING: COMPARING AND CONTRASTING PHOTOS

- If you cannot think of things to say, use the questions *What? Who? Where? Why? When?* etc. to give you ideas.
- Think of possible questions that the examiner will ask you about the photo. If you don't know a word, don't worry. Think of similar words, more basic or general words, or explain the word.
- Use words and expressions like *Both of the photos show, One similarity is that ... , One thing they have in common is ...* to say things that are similar in the two photos.
- Use words and expressions like *but, whereas, however, One difference between the photos is that ...* to say things that are different in the two photos.
- Use fillers like *Well, Hmm* or *Let me think* to give yourself time to think of what you are going to say next.
- If you aren't 100% sure of what you can see, speculate using expressions like *It may/might be, I'm not sure but I think, It looks like, It seems that,* etc. Don't be afraid of saying simple, obvious things. The important thing is to say something because the examiner basically wants to hear you speaking English.

Communication activities

Unit 2

GRAMMAR IN CONTEXT

Exercise 7b, page 21

Student B: look at the information below. Prepare questions to ask your partner to find the missing information.

> Sir Arthur Conan Doyle was the creator of the world-famous detective, Sherlock Holmes. He was born in 1859 in **(a)** ....
> Conan Doyle was a doctor. He began writing stories when **(b)** .... When he began work he didn't have many patients. He started writing stories again. Conan Doyle wrote the first Sherlock Holmes novel in **(c)** .... The title was *A Study in Scarlet*.
> The idea for Sherlock Holmes came from one of Conan Doyle's teachers at university. The teacher's name was Joseph Bell. Apart from Sherlock Holmes, Conan Doyle created another interesting character, Sherlock's great friend, **(d)** ....
> Sherlock Holmes was always a very popular character. He appeared in **(e)** .... short stories and four novels. Conan Doyle tried to **(f)** .... in 1893. But the public wanted more Sherlock Holmes stories and Conan Doyle **(g)** .... in 1903.
> Conan Doyle died when he was 71 years old. But his famous character Sherlock Holmes is still very much alive. He continues to appear in new films, TV series and novels.

Unit 3

DEVELOPING SPEAKING

Exercise 6b, page 40

Student B: You are the receptionist at the San Francisco English Centre, USA.

THE SAN FRANCISCO ENGLISH CENTRE, USA

Course begins: 21ˢᵗ July

Course lasts: One month

Accommodation organised

Price: 4,325 US dollars

Other activities include: mountain biking, excursion to a theme park, karaoke evenings

Gateway to exams: Units 3–4

Exercise 6, page 57

Photo A:

Unit 3

GATEWAY TO LIFE SKILLS

Exercise 1b, page 36

1 B 2 A 3 A

DEVELOPING SPEAKING

Exercise 6a, page 40

Student A: You are the receptionist at the Sydney English Centre, Australia.

THE SYDNEY ENGLISH CENTRE, AUSTRALIA

Course begins: 16ᵗʰ August

Course lasts: 12 days

Accommodation organised

Price: 930 Australian dollars

Other activities include: swimming, surfing, excursion to the Blue Mountains

Unit 7

GATEWAY TO LIFE SKILLS

Life task, page 89

Give yourself a mark from 5 (brilliant) to 1 (poor) for each skill.

TRANSFERABLE SKILLS

PERSONAL SKILLS

Ambitious ....
Responsible and reliable ....
Well-organised ....
Other: ....

INTERPERSONAL SKILLS

Friendly and caring ....
Good at leading, motivating and organising others ....
Good at working with others and taking orders ....
Patient ....
Other: ....

OTHER SKILLS

Good communication skills ....
Good with your hands ....
ICT skills ....
Maths, money and numeracy ....
Problem-solving skills ....

OTHER:

....

Unit 7

DEVELOPING SPEAKING

Exercise 5a, page 92

Student B:

CINERAMA CINEMAS

No experience necessary
Job is from 20th June to 20th September
Part-time work: 24 hours a week
Don't work Mondays
Wages: £7.80 an hour
Need to be reliable and sociable
Don't need to be an expert in films
Email letter and CV to: jdoors@cineramacinemas.co.uk

Unit 10

DEVELOPING SPEAKING

Exercise 5a, page 130

Student B:

Gateway to exams: Units 3–4

SPEAKING

Exercise 6, page 57

Photo B:

Gateway to exams: Units 9–10

SPEAKING

Exercises 6a & 6b, page 135

Photo A: Photo B:

Unit 7

DEVELOPING SPEAKING

Exercise 5b, page 92

Student A:

SPORTS STAR CAMP

Good to have experience of sports camps, but not essential
Job is for July and September
Full-time work only: residential, living with the children doing the camp
Salary: £8.90 an hour
Need to be fit, interested in sport, caring, responsible
Don't need to speak foreign languages
Email letter and CV to: cjones@sportsstarcamp.co.uk

Unit 8

LISTENING

Exercise 2, page 102

Count how many ticks you have in each section (1-4) on page 102. Read below about the section where you have most ticks. Do you agree with the result?

MOSTLY SECTION 1: YOU ARE A PERFECTIONIST.

Personality: You're very hard-working and always want to do your best, but sometimes you're too serious.
Romance: Your relationships are intense but short. If your partner isn't perfect, you always have arguments.
Ideal jobs: Fashion designer, TV producer, journalist
Advice: You should be more relaxed. Not everybody is as perfect as you.

MOSTLY SECTION 2: YOU ARE A ROMANTIC.

Personality: You're very caring and get on well with others, but you can get very sad when people don't think about you.
Romance: You're a total romantic and believe in true love. You need your partner to be 100% in love with you.
Ideal jobs: Artist, novelist, actor
Advice: You shouldn't get too unhappy if things go wrong.

MOSTLY SECTION 3: YOU'RE A THINKER.

Personality: You're a reliable friend because you're good at listening to people and helping them with problems. But sometimes you spend too much time alone, thinking about things.
Romance: You're very practical about relationships but you need to relax and enjoy yourself more.
Ideal jobs: Politician, teacher, computer programmer
Advice: You have to do more and think less. Don't worry about the consequences of your actions – just do it!

MOSTLY SECTION 4: YOU'RE A LEADER.

Personality: You have to be in control. You're strong and ambitious. But that can be a weakness too because some people will think you are too interested in being the boss.
Romance: You think it's easy to make somebody fall in love with you. But some people may think you are frightening!
Ideal jobs: Company director, police officer, bank manager
Advice: You should think of others. Be more tolerant of people who aren't as direct as you.

Unit 10

DEVELOPING SPEAKING

Exercise 5a, page 130

Student A:

Irregular verbs

Infinitive	Past simple	Past participle
be	was/were	been
beat	beat	beaten
become	became	become
begin	began	begun
break	broke	broken
bring	brought	brought
build	built	built
burn	burnt	burnt
buy	bought	bought
catch	caught	caught
choose	chose	chosen
come	came	come
cost	cost	cost
cut	cut	cut
do	did	done
draw	drew	drawn
drink	drank	drunk
drive	drove	driven
eat	ate	eaten
fall	fell	fallen
feel	felt	felt
find	found	found
fly	flew	flown
forget	forgot	forgotten
forgive	forgave	forgiven
get	got	got
give	gave	given
go	went	gone
grow	grew	grown
hang out	hung out	hung out
have	had	had
hear	heard	heard
hide	hid	hidden
hit	hit	hit
hurt	hurt	hurt
keep	kept	kept
know	knew	known
lay	laid	laid
leave	left	left
learn	learned/learnt	learned/learnt

Infinitive	Past simple	Past participle
let	let	let
lie	lay	lain
lose	lost	lost
make	made	made
mean	meant	meant
meet	met	met
pay	paid	paid
put	put	put
read	read	read
ride	rode	ridden
ring	rang	rung
run	ran	run
say	said	said
see	saw	seen
sell	sold	sold
send	sent	sent
set up	set up	set up
shine	shone	shone
shoot	shot	shot
show	showed	shown
sing	sang	sung
sit	sat	sat
sleep	slept	slept
speak	spoke	spoken
speed	sped	sped
spell	spelt	spelt
spend	spent	spent
split up	split up	split up
stand up	stood up	stood up
steal	stole	stolen
swim	swam	swum
take	took	taken
teach	taught	taught
tell	told	told
think	thought	thought
understand	understood	understood
wake up	woke up	woken up
wear	wore	worn
win	won	won
write	wrote	written

Writing bank

Unit 1

AN INFORMAL EMAIL

p15

Style: Use contractions. We can also use emoticons (e.g. ☺).

Start: *Hi, Dear …, Hello*

Useful expressions: To begin, ask questions like *How are you?, How are things?, Are you doing exams/on holiday at the moment?*. Use *Anyway* or *By the way* to change the subject.

End: *That's all for now, Bye for now!, Write back soon, All the best, Best wishes.*

Content in informal emails giving basic personal information:

Suggested paragraph plan:

Paragraph 1: Basic personal information

Paragraph 2: Family

Paragraph 3: Main hobby/hobbies

Paragraph 4: Favourite subject(s) at school

Paragraph 5: Ask for a reply

Unit 2

A BLOG POST

p27

Style: Informal. Use contractions.

Start: Have a name for your blog. Have a title for the blog post.

Useful expressions: To explain the sequence of events when talking about past events use *At first, First of all, Then, Next, In the end, Finally.* To say when things happened use *Yesterday, When, Suddenly, A few minutes/hours/days later, The next day.*

Unit 3

A LANGUAGE BIOGRAPHY

p41

Style: (Semi-) Informal. We can use contractions.

Useful expressions: To explain the sequence of events use *At first, First of all, Next, Then, After that.*

Content of a language biography:

Suggested paragraph plan:

Paragraph 1: Basic personal information

Paragraph 2: Language-learning experiences at primary school

Paragraph 3: Language-learning experiences at secondary school

Paragraph 4: Language-learning experiences outside school, including trips

Paragraph 5: How you prefer to learn a language

Unit 4

NOTES AND MESSAGES

p53

Style: Informal. Use contractions. Write short, direct sentences. We often use imperatives like *Call me*, rather than *Could you call me?* Use abbreviations (see below).

Start: Simply write the name of the person you are writing to.

Useful abbreviations: *PS, e.g., NB, asap, i.e., etc.*

Useful expressions: *I was really sorry to hear that …* (bad news), *Get well soon* (for sickness and accidents), *Congratulations* (good news).

End: Write your name.

Content: Include all the practical information that the reader needs to know.

Unit 5

A REVIEW

p67

Useful expressions: To give your opinions use *Personally, I …, In my opinion, I think …, I would recommend (…) to …, As far as I'm concerned, …*

Content of a review:

Suggested paragraph plan:

Paragraph 1: Basic information about what you are reviewing

Paragraph 2: A more detailed description of what you are reviewing

Paragraph 3: Why you like/don't like it

Paragraph 4: A recommendation

Unit 6

A FORMAL LETTER

p79

Style: Do not use contractions.

Start: When we do not know or use the name of the person we are writing to, we write *Dear Sir* or *Madam* or *Dear Editor* (to a newspaper). Begin *I am writing about/in response to …*

Useful expressions: Use *Personally, I …, In my opinion, I think …, I believe …, As far as I'm concerned …* Ask for other people's opinions with *I will be interested in hearing other readers' opinions on this subject.*

Useful linkers: To put opinions and ideas in sequence use *Firstly, Next, Finally.* To add opinions and ideas use *Furthermore, What is more.* To contrast ideas and opinions use *However, Nevertheless.*

End: When we don't know the name of the person we are writing to, use *Yours faithfully.*

Content of a formal letter of opinion:

Suggested paragraph plan:

Paragraph 1: Begin by explaining why you are writing.

Paragraph 2: Express your opinion and explain your main reason for it.

Paragraph 3: Give additional reasons for your opinion.

Paragraph 4: Ask for other people's opinions and end your letter.

Unit 7

A LETTER OF APPLICATION AND CV

p93

Style: Formal. Do not use contractions.

Start: Write your address and the date in the top right-hand corner. Then write *Dear Mr (Smith)* (for a man), *Dear Mrs (Smith)* (for a married woman), or *Dear Ms (Smith)* (when we make no distinction if a woman is married or not). When we do not know the name of the person we are writing to, we write *Dear Sir or Madam.*

Useful expressions: Begin *I am writing in response to the advertisement in ….* Use *I would like to apply for the job of … , I enclose a CV with information about myself, I have experience of …* End *I look forward to hearing from you.*

End: When we know the name of the person we are writing to use *Yours sincerely.* When we don't know the name of the person we are writing to use *Yours faithfully.*

Content in job applications: Begin by saying what job you are applying for. Explain why you would be good for this job by saying what experience you have. Give details of some of your personal qualities that make you a good candidate.

Unit 10

TEXT MESSAGES

p131

Style: Informal

Useful abbreviations: *PLS, @, L8R, B, BCZ, L8, MSG, SPK, THX, 2DAY, 2MORO, WKND, XLNT, 2nite, 2, YR, C, U, WOT, R, B4, GR8*

Unit 8

AN EMAIL OF ADVICE

p105

Style: Use contractions.

Start: Write *Dear* or *Hi* and the name of the person you are writing to.

Useful expressions: Begin *I'm writing to tell you about/because …, I hope you're well, Thanks for your letter, It was good to hear from you.* Ask questions like *How are you?, How are things?* Use *Anyway* or *By the way* to change the subject.

End: Use *Please write back soon, That's all for now, All the best.*

Useful linkers: To put ideas in order use *First, Firstly, First of all, Then, Next, After that, Finally, Lastly.*

Useful grammar: Use *should/ shouldn't* to give advice.

Unit 9

A STORY

p119

Useful expressions: Use adjectives (*young, famous, beautiful*) and adverbs (*quietly, immediately, quickly*) to make your writing more descriptive. To say when things happened use for example: *One day, Last weekend, Two weeks ago, On Friday, On Saturday night, Suddenly, Two weeks later.* To explain the sequence of events use *At first, First of all, Next, Then, After that, Finally, In the end.*

Useful grammar: Use a variety of past tenses.

- Past simple (a completed action in the past)
- Past continuous (an activity in progress at a moment in the past. We often use it to describe scenes in the past)
- Past perfect (an activity that happened before another action in the past)

Content in a story:

Suggested paragraph plan:

Paragraph 1: Explain where and when the story begins. Introduce the characters.

Paragraphs 2 and 3: Explain the main events in the story.

Paragraph 4: Explain how the story ended and what the consequences were.

CHECKING YOUR WRITING

Check for mistakes with:

- Punctuation
- Capital letters
- Word order
- Spelling
- Tenses
- Vocabulary
- Missing words
- Agreement between the subject and verb (e.g. *He goes …* not *He go.*)
- Style
- Content

Macmillan Education
4 Crinan Street
London N1 9XW
A division of Macmillan Publishers Limited

Companies and representatives throughout the world

ISBN 978-0-230-47090-3

Text © David Spencer 2016
Design and illustration © Macmillan Publishers Limited 2016
The author has asserted his right to be identified as the author of this work in accordance with the Copyright, Designs and Patents Act 1988.

This edition published 2016
First edition entitled Gateway B1 Student's Book published 2011

Designed by emc design ltd
Illustrated by A Corazón Abierto (Sylvie Poggio Artists Agency) pp8, 24, 25, 26; Monica Auriemma (Sylvie Poggio Artists Agency) p19; Tim Bradford (Illustrated Ltd) pp13, 21
Cover design by emc design ltd and Macmillan Publishers Ltd
Cover illustration/photograph by Getty/Valentin Casarsa, Getty/Leonardo Patrizi
Picture research by Catherine Dunn

Author acknowledgments
I would like to give a big thank you to the whole Macmillan team in the UK for their dedication, hard work and enthusiasm throughout the writing of this course. Thanks also to all the other Macmillan teams around the world for their help, encouragement and always making me feel welcome. Very special thanks to Colegio Europeo Aristos in Getafe, Spain. The daily contact with my students there continues to be a main source of inspiration and I am sincerely grateful to every one of my students, past and present. Massive thanks, as always, to Gemma, Jamie and Becky for their unending love and support.

This book is dedicated to Emily Rosser.

The publishers would like to thank the staff and pupils at the following schools in Mexico and Spain for helping us so enthusiastically with our research for the course: Concha Campos, IES Burgo de Las Rozas, Las Rozas, Madrid; Félix Gaspar, IES Las Encinas; Villanueva de la Cañada, Madrid; Cristina Moisen, IES Joaquín Turina, Madrid; Colegio Montessori Cuautitlán; Colegio Conrad Gessner; Colegio Erasmo de Rotterdam; Colegio Kanic, Centro Educativo Erich Fromm; Universidad Franco Mexicana; Centro Pedagógico María Montessori de Ecatepec; Instituto Cultural; Escuela Maestro Manuel Acosta; Liceo Sakbé De México.

The publishers would also like to thank all those who reviewed or piloted the first edition of Gateway:
Benjamin Affolter, Evelyn Andorfer, Anna Ciereszynska, Regina Culver, Anna Dabrowska, Justyna Deja, Ondrej Dosedel, Lisa Durham, Dagmar Eder, Eva Ellederovan, H Fouad, Sabrina Funes, Luiza Gervescu, Isabel González Bueno, Jutta Habringer, Stela Halmageanu, Marta Hilger, Andrea Hutterer, Nicole Ioakimidis, Mag. Annemarie Kammerhofer, Irina Kondrasheva, Sonja Lengauer, Gabriela Liptakova, Andrea Littlewood, María Cristina Maggi, Silvia Miranda Barbara Nowak, Agnieska Orlińska, Anna Orlowska, María Paula Palou Marta Piotrowska, N Reda, Katharina Schatz, Roswitha Schwarz, Barbara Ścibor, Katarzyna Sochacka, Joanna Spoz, Monica Srtygner, Marisol Suppan, Stephanie Sutter, Halina Tyliba, Prilipko, Maria Vizgina, Vladyko, Pia Wimmer, Katarzyna Zadrożna-Attia and Katarzyna Zaremba-Jaworska.

The authors and publishers would like to thank the following for permission to reproduce their photographs:
Alamy/ableimages p14(Phillipa), Alamy/Chris Batson p27(tr), Alamy/Aleksey Boldin p78(br), 131(cll, clr), Alamy/Blend Images – KidStock p148(internet shop), Alamy/Cultura Creative p52(a), Alamy/Daisy-Daisy pp30, 49(c), Alamy/Flvele Images Ltd p51(f), Alamy/imageBROKER p51(a), Alamy/Image Source p84(c), Alamy/LJSphotography p50(d), Alamy/mediacolor's p74(3), Alamy/OJO Images Ltd pp14(Emma), 148(bc), Alamy/Andrew Paterson p14(Oliver), Alamy/PhotoAlto sas p14(Liam), Alamy/Purestock p98, Alamy/Kumar Sriskandan p40(tll), Alamy/TomBham p128(tl), Alamy/Tony Tallec p84(br), Alamy/Angus Taylor p51(b), Alamy/Westend61 GmbH p99(bl); **Corbis/**Andersen-Ross p66(c), Corbis/Jim Edds p79(tr), Corbis/Valentin Flauraud p123(cr), Corbis/Jon Hicks p15(bl), Corbis/Elliott Kaufman/Beateworks p101(room), Corbis/Sharie Kennedy p66(a), Corbis/Latin Stock Collection p23(a), Corbis/Samantha Mitchell p25, Corbis/moodboard p130; **DIGITAL VISION** p83; **Eric Fischer/** Map by Eric Fischer, using data from the Twitter streaming API/p32(cr); **Getty/**Franz Aberham p59(tr), Getty/Daniel Allan p27(tl), Getty/Kaori Ando p66(b), Getty/Akiko Aoki p131(t), Getty/artpartner-images p124(tr), Getty/Andrey Artykov p78(tln), Getty/Mark Edward Atkinson p84(d), Getty/Thomas Barwick p87(e), 104(b), Getty/Michael Blann p51(e), Getty/Blend Images – KidStock p148(shopping), Getty/Blend Images - Take A Pix Media p87(c), Getty/Tom Bonaventure p35(Japan), Getty/Brand New Images p6(a), Getty/Natalie Behring p82(r), Getty/Blend Images - Moxie Productions p96(tr), Getty/Hilary Brodey p70(header dunes), Getty/Pascal Broze p58(header boy), Getty/Nigel Carse p84(Header background), Getty/Colleen Butler p70(a), Getty/A. Chederros p11(b), Getty/Steve Cicero p23(bl), Getty/Clerkenwell p6(e), Getty/Comstock p105, Getty/ColorBlind Images p36(br), Getty/CARL COURT / Stringer p87(br), Getty/dalton00 p70(a), Getty/Daly and Newton p59(tc), Getty/WLDavies p58(c), Getty/Peter Dazeley p87(b), Getty/Digital Vision p15(tr), p79(tr inset), Getty/George Doyle p58(d), Getty/DreamPictures p85(2), Getty/Dual Dual p23(b), Getty/DreamPictures p58(f), Getty/Sam Edwards p51(d), Getty/ fstop123 p126(br), Getty/Jon Feingersh p104(a), Getty/Giorgio Fochesato p70(Header prickly pear), Getty/franckreporter p148(reading ebook), Getty/Salomé Fresco p15(cl), Getty/Rob Friedman p50(tl), Getty/Christopher Futcher p88(br), 89(bl), Getty/Ron Galella p61(a), 103, Getty/Andrew Geiger p91, Getty/John Giustina p66(d), Getty/Michael Graham p70(b), Getty/Fuse p6(d), 12(cl), Getty/Chris Gramly p6(tr), Getty/Tom Grubbe p70(d), Getty/Charles Gullung p6(c), Getty/Barnaby Hall p18(tr), Getty/Hero Images p113(cr), Getty/Andrew Hobbs p62(bl), Getty/Dave J Hogan p111(a), Getty/Bill Holden p130(tr), Getty/Justin Horrocks p46, Getty/Corinne J. Humphrey p85(1), Getty/Image Source pp82(newsreporter), 101(football), 118(t), Getty/Maya Karkalicheva p148(br), Getty/Jonathan Knowles p74(4), Getty/Kevin Kozicki p41(d), Getty/Mike Marsland p111(d), Getty/Photodisc p101(brownies), Getty/Julian Elliott Photography p41(a), Getty/Mike Kemp pp11(cl), 74(2), Getty/Michaa Krakowiak p74(1), Getty/Jason LaVeris p61(b), Getty/Michael Langford p71(c), Getty/Hans Laubel p18(header), Getty/Rob Lewine p12(tl), Getty/Matthew G Lloyd/Contour by Getty Images p64, Getty/Ghislain & Marie David de Lossy p84(a), Getty/David McGlynn p18(cr), Getty/Tim Macpherson p96(tl), Getty/Luis Sandoval Mandujano p58(e), Getty/mediaphotos p62(bl), Getty/Tom Merton p148(bl), Getty/Buero Monaco p6(f), Getty Laurence Monneret p66(d), Getty/Melinda Moore P35(Switzerland), Getty/Tara Moore p88(cl), Getty/Morsa Images p6(b), Getty/Multi-bits p75(tap), Getty/OJO Images p113(cl), Getty/White Packert p66(f), Getty/Cevdet GAkhan Palas p67, Getty/Pali Rao p58(a), Getty/Ragnar Schmuck p90, Getty/Ron Royals/Fuse p129, Getty/Compassionate Eye Foundation/Chris Ryan p147, Getty/Gregor Schuster p123, Getty/William Shaw p45(cr), Getty/Ariel Skelley p87(d), Getty/Nicho Sodling p24(br), Getty/Stephen Stickler p50(c), Getty/sturti p88(bl), Getty/Justin Sullivan p58(b), Getty/Stewart Sutton p111(b), Getty/images by Tang Ming Tung p148(bookshop), Getty/Tetra Images – fotog pp99(blc), 101(camera), Getty/TommL p117, Getty/Vetta p134(bl), Getty/VisitBritain p85(3), Getty/Jeremy Walker p36(Rio), Getty/Warchi p58 (header screens), Getty/Westend61 p45(tr), Getty/mark wragg p45(cl), Getty/Zero Creatives p50(b); **GOODSHOOT** p35(Egypt); **Macmillan Publishers Ltd** pp110(a-g), p115(covers); **Hanbury Agency/** Picture of Anna Caltabiano used with permission of The Hanbury Agency p113(anna); **Hartswood Films Ltd**/Sherlock p21(bl); **NASA**/ Image courtesy NASA GSFC Scientific Visualization Studio, based on data provided by the TOMS science team. P70(c); **Photodisc** p78(tll), PhotoDisc/Getty Images p73; **Rex Features** p51(c), REX/Mark Campbell p65(cl), REX/Broadimage p38(br),REX/Freemantle Media International p111(c), REX/Jonathan Hordle p50(tc), REX/The Lighthouse / Universal Images Group p71(br), REX/c.Lions Gate/Everett pp41(b), 116, REX/Ken McKay p31, REX/Tina Norris p108, REX/Startraks Photo p39; **Thinkstock/**akiyoko p10, 11(border), Thinkstock/alexaldo pp122(header), 126, 127 (background), Thinkstock/Mark Edward Atkinson p7(bl), Thinkstock/Belyaevskiy p22(br), Thinkstock/Boarding1Now p110(tr), Thinkstock/Robert Churchill p33, Thinkstock/claudiodivizia p48(plaster), Thinkstock/Creatas p92(tll), Thinkstock/dk_photos p74(header cracking), Thinkstock/Dan Grannum Photo p48/49(first aid box), Thinkstock/defun p44(header), Thinkstock/Denniro p49(thermometer), Thinkstock/decisiveimages p135, Thinkstock/DivVector p114(border), Thinkstock/Dmitry-Fisher p75(b), Thinkstock/Murat Domkhokov p48(header), Thinkstock/eskaylim p11(tr), Thinkstock/eyemrs p56, Thinkstock/everythingpossible p44(header r), Thinkstock/Fuse p10(br), Thinkstock/g-stockstudio p36(2, 3), Thinkstock/GooDween123 p84(header hand), Thinkstock/Antonio Guillem p22/23, Thinkstock/hjalmeida pp114,115(boy reading), Thinkstock/iconion_th p49(scissors), Thinkstock/ivosar pp32(tr), 38(tl), Thinkstock/Jacek27 pp62(bl), 63(cr), Thinkstock/Brian Jackson p82(newspapers), Thinkstock/JumpStock p49(bc), Thinkstock/Noam Kahalany p128(br), Thinkstock/R Kaulitzki p36(background), Thinkstock/David Kam p36(1), Thinkstock/OlgaLebedeva P62/63, Thinkstock/Huchen Lu p122(tr), Thinkstock/Ryan McVay p75(border), Thinkstock/marigold_88 pp36,37(border), Thinkstock/Mega_Pixel p49(plaster), Thinkstock/michaeljung p87(a), Thinkstock/Minerva Studio p100(bl),101(br), Thinkstock/miszaqq p127(bl), Thinkstock/Thomas Northcut pp52(c), 92(cr), Thinkstock/Pixland p27(cl), Thinkstock/Purestock p110(header), Thinkstock/Rach27 p127(tl background), Thinkstock/RamCreativ p62(header), Thinkstock/ramzihachicho(border, br, bl), Thinkstock/richiesd p92(tc), Thinkstock/Ridofranz pp 40(tlr),100(cr), Thinkstock/robertsrob p114(tr), Thinkstock/Rosmizan Abu seman p127(tl), Thinkstock/scanrail p82(radio), Thinkstock/scyther5 p82((internet news), Thinkstock/shipfactory p37(tc, tl, cb,clt,bl), Thinkstock/GenaroSilva p124(cr), Thinkstock/somchaij p6(header), Thinkstock/Siri Stafford p48(bandage), Thinkstock/Stockbyte p93, Thinkstock/Sergii Telesh p41(c), Thinkstock/Klaus Tiedge p76, Thinkstock/Paolo_Toffanin p92(tr), Thinkstock/topform84 p7(bl background), Thinkstock/tuja66 p36/37(background), Thinkstock/Karl Weatherly p100, 101(border), Thinkstock/Wong_A p100, 101(background), Thinkstock/Catherine Yeulet p13, Thinkstock/yewkeo p10(header), Thinkstock/Lisa F. Young p52(b), Thinkstock/Wavebreakmedia Ltd p126(header), Thinkstock/Michael-john Wolfe p63(bl), Thinkstock/James Woodson p15(tl), Thinkstock/Zoonar RF p32(Header background).

Cover image from THE SEVENTH MISS HATFIELD by Anna Caltabiano reproduced with permission from the Orion Publishing group London p113(cover)
Cover Image of 'Maximum Ride: The Angel Experiment' reproduced with permission from Headline Publishing Group p114
Cover image from Holes by Louis Sachar published by Bloomsbury Publishing PLC, cover reproduced with permission p118(tr)
Images 'Making a silicon chip' used with permission from Intel p124(b)

The author and publishers would like to thank the following for permission to reproduce the following copyright material:
p13 Extract from 'Talk at mealtimes' by Christina Clark © National Literary Trust, 2013. Reprinted with permission.
p19 Extract from 'Europe at a Glance' © The Week, 2012. Published in The Week 22 December 2012. Reprinted with permission.
p33 Extract from 'Twitter map of London shows 66 languages' by Shane Richmond. Originally published in the Daily Telegraph on 26 October 2012 © Telegraph Group Limited, 2012. Reprinted with permission. www.telegraph.co.uk
p33 Extract from 'The language of Twitter' by Christian Arno. Originally published in Lingo24 on 25 April 2012 © Lingo24, 2012. Reprinted with permission.
p39 Extract from 'Learn to speak Dothraki and Valyrian From the Man who invented them for Game of Thrones' by Denise Martin. Originally published in Vulture on 23 April 2014 © New York Media LLC 2014. Reprinted with permission.
p50 Extract from 'I am Jackie Chan: My Life in Action' © Ballantine Publishing Group, 1998.
p62 Extract from 'Addicted to Fame' by Hannah Frankel. Originally published in the Times Educational Supplement on 12 May 2008 © TES Global Limited, 2008. Reprinted with permission.
p74 Extract from 'You Can Save the Planet' by Rich Hough © Rich Hough. Published by A & C Black Publishers Limited and The Guardian. Reprinted by permission of the publishers.
p76 Extract from 'Run, don't walk: The school that gets pupils to generate electricity' by Richard Garner. Originally published in The Independent on 05 September 2013 © The Independent, 2013. Reprinted with permission. www.theindependent.co.uk
p97 Extract from 'A short story – True friends' © Dr Prem. Reprinted with permission.
p108 Extract from 'Fraser Doherty: The Adventures of JamBoy' © Fraser Doherty. Reprinted with permission.
p113 Reproduced with permission of Anna Caltabiano, care of The Hanbury Agency, 28 Moreton Street, London SW1V 2PE. Copyright, © Anna Caltabiano 2011, All Rights Reserved.
p114 Extract from 'Maximum Ride: The Angel Experiment' by James Patterson © James Patterson, 2005. Reprinted with permission of Hodder & Stoughton Publishers and Hachette Book Group.
p126 Extract from 'More Employers finding reasons not to hire candidates on social media, finds careerbuilder survey'. Originally published on careerbuilder on 27 June 2013 © CareerBuilder LLC, 2013.
p134 Extract from 'Q: How do you make 1.6m a year and drive a Ferrari? A: Sell essays for £400' by Matthew Taylor. Originally published in The Guardian on 29 July 2006 © Guardian News and Media Limited, 2006. Reprinted with permission. www.theguardian.com/uk

These materials may contain links for third party websites. We have no control over, and are not responsible for, the contents of such third party websites. Please use care when accessing them.

Printed and bound in Thailand
2020 2019 2018 2017 2016
10 9 8 7 6 5 4 3 2 1